Related Books of Interest

Disciplined Agile Delivery
A Practitioner's Guide to Agile Software Delivery in the Enterprise

By Scott W. Ambler and Mark Lines

ISBN-13: 978-0-13-281013-5

It is widely recognized that moving from traditional to agile approaches to build software solutions is a critical source of competitive advantage. Mainstream agile approaches that are indeed suitable for small projects require significant tailoring for larger, complex enterprise projects. In *Disciplined Agile Delivery*, Scott W. Ambler and Mark Lines introduce IBM®'s breakthrough Disciplined Agile Delivery (DAD) process framework, which describes how to do this tailoring. DAD applies a more disciplined approach to agile development by acknowledging and dealing with the realities and complexities of a portfolio of interdependent program initiatives.

Ambler and Lines show how to extend Scrum with supplementary agile and lean strategies from Agile Modeling (AM), Extreme Programming (XP), Kanban, Unified Process (UP), and other proven methods to provide a hybrid approach that is adaptable to your organization's unique needs.

A Practical Guide to Distributed Scrum

By Elizabeth Woodward, Steffan Surdek, and Matthew Ganis

ISBN-13: 978-0-13-704113-8

This is the first comprehensive, practical guide for Scrum practitioners working in large-scale distributed environments. Written by three of IBM's leading Scrum practitioners—in close collaboration with the IBM QSE Scrum Community of more than 1,000 members worldwide—this book offers specific, actionable guidance for everyone who wants to succeed with Scrum in the enterprise.

Readers will follow a journey through the lifecycle of a distributed Scrum project, from envisioning products and setting up teams to preparing for Sprint planning and running retrospectives. Using real-world examples, the book demonstrates how to apply key Scrum practices, such as look-ahead planning in geographically distributed environments. Readers will also gain valuable new insights into the agile management of complex problem and technical domains.

Related Books of Interest

Agile Career Development
Lessons and Approaches from IBM

By Mary Ann Bopp, Diana A. Bing,
Sheila Forte-Trammell
ISBN-13: 978-0-13-715364-0

**Supercharge Performance by Linking
Employee-Driven Career Development with
Business Goals**

How do you make career development work for
both the employee and the business? IBM® has
done it by tightly linking employee-driven career
development programs with corporate goals. In
Agile Career Development, three of IBM's leading
HR innovators show how IBM has accomplished
this by illustrating various lessons and approaches that can be applied to other organizations as
well. This book is for every HR professional, learning or training manager, executive, strategist, and
any other business leader who wants to create a
high-performing organization.

Patterns of Information Management

By Mandy Chessell and Harald Smith
ISBN-13: 978-0-13-315550-1

**Use Best Practice Patterns to Understand
and Architect Manageable, Efficient
Information Supply Chains That Help You
Leverage All Your Data and Knowledge**

In the era of "Big Data," information pervades
every aspect of the organization. Therefore,
architecting and managing it is a multi-
disciplinary task. Now, two pioneering IBM®
architects present proven architecture patterns
that fully reflect this reality. Using their pattern
language, you can accurately characterize the
information issues associated with your own
systems, and design solutions that succeed
over both the short- and long-term.

Related Books of Interest

Implementing the IBM® Rational Unified Process® and Solutions

By Joshua Barnes

ISBN-13: 978-0-321-36945-1

This book delivers all the knowledge and insight you need to succeed with the IBM Rational Unified Process and Solutions. Joshua Barnes presents a start-to-finish, best-practice roadmap to the complete implementation cycle of IBM RUP—from projecting ROI and making the business case through piloting, implementation, mentoring, and beyond. Drawing on his extensive experience leading large-scale IBM RUP implementations and working with some of the industry's most recognized thought leaders in the Software Engineering Process world, Barnes brings together comprehensive "lessons learned" from both successful and failed projects. You'll learn from real-world case studies, including actual project artifacts.

Work Item Management with IBM Rational ClearQuest and Jazz

A Customization Guide

Shmuel Bashan, David Bellagio

ISBN-13: 978-0-13-700179-8

Software Test Engineering with IBM Rational Functional Tester

The Definitive Resource

Davis, Chirillo, Gouveia, Saracevic, Bocarsley, Quesada, Thomas, van Lint

ISBN-13: 978-0-13-700066-1

Enterprise Master Data Management

An SOA Approach to Managing Core Information

Dreibelbis, Hechler, Milman, Oberhofer, van Run, Wolfson

ISBN-13: 978-0-13-236625-0

An Introduction to IMS

Your Complete Guide to IBM Information Management Systems, 2nd Edition

Barbara Klein, et al.

ISBN-13: 978-0-13-288687-1

Outside-in Software Development

A Practical Approach to Building Successful Stakeholder-based Products

Carl Kessler, John Sweitzer

ISBN-13: 978-0-13-157551-6

Being Agile

Being Agile

Eleven Breakthrough Techniques to Keep You from "Waterfalling Backward"

Leslie Ekas

Scott Will

IBM Press
Pearson plc
Upper Saddle River, NJ • Boston • Indianapolis • San Francisco
New York • Toronto • Montreal • London • Munich • Paris • Madrid
Cape Town • Sydney • Tokyo • Singapore • Mexico City

ibmpressbooks.com

IBM Press Program Managers: Steven M. Stansel, Ellice Uffer

Cover design: IBM Corporation

Executive Editor: Bernard Goodwin

Marketing Manager: Stephane Nakib

Publicist: Heather Fox

Managing Editor: Kristy Hart

Designer: Alan Clements

Project Editor: Elaine Wiley

Copy Editor: Apostrophe Editing Services

Indexer: Erika Millen

Senior Compositor: Gloria Schurick

Proofreader: Jess DeGabriele

Manufacturing Buyer: Dan Uhrig

Published by Pearson plc

Publishing as IBM Press

IBM Press offers excellent discounts on this book when ordered in quantity for bulk purchases or special sales, which may include electronic versions and/or custom covers and content particular to your business, training goals, marketing focus, and branding interests. For more information, please contact

U. S. Corporate and Government Sales
1-800-382-3419
corpsales@pearsontechgroup.com.

For sales outside the United States, please contact

International Sales
international@pearsoned.com.

Library of Congress Control Number: 2013946079

ISBN-13: 978-0-13-337562-6
ISBN-10: 0-13-337562-5

Text printed in the United States on recycled paper at Courier in Stoughton, Massachusetts.

First printing: October 2013

Contents

Preface   **xviii**

Acknowledgements   **xxi**

Introduction *By Leslie Ekas*   **1**
    Who This Book Is For   1
    What Is Our Approach?   1
    What Does This Book Cover?   3
    An Overview Of The Content   4
    What Do You Have To Do?   6
    What Benefits Can You Get from Reading This Book?   6
    Who Are We?   6
    Join the Conversation   7

Chapter 1   Whole Teams   **9**
    Being agile requires whole teams because the synergy derived
    from cross-disciplined and cross-component
    teams working together enables teams to be more
    productive than working in isolation.
    By Leslie Ekas

    Principles   10
        What Is a Whole Team?   10
        Why Are Whole Teams Hard to Create?   11
        Cross-Component Teams   11
        Cross-Discipline Teams   12
        Cross-Geographical, Cross-Cultural, Large Teams   13
        Stable, Dedicated, and Protected   14
    Practices   16
        Start with Whole Teams   16
        Maintain and Protect Dedicated Teams   16
        The Conversation   17
        Share the Same Truth   19
        No Partial Credit   19
        Offer Help   20
    Metrics   20
    Breakthrough   21
    Summary   22

Chapter 2   **Active Stakeholder Interaction**   **25**

Being agile requires active stakeholder interaction
because only your stakeholders can confirm that
what you create actually meets their needs.
By Scott Will

Principles   26
What Is Active Stakeholder Interaction?   26
Why Can It Be Hard to Get Active Stakeholder Interaction?   27
Stakeholder Interaction Is Not a New Idea   29
Stakeholder Interaction Is Not Optional   29
Do What's Needed—And No More   30
Practices   31
Identifying Stakeholders   31
Review Epics with Stakeholders   33
Set Expectations   33
Stakeholders Should Have *Skin in the Game*   34
Make Stakeholder Interaction Compelling for Your Customers   35
Doing Regular Demonstrations   35
Reacting to Feedback Received   36
When Is the Development Organization a Stakeholder?   37
Customer Support Teams as Stakeholders   38
Working with Customers in Countries Other Than Your Own   39
Metrics   39
Breakthrough   40
Summary   42

Chapter 3   **Queuing Theory**   **43**

Being agile requires embracing queuing theory
practices because teams achieve greater efficiency
and throughput by leveraging a steady flow of small
work items.
By Scott Will

Principles   44
Why Does Waterfall Thinking Still Linger?   44
Small Batches of Coordinated Work   45
Frequent Feedback   46
Ensure Sufficient Capacity   46
Practices   47
Small Task Sizes: 4 Hours, 8 Hours, 16 Hours   47
One User Story at a Time   48
Short Iterations   49
Metrics Should Support the Focus on Working Software   50
Metrics   50
Breakthrough   51
Summary   51

Chapter 4 No Multitasking   **53**

*Being agile requires teams to avoid multitasking
because teams are more productive when they focus.
By Scott Will*

Principles   55
    One Thing at a Time Is More Efficient   55
    Flow   56
    Stop Starting; Start Finishing   57
Practices   57
    Team Members Are Dedicated to a Project 100% of the Time   57
    One Project at a Time   58
    Be a "Firewall" and Stop Being a "Fast-Forward" Button   58
    Pair Programming; Pair Testing   59
    Calendar Ruthlessness   59
Metrics   60
Breakthrough   61
Summary   62

Chapter 5 Eliminate Waste   **63**

*Being agile requires eliminating waste to realize
significant efficiency, productivity, and quality gains.
By Leslie Ekas*

Principles   64
    What Is Eliminating Waste?   64
    Why the Focus on Eliminating Waste?   65
    Technical Debt   65
    Project Debt   67
    Why Is It Hard to Eliminate Waste?   67
Practices   69
    Get Rid of Waste... One Way or Another   69
    Small Tasks   70
    Build Quality In   71
    Focus on Customer Value   72
    Expand "Done!" Criteria   73
    Handling Latent Defects   74
    Stop Writing Defect Records   74
Metrics   75
Breakthrough   76
Summary   77

Chapter 6   Working Software   79

Being agile requires always having working software because it
validates progress, ensures the highest
levels of quality, and enables regular feedback.
By Leslie Ekas

Principles   80
  What Is Working Software?   80
  Why Is It Hard to Regularly Have Working Software?   82
  Working Software Extends Test Suites   82
Practices   83
  Short Iterations   83
  Continuous Integration and Automation   84
  Vertically Sliced Stories   85
  Evolutionary Architecture and Emergent Design   86
  In-House Deploys   88
Metrics   89
Breakthrough   89
Summary   91

Chapter 7   Deliver Value   93

Being agile requires delivering real value so that
customers succeed with your product.
By Scott Will

Principles   94
  Why User Stories?   94
Practices   97
  The "So That" Clause   97
  Vertically Sliced Stories   98
  Acceptance Criteria   99
  Using Velocity Effectively   100
Metrics   103
Breakthrough   103
  What Exactly Is a Zero-Gravity Thinker?   104
  A Real Example   106
  Zero Gravity Thinking in Sum...   106
Summary   107

Chapter 8   **Release Often**   **109**

Being agile requires releasing software often so
that teams learn fast and customers succeed sooner.
By Leslie Ekas

Principles   112
     Why Release Often?   112
     Do Just Enough   113
     Defer Commitment   114
     Why Can It Be Hard to Release Often?   116
Practices   117
     Start with Shorter Release Cycles   117
     Epic Stories   117
     Evolutionary Product Design   119
     High Value First   120
     High Risk First   121
     Value-Driven Development: the Outworking of Frequent Code Drops   123
Metrics   124
Breakthrough   125
Summary   128

Chapter 9   **Stop the Line**   **129**

Being agile requires that teams stop the line to
solve critical problems at their core so that they
do not lose time by dealing with the same problem
again and again.
By Leslie Ekas

Principles   130
     What Is Stop the Line?   130
     Why Is Stop the Line Hard?   131
Practices   133
     Fix Blockers   133
     Reflections as a Guide   133
     What if the Problem Is Too Big to Stop the Line?   133
Metrics   134
Breakthrough   139
Summary   141

Chapter 10   Agile Leadership   **143**

*Being successful with agile requires leaders who
learn, participate in, and experiment with agile so
that they lead with an agile mindset and react with
agile instincts.*
By Leslie Ekas

Principles   145
   Agile Leadership   145
   Why Is Agile Leadership Hard?   146
Practices   147
   Learn Agile, Experience Agile, Develop Agile Instincts   147
   Enable and Protect   148
   Help Your Team Learn, Let Your Team Fail   149
   Set Priorities, Provide Boundaries, and Let the Team Figure Out How   151
   A Single, Visible View of the Truth   153
Metrics   154
Breakthrough   154
Summary   155

Chapter 11   Continuous Improvement   **157**

*Being agile requires continuous improvement
because teams that continue to learn, adapt, and evolve
are more productive and competitive. Agile is a
never-ending journey of getting better.*
By Scott Will

Principles   158
   Why Is Continuous Improvement Important?   158
   Why Is Continuous Improvement Hard?   159
   There Is No Such Thing as "100 Percent Agile"   159
   Realize That You Will Learn New Things as a Project Progresses   160
   You Need to Set Time Aside to Sharpen Your Axe   160
   Focus on Small, On-Going Improvements   161
   Learn from Your Mistakes; Don't Make Them Again   162
   Fail Fast   162
   Management Needs to Actively Promote Innovation   162
Practices   164
   Reflections   164
   Value Stream Mapping   166
   Addressing Reluctance   167
   The "Art" of Continuous Improvement   167
   Share   169
Metrics   169
Breakthrough   169
Summary   170

Appendix   *By Scott Will*   **173**

   Exploring Your Agility: A Brief, Annotated Questionnaire   173

   What Would You Be Willing to Give Up?   174

   Questions on Various Agile Practices   175

      How Long Are Your Iterations?   175

      How Often Do You Build?   176

      What Disciplines Are on Your Teams?   176

      Do You Carry a Defect Backlog?   176

      What Do You Automate?   177

      Do You Conduct Status Meetings?   177

      Are You Delivering Value to Your Customers?   178

      Do You Get to "Done!" Each Iteration?   178

      Are You Getting Better?   178

   Concluding Thoughts   178

Index   **179**

Preface

By Leslie Ekas

Your team embarked on adopting agile a while ago, but the results you expected to see by now just haven't materialized. To be honest, you're kind of surprised, especially given all the hype about agile, the stories of wild success you've seen online, and the tremendous enthusiasm expressed by the team early on. There might even be some whispered talk in the hallway about "chucking this agile thing" and going back to waterfall. If you find yourself in a situation similar to this, then this book is for you.

The target audience is software engineers and leaders who understand how to apply agile to software development but may find their teams falling back into old habits when the going gets tough or because an old waterfall approach seems like the right thing to do. It is also for those teams that have adopted agile but do not feel like there has been a significant improvement. Our goal in writing this book is to give you the means to *be agile* as well as to help keep you from "waterfalling backward."

Transforming to agile from waterfall is no small undertaking. Resorting to old habits when trouble hits is what our instincts tell us to do. When I started to learn agile, the first organization I led experienced challenges adopting agile but, fortunately, I got some unwavering encouragement and then some timely help. Let me explain: I first learned about agile in early 2007 in a class led by Tom and Mary Poppendieck. Following the class one of my teams jumped into agile and after approximately 6 months concluded that it was enabling us to deliver better value to our customers. However, the change was not compelling, we were not getting all the practices to succeed, and we were wondering when "the big moment" would happen when significant benefits became obvious. My team leaders and I had the opportunity to get additional coaching from Tom and Mary after the class to help our team address our specific problems. We described the challenges we faced with our agile adoption: not getting to "Done!" each iteration, not working well together as a team, failing to break our pattern of building up project debt, and so forth. We were discouraged and hoped that they would give us the key to resolving our problems. Tom and Mary both smiled and said, "You'll do fine." I wanted to scream! "What do you mean by 'fine'?!?!? We can't get it right! And you can't believe how many problems we have to fix!"

It took me a while to understand their reaction. They did give us the key to resolving our problems, or at least they told us that we already had the key. They knew we were trying new ideas and wanted to have more success than we had experienced. They knew that with more success, we would try harder and get better—and they were right. Teams that are actually trying to get better are well on their way to becoming agile.

In our quest to get better, my team did finally experience a pivotal moment that not only fixed a significant waterfall problem that we had but also changed the way that we thought about working together. We wrote this book for anyone who wants to break through old ways of thinking—but may need a few tricks to get there.

Now let me start from the beginning and describe the events that led Scott and me to write this book. I worked for years as a software developer and then as manager in typical waterfall-style projects. Our teams had good engineering discipline and shipped good products; however, I did not think that we were delivering high enough value or quality to our customers. I was frustrated because I did not know how to fix the problems. We looked at several popular approaches but none of them got my attention until I learned about agile. When I started practicing agile in 2007, I was excited because this approach made sense, and the literature indicated that adopting agile produced some believable and compelling results.

My team started its agile journey implementing daily standup meetings, using 1-month iterations, completing iteration planning, demonstrations, and reflections, and even trying to build a product backlog. I noticed several positive changes taking place within the team—but did I think the move to agile was compelling? To be honest, no. Our results were not earth shaking. We were productive before moving to agile and that had not changed significantly.

At first, my team was organized like many traditional teams are—by discipline. We had very skilled teams working on the product; however, they were used to working in their silos—and that is where they stayed. They met as a group but worked in their individual disciplines. This same problem kept surfacing during our reflections at the end of each iteration—we were not working well together. We tried to fix this problem in a variety of ways but nothing worked, and most of us sensed that not solving this problem would lead to defeat with agile. An outside consultant suggested that we try *bullpens* (more on this in Chapter 1, "Whole Teams")—and it worked. I mean, it really worked, immediately. Our team started to become a whole team, and it made a difference in our results. The change was so compelling that we never looked back. This was our breakthrough. Given how eye opening my team's first breakthrough was, it prompted us to continually look for other breakthroughs. This book is the result of our efforts and experiences in discovering other breakthroughs.

The goal for this book is to help teams that have adopted agile but are struggling to make it stick, or struggling to get compelling value from it, or both. Old habits die hard, and in those instances when agile does not stick, it is often because teams have not experienced an "Ah-ha!" moment that changes the way they think. When no compelling improvements are noted, teams tend to "waterfall backward" one compromise (or excuse) at a time. Symptoms of waterfalling backward include moving to longer iterations, resetting iteration end dates, not breaking down user stories to fit into an iteration, measuring project progress based on individual disciplines instead of focusing on "working software," and an inability to share the work due to limited domain expertise.

In this book we offer several breakthrough techniques that enable teams to experience enough of an "Ah-ha!" moment that it breaks typical, reflexive waterfall thinking, thus allowing agile thinking which, in turn, helps transform software engineering teams from simply "doing agile" to actually "being agile"—with the resulting increase in realized benefits.

So back to my opening comments: If you're looking for ways to get better, you've passed the first hurdle to actually getting better. In addition, if you know that your team needs to get better but have difficulty convincing others that more benefits can be gained from moving further down the agile path, this book is also for you. Our hope is that you discover valuable techniques and gain new insights that help you continually improve. We also hope that your successes excite other teams in your organization (especially those on the verge of giving up) to press on. We like to see teams not only adopt agile, but also make it stick. Agile is fun and it helps teams produce higher value and higher quality software.

Join the Conversation

We encourage you to join the agile conversation on our blog: "Being Agile." You can find it at www.ibm.com/developerworks/community/blogs/beingagile/?lang=en.

Acknowledgments

We really enjoyed writing this book because it helped us to distill our years of thinking about these topics. We have had many discussions through our work with various teams on what is required to help them succeed and our hope is that we can help even more teams with this book.

We received our initial education on agile software development from Tom and Mary Poppendieck. In addition to their education, the Poppendiecks gave IBM® tremendous support that we have leveraged in our coaching over the years. The Poppendiecks certainly gave Leslie and her team the motivation early on to stick with their efforts to make agile work and to get better in the process of doing so. We also want to thank Tom in particular for providing a review of our initial book proposal and his subsequent reviews of various chapters.

Leslie would also like to thank Stan Rifkin whose guidance early on helped her team achieve an "Ah-ha!" moment that really made its agile transformation become permanent.

Also, we want to thank Pramod Sadalage who provided reviews on every chapter. He helped us clarify and improve our explanations of several topics that, otherwise, might have been a little too IBM-centric.

We thank Scott's daughter Karoline Strickland for her review of our chapters in the final weeks. Her strength in writing combined with her lack of subject matter expertise made her an outstanding reviewer because she could quickly detect when our thoughts were not coming across clearly. Karoline now calls herself a "zero-gravity reviewer" (you'll just have to read the Deliver Value chapter to get the joke).

Mark Wainwright was a fellow coach in the IBM Software Group Agile Center of Competence prior to retiring from IBM. He provided very useful feedback early in the process of writing our proposal that helped us redesign our approach in conveying the material in the book. We had many great times working with Mark and his insights always kept us on track. We thank him for all his support, the things we learned from him, and for his friendship.

Dibbe Edwards, a Vice President in the IBM Rational Software organization, provided IBM executive sponsorship for this book. She has championed the agile mission in IBM for a long time and has supported our efforts to help teams realize the rewards that agile adoption has to offer. Dibbe willingly supported new approaches to solve some difficult problems and her leadership helped her teams achieve ever-higher levels of productivity when adopting agile.

As we've continued to work with teams across all of IBM, it's always gratifying to see others take up the flag and help drive agile adoption as well. Yvonne Matute is one such person and Matthew Stave is another. We would like to thank Yvonne for letting us use quotes from an email she sent to us describing her team's successes in adopting agile and to Matthew for letting us include his list of items regarding the adoption of short iterations that we've included in the Appendix of the book.

We would also like to thank Carl Kessler for his early and ongoing encouragement to all of IBM to move to agile. We both had the distinct pleasure of working for Carl at various points in our careers and, even though Carl retired from his role as a senior development executive in IBM several years ago, his name still regularly comes up in conversations revolving around helping teams adopt agile. Thank you, Carl!

It should come as no surprise that writing this book took time away from our respective families, so we would both like to publicly thank our families for putting up with late nights, missed dinners, and not doing all the other things we could have been doing with you. The support we received from you all was critical in seeing this dream come to fruition. Thank you so much!

We heartily thank all the teams that we have worked with because they persevered and got better, and they enabled us to learn and leverage their experiences and their unique perspectives for our coaching responsibilities. If it wasn't for your willingness to hear us out and to try new things, this book would never have been written. You know who you are! And now you know how thankful we are to you!

Finally, we would like to thank Steven Stansel from IBM Press, and Bernard Goodwin, Michelle Housley, and Elaine Wiley of Pearson Press for all their incredible help in making this book a reality.

We would also like to acknowledge that, as with any major undertaking, not everything is going to be perfect. Any errors and any lack of clarity you may find while reading the book remain the sole responsibility of the authors.

About the Authors

 **Leslie Ekas** has worked in software development for over 20 years as a developer, manager, and agile coach. Her industry experience ranges from a startup, to a mid-sized company, and now IBM. She has led multiple products to market successfully over the years. She has managed teams of all sizes and many disciplines and across broad geographies. Leslie helped start the IBM Software Group Agile Center of Competence after her team's early success transforming to agile. After coaching for several years, she returned to development to lead the worldwide Rational ClearCase team. In her new job as the Smarter Infrastructure Portfolio Manager, she is helping the business team adopt an agile operational approach.

 **Scott Will** has been with IBM for more than 22 years, the last six as an agile consultant. His experience ranges from providing consulting for small, co-located teams to teams with hundreds of engineers scattered across the world. Previously Scott was a successful programmer, tester, and customer support team lead, and he was in management for years. He is a contributing author to the book *Agility and Discipline Made Easy*, an IBM Master Inventor with numerous patents, a former Air Force combat pilot, and a graduate of Purdue University with degrees in Computer Science, Mathematics, and Numerical Analysis. He also completed his MBA while in the Air Force.

Introduction

By Leslie Ekas

Who This Book Is For

Transforming from a waterfall-based methodology to agile is no small undertaking. This book is for people who may find their team falling back into old habits when the going gets tough or just because an old waterfall approach seems like the right thing to do. It is also for those teams that have adopted agile but do not feel like there has been a significant improvement. The target audience includes both leaders and members of agile teams. The goal in writing this book is to give you the means to react to situations and challenges in an instinctively agile way and, thus, secure the real benefits that agile promises.

What Is Our Approach?

Adopting agile requires a change in thinking—it's not just adopting a set of practices. Too many teams have adopted a list of practices and called themselves "agile." This book can help teams get past a typical, rote approach to adopting agile and start gaining the real benefits that agile promises. Even if you are already experienced and successful with agile, you can gain additional insights that can help you and your teams be even more successful. (*Continuous improvement* is one of the fundamental concepts of agile.) Basically, we don't care what specific agile practices you've adopted—what we're concerned with in this book is whether you've gained the *benefits* from adopting those practices and, if not, we can provide some help in showing you how to do so.

Agile continues to grow in popularity because the benefits promised are substantial. As markets grow more competitive, and products become more sophisticated, software development teams need to become more efficient and effective while still ensuring high product quality and delivering real customer value. Agile gives teams a proven way to address these challenges. However, being an agile team is more than having daily standups, chunking up work into short, time-boxed iterations, and always having working software. Agile means thinking differently:

focusing on customer-value, continuous high-quality development, constant improvement, and more. If teams simply adopt some practices—without understanding the principles behind them—they may never get the full value of agile.

Through our years of working with teams, we've found that teams need ways to overcome their reflexive waterfall habits to really understand and benefit from agile. In our experience, if teams couldn't break an old habit, they would typically wind up with a modified waterfall approach instead of truly becoming agile.

This book reviews several of the foundational concepts in agile, covers the principles that undergird each of the concepts, and then discusses the corresponding practices that complement the principles. At the end of each chapter we offer a breakthrough technique that can provide a mechanism for teams to move toward the goal of "being agile" instead of just "doing agile."

And now for a warning: To make a breakthrough, we recommend techniques that are radical enough that you CANNOT fall back into a waterfall habit. You have to remove the safety net—no "cheating" allowed. One of the differentiators between this book and other agile books is that we cover more than just agile practices; we discuss the principles on which the practices are built and also offer breakthrough techniques that can help break old, bad habits. We broke through ourselves and have seen many other teams succeed with these methods.

This may sound funny, but it is our hope that when you read any of the breakthrough techniques in this book, your first reaction is to tell us that we're nuts! We want the ideas to feel edgy enough that they make you feel uncomfortable. Getting out of your comfort zone is how it works. Not all the ideas may strike you this way depending on how your team works currently—and that's OK.

AN EXAMPLE OF A BREAKTHROUGH

The following is an example of the type of habit-breaking we're referring to, but it comes from outside the realm of software engineering. Scott is a competitive marksman, as is his wife and several family members. However, his oldest daughter always had problems with flinching when she would shoot—she was anticipating the recoil of the firearm and it would inevitably cause her shots to be off the mark. Scott had tried numerous ways to help his daughter overcome the flinching habit, but often with little improvement noted. One day he suggested that his daughter try shooting with both eyes open. (Note that most shooters will shoot with only their dominant eye open, focusing primarily on the firearm's front sight. When shooting with both eyes open, the focus must transition to the target instead of the front sight.) When his daughter tried shooting with both eyes open, suddenly the flinching stopped and she started hitting the target right where she was aiming. The radical change in the shooting fundamentals likely "overloaded" her reflexive, flinching response and helped her instead to become an excellent shooter, almost immediately. It truly was a *breakthrough...*

What Does This Book Cover?

In this book, Scott and I have distilled our collective 12 years' experience in both leading software teams through adopting agile and subsequently coaching many, many additional teams. The book is divided into chapters that focus on 11 crucial topics for agile organizations. Chapter 1, "Whole Teams," explores the vital need for developers, testers, and product documentation writers to work together during each iteration to accomplish a small but valuable slice of functionality. Each small portion of functionality can—and should—be regularly demonstrated to customers, as described in Chapter 2, "Active Stakeholder Interaction," where we provide guidance on how to get the most from these regular interactions.

You may be challenged with getting to "Done!" every iteration. In Chapter 3, "Queuing Theory," you'll see how working on—and regularly completing—some small amount of functionality allows teams to be much more productive and efficient than has ever been possible with typical waterfall approaches. A common refrain in agile circles is, "Stop starting and start finishing!"

One of the primary obstacles to regularly finishing small amounts of work is the pervasiveness of multitasking, and in Chapter 4, "No Multitasking," we help you see why multitasking (sometimes referred to as task-switching) is inherently inefficient. Here we help you see the difference between *busyness* and *productivity*.

One of the principles of the Agile Manifesto is "Simplicity—the art of maximizing the amount of work not done—is essential."[1] To maximize the amount of work *not* done, there has to be an intense focus on eliminating waste. Waste can take many forms in software development. Chapter 5, "Eliminate Waste," provides numerous ways to help you both to see waste and to get rid of it.

The flip-side of eliminating waste is ensuring that what is created is valuable—especially with respect to your stakeholders. Chapter 2 covers how to engage with your stakeholders during a release. In Chapter 7, "Deliver Value," we discuss ways to ensure that what your team is creating actually provides value to your stakeholders.

And the best way to engage with your stakeholders regularly is to always have working software. Two-hundred lines of code that provide some small amount of functionality, that are "release-ready," and that can be demonstrated to customers to get their feedback is far more valuable than 2,000 lines of code that haven't been tested and can't be shown to customers. Teams should focus on always having working software, and Chapter 6, "Working Software," covers just how important of a practice this is for agile teams.

Always having working software allows teams to have much greater flexibility for actually releasing a product. Scott and I come from the enterprise application software world in which it is common for products to release once every 2 to 3 years. Given the rapid changes going on in the industry today, with the advent of cloud technologies and continuous delivery approaches, shorter release cycles are becoming the norm. But even apart from these, shorter release cycles

---

1. http://agilemanifesto.org/principles.html

are more efficient and provide more flexibility to teams than longer release cycles. Chapter 8, "Release Often," provides much food for thought on this topic.

What do you do when a critical problem surfaces? Do you just address the symptoms and move on? Chapter 9, "Stop the Line," encourages teams to immediately stop work when a critical problem surfaces and fix the problem at its root. Doing so means that the problem will never surface again.

As with stop the line behavior, many things covered in the book will likely seem counterintuitive, especially given the hold that waterfall thinking has had on software development for decades. Real transformation requires both a technical and executive leadership that genuinely understands agile principles and practices, is willing to learn more, encourages continuous improvement, and provides a penalty-free environment. Chapter 10, "Agile Leadership," shows that meaningful transformation cannot occur without leaders who engage with their teams when embarking on an agile transformation.

Perhaps the most important chapter in this book is Chapter 11, "Continuous Improvement." We frequently tell teams that there is no such thing as "100 percent agile" because "being agile" means always looking for ways to get better. The best teams we've worked with are those that continually look for ways to get better. Chapter 11 provides a lot of encouragement to adopt a continuous improvement mindset as part of your day-to-day thinking.

The chapters are organized so that they can act as a ready reference for each topic. In addition, the chapters can be read in any order; in general, one chapter does not build on any previous chapter. However, because many of the concepts and principles have a lot of affinity with each other, you can see that we've emphasized some items in more than one place in the book. Adopting one agile concept or practice tends to pull other concepts and practices along with it. For instance, the concepts of Stop the Line, Eliminate Waste, and Continuous Improvement overlap in both intent and practice. However, they are separated in the book in order to reinforce the value of each concept in isolation.

As a side-note, Scott and I firmly believe that teams should not try to "tip-toe" into adopting agile. We recommend jumping in with both feet. Yes, it will be messier and more chaotic than tip-toeing in, but the benefits will accrue faster because teams will learn faster. Pulling stuff in slowly delays many of the benefits and can often actually derail motivation for going further. ("We haven't seen much benefit yet, why should we take on something else? Why not just go back to waterfall...?") Jumping into agile allows you to change your thinking, and consequently your reflexive habits much more quickly.

An Overview Of The Content

Each chapter is divided into four main sections: Principles, Practices, Metrics, and Breakthrough. The Principle section provides the conceptual foundation upon which the topic is built and shows how the ensuing practices support the concept. These principles often provide the necessary insight to help teams understand the "why" of adopting any given practice. Each principle is described in terms of why it is important for agile thinking. The practices described are those necessary for really making a transformation in an agile way. There is not a one-to-one mapping between the principles and the practices—there is actually a lot of overlap between all the principles and practices. In fact, in some cases it can be hard to classify an item as either a principle or a practice because it can easily fit into both categories. So if this seems a bit confounding, don't worry about it. The content of the concept matters more than the context.

If things are working well you generally know it, but it might be useful to have a way to measure progress. Metrics are often useful to entice another team to try something similar, or just to give you some context for your own results. The metrics section provides possible ways to evaluate if the principles are sticking. Be careful, though, to not let them be your only guide in understanding improvement.

The set of concepts, principles, and practices that we've selected are ones that we have found to be critical in helping our teams succeed. We are not trying to be exhaustive—there are much better references for that. Our intent is to build a better understanding of each concept so that you understand the thinking that is achieved by the breakthrough method. At the end of each chapter we introduce a breakthrough technique to help make lasting transformations. Each technique is intended to help teams break their traditional, reflexive (waterfall) thinking patterns. We did not invent all the breakthrough techniques—some have been adopted from our interaction with other agile practitioners (such as the bullpen technique mentioned in the Preface). The others are ones we've discovered through our coaching experiences. We know there are more techniques out there and hope that this book will encourage teams to share what's worked for them.

We've also included a number of stories from teams with which we have worked. Some of the stories are of successes. Others describe challenging situations we faced when first working with a team—situations that forced us to think of out-of-the-box ways to help them. Some are simply illustrative.

As mentioned earlier, the focus of much of our coaching experience has been in helping enterprise application software development teams. Enterprise application software is generally defined as software that enables organizations to run their businesses better. It is not intended just for individual usage. As such, it is expected to have a life cycle of up to 20 years or more in some cases, is deployed to thousands of users, can run on a variety of hardware and software platforms, can typically be enhanced via supported interfaces such as APIs, and generally is built with millions of lines of code. Examples include Facilities Management for global companies, Enterprise Content Management that protects intellectual property, and Business Process Management that guarantees audit-ready process compliance for regulated industries. Enterprise software obviously needs to operate continuously, needs to provide the ability to scale, must ensure that the business value offered is secure, and more. For these reasons, enterprise software development environments have tended to have heavier-weight processes as well as long-entrenched waterfall practices. Teams tend to be large and are often spread out geographically and functionally. However, we are convinced that if these principles, practices, and breakthroughs work in enterprise application software development, they can easily be applied to smaller development projects.

What Do You Have To Do?

For this book to be useful, teams have to be willing to "jump off the cliff" (so to speak) and give these breakthrough techniques a try. Many of the techniques can be tackled in a couple of weeks, but adopting one or more means removing other distractions and staying focused so that the techniques get the attention they require. Everyone on the team needs to have "skin in the game" and make a conscious effort to succeed. Such a mindset can serve the team well on its agile transformation journey.

Making agile stick is hard work. You may have to update your technologies, get rid of your project debt, be rigorous in your planning and execution, learn how to work as a team, listen to your stakeholders when they tell you what you may not want to hear, and keep the focus on getting better. But your efforts will succeed. We can generally tell when teams are doing well with their agile transformation because they are *having fun*.

What Benefits Can You Get from Reading This Book?

In this book, you can

- Learn techniques that will break typical waterfall response patterns learned over many years and which can also help with adopting a new agile way of thinking.
- Learn why agile recommends various practices and why they are key to being successful.
- See how to gain the real benefits that agile promises.
- Benefit from the authors' combined 12 years' experience at IBM® in coaching IBM enterprise software teams in agile.
- Benefit from the experiences of other teams who have adopted agile.
- Use a short questionnaire at the end of the book to assess whether your team is just "doing agile" or if you are actually "being agile."
- Add a useful, continually referenced agile book to your library.

Who Are We?

As with adopting agile, learning how to coach effectively requires years of experience and continuous improvement. Both Scott and I became agile coaches and have spent many hours discovering how to help teams get better. Just like agile adoption, coaching is a journey. Scott's years as an instructor pilot in the Air Force trained him to communicate techniques effectively, often requiring him to find different ways to communicate the same principle to people who learned and understood things differently. One of Scott's favorite sayings is, "Communicate, communicate, communicate!" This book has the same intention: to give you different ways to understand critical agile concepts so that they can be communicated to a wide spectrum of teams.

After leaving the Air Force in 1991, Scott joined IBM and has been a developer, Chief Programmer, Customer Support team lead, Development Operations manager, System Test manager, Quality Engineering manager, and had responsibility for the Quality Management System for all IBM Software Group—all prior to becoming an agile coach.

In addition to coaching agile teams, Leslie has been the senior development manager for several organizations in IBM making the transition to agile. Her efforts started with her heritage teams in FileNet® working on Enterprise Content Management and continued to Rational® working on the ClearCase® and ClearQuest® products, and then onto the Cloud and Smarter Infrastructure organization focusing on the Smarter Infrastructure products. She worked for several companies prior to joining IBM, including Boeing, Tandem, the Saros Corporation, and FileNet (acquired by IBM in 2006). Teams are often tasked with "adopting agile" without much management participation and, given her management background, her perspective is that successful adoption starts with leadership—and Scott is in complete agreement. We drive this point throughout the book.

As agile coaches, we enjoy the "I get it!" moments that people experience after they make a breakthrough in their thinking. This is the goal we have for you. And if you don't "get it" from reading this book, hopefully you'll "get it" from trying the breakthrough techniques. After you do get it, it feels good—and you will want to find yet more new ways to drive improvement. And that, in turn, is fun!

Join the Conversation

We encourage you to join the agile conversation on our blog: "Being Agile." You can find it at: https://www.ibm.com/developerworks/community/blogs/beingagile/?lang=en

Whole Teams

Being agile requires whole teams because the synergy derived from cross-disciplined and cross-component teams working together enables teams to be more productive than working in isolation.

By Leslie Ekas

Do any of these phrases sound familiar?

- "When are you going to get your problem solved?"
- "Oops, I forgot to copy John on the email that discussed our proposed solution."
- "The test team can't start working on this release yet, so we will have to start writing code without them."

These are phrases typical of teams that work in silos. If you regularly hear such comments from your team, you are likely not experiencing the benefits of whole teams. Whole teams are composed of people who work together to deliver a product.

The first time I saw the power of whole teams went something like this: While we were building a product, our entire team met together to discuss various challenges. One developer was working on a search interface, and innocently brought up a usability problem he was tackling. This search interface showed various related fields that the user could select. (Just to describe the scenario, think of one field being the state selection and another field being the city selection. The city selection contents would change based on which state the user selected.) The developer casually mentioned that if a user selected the state and city but then changed the state, he would receive an error dialog alerting him that the city was no longer valid. One of the testers instantly became indignant and complained that she hit this issue all the time and getting an error message would drive her crazy! If she had to close an error message every time she switched the state selection, she would despise the interface and the application. The meeting came to a halt in a stunned silence.

Luckily the whole team was in attendance and that included the user experience (UX) expert. He agreed that the error dialog was a poor choice and recommended using a visual warning that the user could open or ignore. This may not seem like a big deal, but the team had already used error dialogs in the code, so this was a change in the design pattern. But everyone liked it, and after they discussed it, it seemed like it should have been the obvious solution all along. In fact the idea was so well received that over time they updated the application to use it wherever possible.

What occurred to me while I listened was that, had this problem been raised after the entire interface was written and was in test, it would have been considered an enhancement request. As such, it would not likely have seen the light of day because it would have been too late to do anything but fix broken functionality—forget about making the application a little easier to use. The more code that is written before a good suggestion comes in, the harder it is to make a change because it affects more code and subsequently requires more testing. So the team experienced "just in time feedback," which allowed them to make the product better.

But what was so compelling is that the entire team was there. Without the whole team present and working together, this problem would have taken weeks to solve. Using email, we would likely have missed a few critical team members needed to "seal the deal." As it was, in a few hours a problem was solved, the customer got more value from the solution, and the team did not have to revisit the issue again. During the meeting, feedback was given fearlessly and feedback was taken constructively. For me, this was an early, albeit unintentional, demonstration of the power of whole teams.

Principles

What Is a Whole Team?

In the context of agile development, whole teams are teams that are both cross-component and cross-discipline teams that work together throughout a product life cycle. The whole team is responsible for the success of its work. By cross-discipline I mean a team that includes developers, testers, and user documentation professionals (writers). By cross-component I refer to teams that are responsible—not for just a single component out of a larger project—but which have the necessary expertise to work on all the affected components. The whole team concept goes beyond just team composition though: The whole team concept is a way of thinking and acting that must become the norm. In fact, until a team starts to be a true whole team, the team may experience limited success with agile and may feel continually stuck in a beginner's rut.

Being agile requires whole teams because the synergy derived from cross-disciplined and cross-component teams working together is more productive than when each discipline works in isolation and/or when components are developed in isolation. Whole teams succeed because they capitalize on the combined skills of each team member working together to accelerate their deliverables. Working cooperatively, they can leverage each other's insights, instincts, and responses to ongoing work throughout a project.

This chapter describes why whole teams experience better communication, productivity, and collective knowledge sharing than traditional silo'd teams. It makes a case for keeping teams intact as well as protecting them from interruption during a product release.[1]

1. Note that in some agile circles, the term "integrated teams" is used instead of "whole teams."

Why Are Whole Teams Hard to Create?

Traditional software development organizational structures have advocated for teams that specialize in technology and are grouped by a common discipline, for example, development, test, user documentation, and so on. The reasoning goes that teams composed of people with similar skills can help each other within their own domains. Furthermore, it is believed that teams that share a common discipline can be "time-sliced" across various projects as needed instead of focusing on one project at a time. This is the epitome of the "job-shop" mentality in which engineers just do their specific job and lose sight of the bigger picture. Unfortunately, optimizing the efficiency of a particular discipline almost always sub-optimizes the organization—a point that is often not well understood. Lean thinking in particular focuses on process throughput optimization to improve efficiency, versus individual throughput (described more in Chapter 3, "Queuing Theory").

The whole team approach advocates the idea of team members being "generalizing specialists" who have deep skills in specific disciplines, domains, and technologies but who can also work outside their area of expertise to help achieve the team's iteration goals. At first, teams shy away from this aspect of the whole team concept because they interpret it to mean that everyone on the team must do everything. In small, high-performing agile teams, this may be the case, but it gets more difficult as projects grow in size and encompass many technology domains. However, teams do not have to achieve the ideal level to become a whole team—but they should at least move in the direction of becoming "generalizing specialists."

Cross-Component Teams

Software composed of multiple architectural components is often built by separate teams that develop their respective components independently. There may be a database team, an application server team, a user interface team, and so forth. After the components are developed, the parts are put together to create the product as a whole and tested during an integration phase. Teams working on a single component find this a convenient way to work because they can easily capitalize on their common knowledge. However, the overall focus of the work becomes rather narrow, and it can be tempting to hand off responsibility for some component to a remote team, further isolating the various parts of an organization. Individual component teams are likely to work together only at the beginning of a project, during initial design, and again at the end of the development cycle when trying to integrate the components (perhaps for the first time).

Building components in isolation rarely produces the best product because the bigger picture is often lost. And although it may seem counterintuitive, building independent components in isolation is less productive than building cross-component functionality from the outset. One of the basic aspects of whole teams is that they include team members from across technology disciplines that are required to develop the software. These integrated teams work together from the beginning of the project and continue together throughout the life cycle of the project. One of the core enablers of teams working together this way is continuous integration, which enables products to be automatically built, tested, and deployed from the beginning of the project. This practice avoids the typical expensive integration problems that arise when large amounts of code get integrated for the first time.

The emphasis on cross-component team composition also facilitates the practices of evolutionary architecture and emergent design.[2] Whole teams, using these practices start with a minimal architecture that is "good enough" to enable them to build a "thin slice" of cross-architecture/ cross-component functionality in one of the earliest iterations. All the architectural details will not have been worked out yet, but the team can test the initial, basic architecture right away. This approach enables teams to validate their architecture early in the project and have greater confidence that it is a sound architecture—or adjust it as needed—which can be much easier now rather than later because the amount of work done up to this point is so small. Compare this with finding a major problem in the architecture late in a project when various components are integrated together for the first time.

Working together as a whole team iteratively on the architecture and design enables everyone on the team to understand the strengths and weakness of the software so that the team develops good instincts regarding any noted constraints. A whole team will also have a common history that enables the team to produce more consistent design patterns as more and more features are added. Furthermore, because this evolutionary approach enables real functionality to be manifested earlier, the team can demonstrate this functionality to its customers and get feedback earlier than was possible with waterfall's component-based development approach.

Cross-component, whole teams should be formed around epic stories or product features rather than technology. Agile teams, working together to build cross-component functionality from the beginning require that an end-to-end working environment be ready early in the project life cycle—that is, a continuous integration system that continually builds, validates, and deploys the product build. These are just a few of the items that need to be addressed for cross-component teams to function successfully in short iterations. Getting such an environment in place at the beginning of the project requires cross-component expertise, and this expertise can continue to be required as the project progresses and the environment requirements continue to grow along with the product.

Cross-Discipline Teams

Whole teams also include team members from each of the disciplines required to develop and successfully deliver the product. Teams should include developers, testers, and writers, and may also include a product manager, a build developer, a user interface designer, and so forth. It is important that teams have the collective skills to fill the required roles. Note, however, that a "person per role" is not required.

Teams organized by discipline often operate differently from cross-discipline teams. For instance, in waterfall, testing groups may wait until the design phase is complete before they develop a test plan, and testing itself doesn't typically begin until late in the cycle when a lot of

---

2. Note that we discuss evolutionary architecture and emergent design in Chapter 6, "Working Software," and Chapter 8, "Release Often" as well.

code has been written. Testers may even be prevented from joining the effort on the new release because they are finishing up leftover work from an earlier release. Getting to the point in which whole teams can begin work together on the first day of a project may take a significant amount of effort, and perhaps some behavioral changes as well. All available engineers should focus on completing any work that would prohibit them from starting together on the next release. This means getting the previous release out the door so that everyone can be available on Day 1 of the next project.

Why is it so important that a team actually start a release together? The goal for whole teams is to work together to produce a product, to learn together, and help each other get to "Done!" each iteration. With whole teams, no one gets credit for anything until the team has gotten to "Done!" Only then is any "credit" given for completing work, and it's *the team* that gets the credit. It's an all-for-one, one-for-all approach in which there's no "partial credit" and no "individual credit." For this to work, the team needs to start together so that coding, testing, user documentation, automation, defect fixing, code reviews, and so forth can all be accomplished as part of each iteration, beginning with the first one.

It is common to see the team members charged with system level testing joining an agile team well after the initial iterations have been completed. System level testing typically describes testing that covers scalability testing, failover testing, long-run testing, performance testing, and more. System testers tend to have a unique set of skills, so they tend to move from one project to another, always joining a project long after its start. When system testers actually do join a project, the rest of the team loses valuable time trying to get this set of contributors caught up and, more importantly, the project team misses the opportunity to have things such as scalability testing and performance testing executed early in the project when adjusting the code is much more manageable. If the system testers are not engaged early in the project, it is also harder for them to devise how best to test the software because much of the discussion and early decisions will not be known to them. Thus, system testers should be part of an agile whole team from the very beginning of a project.

One of the benefits of whole teams is that when the team discovers and solves problems together, every team member understands the context and history of the issues and resolutions. Together they gain a shared experience and build a knowledge foundation that will serve them throughout the entire project. As the team builds its working history, it improves its synergy, which allows the team to make decisions faster and even anticipate problems before they actually happen.

Cross-Geographical, Cross-Cultural, Large Teams

In enterprise application software projects, whole teams can consist of engineers from around the globe and from different cultures. Whole teams can work when team sizes are larger than the recommended 7 to 10 engineers. However, it should be no surprise that all the same principles still apply: These types of teams need to start a project together, plan their work together, and get to "Done!" each iteration together. The effort to create a whole team is even more critical in these situations but—we won't sugarcoat it—it is much harder.

The most difficult part of cross-geographical teams usually has to do with the need for daily communication. To establish trust and ensure rich communication channels, regular communication is an imperative. The communication needs to be open, the interaction needs to be constructive, and the focus needs to be on working together to succeed. There are a couple of ways to tackle the cross-geographical problem. The most successful way is for everyone to share a bit of the "pain." By this I mean that some team members may have to stay up late for calls with the other part of the team, or get up early, or perhaps even shift their schedules to align completely with the other part of the team. Teams can meet at different times throughout the week to "share the pain" of difficult meeting times. Some teams record their standups so that the team members separated by time-zones can understand what happened. There are many ways to make this communication successful, and teams should try a variety of mechanisms to determine what works best.

We know that this is not ideal but we encourage you to be creative, try different approaches, and keep experimenting until you find the right combination of changes that make it work for your team. However, please do not dismiss the need for regular communication (whether the team is local or geographically separated)—it's just *too important*.

There are a couple of positive benefits that cross-geographically organized teams can obtain: Teams that span time zones can coordinate work so that one part of the team can start where another part leaves off at the end of their day. In addition, teams that bring different cultural behaviors together can leverage the best from multiple working styles.

Stable, Dedicated, and Protected

Whole teams are more effective when they are committed to the project for the complete duration of the project. With this approach, teams should get new team members or lose team members only on an exceptional basis. Managers and other project leaders should do everything they can to protect teams from all interruptions so that the teams can get to "Done!" (which is very, very hard to do if management acts like a "fast-forward" button, immediately passing along every interruption to the team).

Although this probably sounds like common sense, it's not that common. Companies with multiple products typically juggle people between projects to align with changing schedules and revenue expectations. Engineers with particular knowledge or skills may get "time-shared" between various projects. People may get pulled from doing new development to manage a critical defect discovered at a customer site. And of course all teams are constantly asked to do more with less. Team churn ultimately slows down project progress. Furthermore, if team members slice their time between different projects, their lack of focus for any length of time can negatively affect their productivity and likely the quality of their work as well. The section "Maintain and Protect Dedicated Teams" discusses the evils of task-switching further, as does Chapter 4, "No Multitasking."

THE MYTHICAL MAN MONTH BY FRED BROOKS[3]

Fred Brooks is a former IBMer who came out against the idea of throwing additional bodies at projects that were running behind. In his classic work titled, *The Mythical Man Month*, he discusses his Brook's Law, which reads, "Adding manpower to a late software project makes it later." My corollary to his point is, when throwing bodies at a project that is running behind, "What one engineer can do in one week, two engineers can do in two weeks." ☺

Expecting team members to work on multiple projects may feel like an efficient use of personnel, but it is likely not delivering the best product in the most efficient way. "Protect the team"—this is a cornerstone principle of whole teams, thus management must have as a primary goal protecting the team. Protecting the team means that the team should be shielded from distractions to meet its project goals.

Rotating people between agile teams is a common practice in some organizations. An individual may have a particular expertise that makes him valuable to multiple teams. There are three primary problems with moving an expert around, however. First, if an expert is moved out of an agile team for an iteration, the work the expert would normally have contributed will not be picked up by the rest of the team, thus putting the team behind. Second, if an expert spends limited time on a project, he will not have the shared history enabling him to make well-informed decisions regarding his own contributions. For example, he will have to learn what technology has been developed so that he can determine what to test. This will demand valuable time from the rest of the team. Finally, it will be difficult for others to learn from the expert due to the limited time the expert has available by virtue of being pulled in multiple directions at once.

One development project that I managed included new features that required aggressive performance tuning. Our company had a skilled team to measure product performance and make tuning suggestions, but that team had little time for my project until late in the schedule. We decided to bring the performance testing work inside the scope of our team and get some of our team members skilled with the performance testing tools. This way we could test and tune early in the project as the features were developed. Educating the developers, creating the environments to test, and managing the results took extra time initially for the project. However, by doing this, we had performance information in one of the earliest iterations, and the data showed that we had problems. The team stopped further feature work until it understood and fixed the performance problems. This behavior continued throughout the project, and by the middle of the project, the team felt confident that it had discovered and fixed the most critical performance issues. Furthermore it concluded that had the problems been found later in the cycle, the root causes and the solutions would have been harder to identify. The actual fixes also would have

---

3. Brooks, Frederick P., *The Mythical Man Month*. Boston: Addison-Wesley, 1995: page 232. Print. This is a book that should be on every software engineer's shelf.

been difficult and time-consuming to implement. This is also an example of "stop the line" thinking, which we address more in-depth in Chapter 9, "Stop the Line."

High-performing agile teams have dedicated members and are protected by their management from interruptions and from constant changes in team membership.

Practices

Start with Whole Teams

Agile teams are whole teams. Whole teams are created at the beginning of a project and stay together throughout the project. Whole teams consist of everyone needed to complete the planned product deliverables.

Team members each have unique skills and expertise that they use to contribute to the overall effort, but they are also expected to cross outside of their skill boundaries when required to help the rest of the team reach the iteration goals. Teams new to agile often respond to this notion with anxiety. "We cannot afford to have developers test." "I cannot learn how to develop." "I am not a good writer." Team productivity will obviously increase if the entire team could do any of the tasks; however, this is not the situation for many teams. Getting to the point in which team members can contribute outside of their particular skill area takes time for most teams to achieve, and some teams never achieve the ideal given the size of their projects. Nevertheless, becoming a whole team requires team members who are willing to jump in and help in any way they can and learn new skills as they go. This might mean helping to set up computers, looking over someone's shoulder to help find bugs, writing draft documentation, and so forth. But it does not necessarily require that everyone on the team learn the most complex aspects of each job, such as kernel-level debugging, the use of automated testing tools, or the usage of unique product documentation tools.

Teams willing to adopt a whole team approach can experience productivity growth. Furthermore, team members willing to jump into unfamiliar tasks can expand their domain knowledge and skill sets and also gain satisfaction and job growth as a consequence. And of course, they are making themselves more valuable to the team.

Maintain and Protect Dedicated Teams

Unless you've adopted the practice of self-organizing teams, it's typically management's responsibility to assign team members to a project and then protect the team. It is to management's benefit to protect the team so that the team can get its work done and ultimately deliver the product with customer value and high quality. Protecting the team means preventing any interruptions to the work the team has committed to accomplishing in its current iteration. Furthermore, management must keep each team member focused on and committed to a single project so that team members can maximize their output.

In the real world, teams have to respond to short-term crises and shifting priorities. The easiest way to manage such challenges and continue to protect teams is to keep iterations short. And by short iterations, we mean 2 weeks maximum. It is easier to protect a team during a short iteration than a longer iteration. In fact, this is one of the many reasons iterations should be short. If a critical interruption arises, and the team is halfway through a 1- or 2-week iteration, the manager can make a better case for the team being allowed to complete its work and stay productive, rather than stopping the team and getting nothing "Done!" for the iteration. It can use its next iteration to manage the crisis because the elapsed time is relatively short. Conversely, if the iteration is as long as a month, it is easy for management to believe new work can be absorbed by the team by simply having the team "work a little harder" (which, when translated into reality, implies overtime).

Highly productive agile teams may even adopt a "no iteration" methodology based on a "pull" or a "continuous flow" model. In these scenarios the team is maintaining working software even more aggressively. As teams get better at working together as a whole team, they should consider trying these lean models.

When teams get used to getting to "Done!" in short iterations, and they reliably repeat the pattern, management has a new defensive strategy: It has the data to show that protecting the team from interruption results in higher productivity. Any situations that arise that require immediate attention are added to the top of the backlog and addressed the next iteration. This should remove the typical distractions that are less urgent than maintaining progress on the project. Shorter release cycles also help protect the team. When teams deliver "just enough" capability in a short release cycle, they can better respond to new priorities that would negatively impact longer release plans.

Whole teams can get to "Done!" better by learning how to work together leveraging their unique skills. Each team is unique and develops its own team dynamics because it is made of unique people who have their own combinations of gifts and skills. Changing the team make-up regularly by moving people around disrupts this pattern and hurts a team's long-term effectiveness and predictability. Short release cycles also help enable dedicated teams because it is easier to keep a team together for shorter time periods.

The Conversation

The most critical aspect to succeeding as a whole team is effective communication. Communication is best achieved by interacting, or rather, by having conversations. Agile's primary mechanisms for this necessary communication include release planning, the daily standup, iteration planning, customer demonstrations, and reflections. There are additional ways that encourage increased communication, such as making it a team rule to help each other remove blocking issues, adopting pair programming, and team creation of user stories. Whatever the mechanism, the goal is *the conversation*—live interaction. Conversation enables interaction while ideas are fresh. It also enables collective thinking, that is, one person's input inspires another's feedback.

Furthermore, timely discussion with all the right people contributing (or maybe even just listening), results in faster progress. Working together enables a team to stay informed.

Teams often use documentation to communicate anything that needs to be referenced. For instance, engineers have a tradition of documenting designs, but often they do not review their designs with their team because it is written down—anyone can pick it up and read it. However, even the best writers often struggle to convey their point in written form.[4] So why do we expect that the written document will succeed in socializing the critical points that need to be conveyed? Many have heard the familiar quote from Blaise Pascal that goes like this, "I have made this letter longer than usual, only because I have not had time to make it shorter." Constructing a message that is easy to understand takes time. Documentation is useful and should not be abandoned, but teams need to use live discussions to make sure that they are communicating and that the information is understood.

Email threads often result in failed communication. After you send an email explaining a problem to a coworker, do you think your job is done? Have you ever received a long email thread with a message from the sender saying, "How do you want to handle this?" Do you have emails sitting in your inbox that have been there more than a week? Email is a great storage repository for unfinished business. Find a way to get critical issues out of email and get them handled.

Scott has a great saying, "If a picture is worth a thousand words, then a conversation is worth a thousand emails." Live discussions are necessary to get work completed in a timely fasion. Improving the communication at the daily standup is a great place to start. But it is hard to enable the teaming on work if you do not share enough descriptive information in the standup. Common—but frustrating—daily standup meeting comments we have heard are, "I am doing the same thing that I did yesterday," "I am still testing," and so on. This input is practically useless. The reason that we go through the typical standup protocol, "What I did since the last standup meeting," "What I am going to do next," and "What blocking issues do I have?" is to provide the opportunity to communicate about our work and help each other.

The same conclusions apply to teams that cross geographies and cultures. Everything that is important for local teams is also critical for cross-geographical teams, but communication alone may determine success or failure.

To succeed in agile, and even in your career, learn to communicate and learn to communicate well. Engage in live discussions, be willing to listen to feedback, be informative—but to the point—in your delivery, and most of all, keep trying to communicate better.

---

4. To drive this point home, Scott and I would much rather be having a live conversation with you about the topics covered in this book rather than simply having you read this book. We could cover the material in less time than it would take you to read the book and in a more comprehensive way. Additionally, you'd have the opportunity to ask questions of us and gain additional clarifications that you obviously aren't able to do by just reading the book.

Share the Same Truth

For any team to succeed, sharing the same priorities and the same information is critical because each team member must continually make decisions. The basis for decision making for the team has to be rooted in the same priorities using all the information available. A prioritized backlog of work provides a mechanism to ensure team synchronicity, and good tooling can provide the mechanism for sharing the same information.

One of the most significant tools for keeping teams coordinated is a team dashboard or an information radiator. Good dashboard products provide a flexible way to create widgets that can integrate live data from external tools (such as separate source code management systems, separate test case repositories, separate build environments, and so on). Providing a single view of commonly viewed data gives teams a real-time view of the same "truth," such as how many defects are active, where the latest build is deployed, what delta functionality is in the latest build, and how far along the team is on this iteration's user stories. Several years ago, a team that I was managing—a large team that spanned the globe—started to use such a tool to coordinate our work. We quit using most other mechanisms of reporting information because our online dashboard solution encompassed all aspects of the project and did so in real time. Because the data that was displayed was live data, it was never out of date.

This dashboard capability moved our large team a lot closer to succeeding as a whole team. The Agile Manifesto calls for interaction over tools and processes, but do not discount the power of excellent tooling to help enable necessary team interaction and communication.

No Partial Credit

Whole teams get credit for the work they complete each iteration. Individuals on the team do not get partial credit for the work they accomplish during the iteration. Team members may give each other "high fives" for finishing work as they go, but agile works when teams embody the whole team spirit and succeed or fail together.

Encourage your team to avoid this kind of thinking: "I have my code written and now it's up to the testers to finish testing while I move on to something else." Encourage them to think instead about how to help the testers finish their work so that the team can move on together. Staying tightly coordinated to finish work enables teams to be more productive and achieve working software every iteration. The notion of "no partial credit" drives this point home. Working software is the team's measure of progress. Having working software every iteration requires coordinated work from the whole team. They all get credit for achieving the goal.

This whole team "full credit and no partial credit" concept flies in the face of most companies' Human Resource (HR) practice of reviewing and rewarding individuals for their accomplishments. To enable whole teams to succeed in such an HR environment, managers have to strike a balance between encouraging individuals to grow their own skills and encouraging individuals to be successful team players who encourage and help each other. Many of the best sports teams have demonstrated repeatedly that teams that work well together make it to the championships. Teams dominated by one or two individuals ultimately lose because the burden is too great for just one player or two players. Whole teams leverage the valuable skills of all the players.

Team members need to set their goals around personal growth areas as well as team growth areas. These goals can naturally work together. To get to "Done!" as a team, each person should contribute to the effort using his strongest skills. But to make the team better, team members need to learn new skills so that they can help each other. When team members can help each other, they can better maintain working software, which is *the* measure of progress.

Offer Help

One critical aspect of whole team success is offering help. Each team member should offer to help other team members whenever needed. This may seem obvious, but it is contrary to mandates commonly practiced by development teams. Typically, individuals are instructed to get their own work completed, grow their own skills, and achieve individual feats to differentiate themselves from their peers. However, this focus on the individual has to be paired with the practice of individuals extending their time and skills to help others on the team. Teams that emerge from a traditional development culture may be unaware that their culture is not transforming successfully. They need to pay close attention to warning signs that they might be in trouble. For instance, *silence* should be painful if no one offers to help when a blocking issue is raised during a standup meeting. A whole team culture requires that team members get into the habit of offering help, even if they have to learn something new.

Every team has a go-to person. People usually figure out who it is and start to rely on her. The go-to person knows what the team is doing, how the code works, what the biggest issue is right now, and so forth. If that go-to person does not know the needed information, she will often start looking for it before you even finish asking. Agile's emphasis on whole teams working together should inspire a whole team of go-to people. Go-to people are not afraid to stretch beyond their job descriptions; in fact they enjoy learning and helping teams to work together well. You may be afraid that you do not have the personality for this, but those that try tend to experience additional job satisfaction, which improves their contributions significantly.

Metrics

To validate that you have a whole team, track the team membership each iteration, beginning with the first iteration, and review it regularly. Confirm that the whole team starts together and finishes together. Yes, this may seem like a relatively simple (or even simplistic) thing to track, but if the goal is to have stable, dedicated teams, then having an indicator immediately available to confirm that this happens can be a big incentive to actually having stable, dedicated teams—especially if you need to convince others in the organization that problems with team stability are real.

As another simple metric, make a rough estimate for the time required to coordinate information across the team at the beginning of a release. Find a mechanism to share the same truth with the entire team. Use a dashboard, a common whiteboard, a wiki, an information radiator, or whatever works. Use that mechanism as a way to share information during the daily standup.

Re-evaluate the time required to coordinate information across the team at the end of the several iterations. Compare the results. If significant progress was not made, or rather the time required for coordination did not decrease, try a new mechanism.

Breakthrough

Early in my experience with agile, a development team that I was managing was lucky enough to make a breakthrough with bullpens that transformed its behavior almost immediately. In fact, this breakthrough was so profound for the team that it changed my reflexive, waterfall-oriented thinking permanently. The team I was managing was having communication problems. A project consultant, Stan Rifkin, suggested we try bullpens to fix these challenges.

But let me back up and describe how we got to this recommendation. The first development team I managed that adopted agile got all the basics down quickly. Our daily standups became essential; we defined the work we planned to complete each iteration; and we demonstrated new functionality to our customers almost weekly. Despite our early success with many of the typical agile techniques, we were not working well as a whole team. Several developers would talk to each other in the hall, decide on a new development strategy, and then forget to tell the testers. An email discussing changes to how the product could be customized would go out to a part of the team, but the writers would be left off the email thread. Testers complained among themselves about the usability problems but did not bring them to the rest of the team. Tempers were mounting and disgruntled team members visited me saying, "He said this; she said that."

I took a piece of advice Mary Poppendieck gave me during a conversation about "stop the line" thinking and identified just one problem to fix during each iteration. If we failed to find a solution to the problem, then we worked on the same problem the next iteration, and the next, and so on, until it was fixed. The team agreed that it was not a whole team. We tried everything we could think of but nothing worked. Over time the team was feeling demoralized, members were banding together to place blame, and the whole agile effort was losing ground.

Luckily we got consulting help from Stan Rifkin, a consultant with 40 years' experience in data processing, management consulting, software engineering, and computer science. We reviewed our practices and issues with him. He suggested that we try bullpens. He explained that bullpens were multihour working meetings with the emphasis on *working*. Instead of meeting to discuss status, or to do planning, teams do real work together. Here are the rules for bullpens:

- Everyone on the agile team MUST attend and pay attention.
- Do real work together.

At first we struggled with what this actually meant. Do we write code together, do we test together, do we review documents together? In the end, it did not matter as long as we worked together and solved problems.

Interestingly enough, the majority of the team had a similar response to the suggestion, "No way!" (although a few people said, "Sounds great, let's try it"). After listening to all the reasons we should not do it for more time than I can stand to remember, I pulled management rank and said, "We will try it beginning tomorrow." The team grumbled off and planned for their first 2-hour bullpen.

The team floundered a bit, wondering how to start, but a tester broke the silence by talking about a set of tests that were failing. That quickly led to discussions on how the tests were run, disagreements about the expected behavior, and candid feedback about how the functionality could be more usable. With that, the team was off and running.

The first bullpen worked well. Problems were solved in real time, and the entire team learned what was going on at the same time. The team proceeded to schedule multiple bullpens weekly. Because the entire team was not in the same room, let alone the same country, we had to do this over the phone and with an emeeting—sort of "virtually sitting next to each other." Adopting bullpens had the added benefit that when the team was not in a bullpen, it could get more focused time to work because most of the issues requiring cross-team communication had already been addressed.

Bullpens became so successful that the team started to use them for a variety of purposes. They had bullpens to jointly review code, discuss and solve difficult technology problems, code bash as a team, and more. We observed these positive outcomes: First, the team became a whole team. Accusations ceased and productivity increased. Second, the amount of email in my inbox dropped in size significantly. The team solved problems in real time with the whole team involved, so no additional communication was required.

Small agile teams that work in the same room usually develop a bullpen behavior simply based on their proximity. These may be called team rooms. Teams not residing in the same location can get similar value from bullpens. One advantage of bullpens over team rooms is that with bullpens, the rule is that everyone must attend, and it also leaves nonbullpen time to get focused work done that is less likely to be interrupted.

The story at the beginning of this chapter about the user interface design point that the tester disliked resulted from one of the first bullpens that I attended. The success of the meeting was stunning to everyone in the meeting. It forever changed our team dynamics and we were hooked.

When a team becomes a *whole team*, the team starts to think in a more agile way. When teams share the ownership of problems and their resolution, they can move faster together, leveraging everyone's collective strengths. Most whole teams have more fun working this way and certainly experience higher productivity.

Summary

Being agile requires whole teams because the synergy derived from cross-disciplined and cross-component teams working together enables teams to be more productive than working in isolation.

- Whole teams accelerate delivery and increase team capacity by working closely together to leverage each other's unique skills.

- Agile advocates the idea of "generalizing specialists" who can work outside their regular domains when required to achieve iteration goals.
- Whole teams work across the architecture stack to deliver end-to-end functionality from the beginning of the project and develop a common history so that consistent design patterns emerge.
- Whole teams start the project together; they get to "Done!" each iteration together; and they succeed or fail together. Whole teams may span the globe and cross cultures.
- Management must protect its teams from interruptions to enable them to deliver value to customers sooner.
- Regular, open, and constructive communication is critical to whole team success.
- Dashboards or information radiators enable teams to share the "same truth."
- Aspire to be a go-to team member.
- Bullpens are a mechanism that breaks teams out of silo'd behaviors and enables them to become whole teams. The basic rules of bullpens are 1. Everyone on the agile team MUST attend and pay attention and 2. Do real work together.

Active Stakeholder Interaction

Being agile requires active stakeholder interaction because only your stakeholders can confirm that what you create actually meets their needs.

By Scott Will

Many years ago, one of the first IBM teams to adopt agile started doing regular demonstrations of completed user stories to its customers at the end of each iteration. After the fourth iteration or so, a customer asked a question that wound up significantly changing the direction of the release. The gist of the question was, "When is the accounting and chargeback control feature going to be implemented?" Several other customers on the call also chimed in and wanted to know as well. It turned out that particular feature was not in the plan for the release, and the IBM team told the customers as much. At that point, the customers stated that the feature was definitely needed and all the other planned features wouldn't compensate for the lack of that particular feature. It was not until the customers actually started seeing the implementation of the planned features (via demonstrations) that they realized they needed the accounting and chargeback control feature.

Because that IBM team had started adopting agile, they could immediately begin working on implementing the requested feature. (Note that in adopting agile we recommend teams work on one feature at a time, complete it, and then move on to the next one. Because this team did not have other, partially complete features in progress, it could immediately begin work on this new feature.) At the end of the next iteration, the team demonstrated some initial progress on the requested feature—and the customers were just amazed! This was the first time they had seen an IBM team respond so quickly to a request—and it also solidified in their minds how important it was that they were providing feedback to the team *during* the release (instead of *after* the product had gone out the door as had been typical in the past with the team's waterfall releases).[1]

---

1. Keep in mind that if a new requirement is added during the middle of a release, that other items will be pushed lower on the backlog, meaning those items may not be completed in the current release and/or the release date will have to be moved out to accommodate the additional work.

The story has an even happier ending. As was relayed to me, the release made its *entire first year's* forecast revenue the day after it was released. The customers who actively participated during the release by attending demonstrations and providing feedback *all* bought the product right after it was made available—they *knew* what they were getting because they had seen it undergo development and also had the opportunity to "put their fingerprints on it."

Such an example should provide plenty of motivation for teams to ensure that they adopt active stakeholder interaction as part of their overall agile adoption. Unfortunately, not many teams are as aggressive as they need to be about adopting this aspect of agile.

Principles

What Is Active Stakeholder Interaction?

Just an opening comment: We tend to use the term *stakeholder* interchangeably with *customer* because the bulk of a team's stakeholders will likely be customers. We'll discuss this more later, but we want to let you know this upfront so that there's no confusion as you read this chapter.

Active stakeholder interaction refers to the practice of engaging your product's stakeholders in reviewing the product as it is being developed and allowing them to provide timely feedback. Traditionally, software development starts with active stakeholder engagement in defining the product requirements. In many cases, teams create a "requirements contract" with their customers before the project begins to ensure that they build the right product for their customers. What has been gleaned from many years of following this plan-driven approach, however, is that customers often envision a solution to their problems, but after they see the solution, it turns out to be not quite what they wanted nor envisioned. And in waterfall projects, when customers see the functionality for the first time and provide feedback, it's usually too late to make any significant changes to the current release.

The issue arises not because the customer was "wrong" about what was needed, but because it's often hard to envision how a planned solution will actually work. In many cases, a customer specifies a particular approach to solve a problem. The customer might even describe exactly how he wants the solution to look and behave. And the team might deliver exactly what the customer specified. However, when the customer tries the resulting product in a real-life scenario, only then does the customer figure out that it does not work as well as expected. For an off-the-wall example of how this happens in real life, I recently replaced a faucet in my house and decided to check out the Internet for some help on how to do it before I started. (My forte is woodworking, not plumbing, but I'm always game to try something new.) The video I watched talked about the need for a faucet wrench, and because I was fresh out of faucet wrenches around the house, I went down to my local home improvement store and bought one. When I started working on replacing the faucet, the faucet wrench did not work as expected because my faucet was of a different design than the one in the video I watched. I had great visions of how easy the faucet wrench would make the job of swapping out the faucet, but then I was faced with reality—and the faucet wrench didn't help at all. So, I just wound up using (or perhaps "misusing") some channel-lock pliers to loosen the old faucet and tighten the new one.

Back to software—by the time a solution is created, many of the factors influencing the original design have likely changed. For instance, the development team may discover that the technology used to create the solution does not work as had been expected, so adjustments had to be made that changed the resulting product behavior. The manifestation of the problem at the customer site may change over time, as well as other factors in its environment.

For all these reasons, it is critical to have active stakeholder interaction, which means that the stakeholders need to be actively involved during the development process and provide feedback about how the solution should evolve. This is one of the most essential reasons for agile's success: It provides the flexibility that enables changes to be made easily based on both evolving circumstances and customer feedback.

Why Can It Be Hard to Get Active Stakeholder Interaction?

Why is it that many teams adopting agile do not pursue more aggressive stakeholder interaction? It revolves around three primary issues: isolation on the part of development organizations, over-reliance on the old waterfall practice of "Betas," and concerns over intellectual property rights.

Isolation

Perhaps a subtle, but nonetheless real inhibitor to pursuing active stakeholder interaction is the mistaken belief that development organizations truly understand what customers want: "We know what customers want; they told us!" "We talked to customers during initial project planning, and they were all in agreement that this is *exactly* what they want!" Well, as the opening story demonstrates, customers' minds can change, especially when they begin to see the implementation of requested features. And the longer the release cycles are, the more likely it is that your customers' needs and priorities will evolve. Staying isolated from your customers for long periods of time during a release (because you think you already know what they want) can be quite detrimental, especially in such a highly dynamic and competitive industry as ours.

In one, unfortunately, negative example of this, a team that we know of moved some of their planned work aside to handle a new request from a big (read: *important*) customer. The team was told that the customer "had to have the feature *this year!*" The team scrambled to get the work done. When it delivered the capability many months later, the customer basically said, "Thanks, but we don't need that right now." Say what...? No one on the team had stayed in touch with the customer. Even now it's unclear whether the customer will ever roll out the new feature.

A slight variation of the isolation problem occurs when the team does not think it has accomplished enough to conduct a demonstration at the end of an iteration. The thinking goes something like this: "Why bother having a demonstration? Customers will think we haven't done much at all." The regular demonstrations enable the team to stay closely coordinated with their stakeholders so that they get timely feedback and can discuss any issues they tackled to make the functionality work. Customers get the chance to hear some of the "triumphs" and the "heartbreaks" that teams go through when working on a project. Teams can also use a demonstration as an opportunity to ask questions of customers, especially questions that relate to functionality that the team plans to start working on next. Some of these discussions can be quite useful because they can provide additional insights from customers that would otherwise have gone unstated. So, even if you don't have that much functionality to demonstrate (and there will be times when this does happen), you can still engage customers in thoughtful discussions to gain a deeper understanding of their perspectives and environments, and how your solution can be better tailored to meet their needs. And remember, if customers do not get enough value from regular meetings, they will let you know!

Betas

Beta programs have been part of waterfall projects for years (especially at the enterprise software level). Traditional Beta releases often occur just prior to the product's scheduled ship date and this is because, in waterfall, it is not until late in the project that the development organization typically has anything available that is remotely usable by a customer. Betas do serve a good purpose for waterfall projects, and they are also useful to agile teams, but the inherent problem with traditional Betas can readily be seen: Betas occur quite late in the project, and if they are the only means of obtaining customer feedback, and if there are major issues that customers uncover during a Beta, the likelihood that those issues can be addressed before the scheduled release date is quite small. Thus, feedback that customers provide via Beta programs is often not acted on until a subsequent release (which is bad for the customers). In addition, waiting to act on substantive feedback until a later release ensures that it is much more difficult to make changes (which is bad for the development team).

Many agile teams move away from traditional Betas and adopt the practice of providing regular *code drops* (sometimes called *Alphas*). Regular code drops (in whatever form) enable customers to get their hands on the software and potentially try it in their unique environments before a product is formally released. This practice not only provides a useful check on quality but also, more importantly, customers can confirm that the solutions provided solve their problems.

Code drops are quite useful to agile teams, but they should not be considered a replacement for demonstrations. Both serve useful and different purposes. Demonstrations encourage an active discussion as part of the process, and getting customer reactions is critical. Code drops enable customers to actually try the software, which may produce a different set of reactions. If your customers take regular code drops, the team should work with such customers to meet regularly and get their feedback so that both the team and the customer are committed to the process, and so the feedback can be timely enough to drive any necessary changes.

Intellectual Property Concerns

IBM has a long history of being a leader regarding intellectual property. (Nearly $1 billion a year in revenue is generated each year just from IBM's patent portfolio.) So it is no surprise that teams are concerned about demonstrating new features that may disclose recent innovations.[2] Most of the time, those concerns can be mitigated through judicious use of Non-Disclosure Agreements, where customers agree to not disclose anything they have seen in order to participate in the active stakeholder engagement process. But, of course, this requires some additional effort, both in engaging your corporate legal team and in discussions with your customers. If your organization isn't concerned with intellectual property rights, this may not be as much of an issue for you as it is for others; but if it is a concern, realize that there are ways to address it. And effort associated with executing Non-Disclosure Agreements is well worth it—active stakeholder engagement is that important!

Stakeholder Interaction Is Not a New Idea

The best way to ensure you understand your customers' needs and wants is to have on-going interaction with them—and this idea is not new. The principle of stakeholder interaction is formalized in the rules of Extreme Programming (commonly referred to as XP):

THE CUSTOMER IS ALWAYS AVAILABLE

One of the few requirements of extreme programming (XP) is to have the customer available, not only to help the development team, but also to be a part of it as well. All phases of an XP project require communication with the customer, preferably face to face, on-site.[3]

There's no doubt that having a customer on-site all day, every day, throughout the development cycle is optimal (as XP advocates). However, in the world Leslie and I live in, our company primarily builds enterprise application software—and our products can have thousands of customers. There's just no way that the XP model can work for us (nor for you if you face similar circumstances). However, this reality does not lessen the need for stakeholder interaction—it just changes the way we go about it.[4]

Stakeholder Interaction Is Not Optional

Do we really need to say any more on this point? Hopefully no! However, we will point out that the principles of the Agile Manifesto are clear regarding focus on customer's needs: "Our highest priority is to satisfy the customer...," and "...Agile processes harness change for the customer's

---

2. At IBM we've created an expedited patent process that can take a patent disclosure from initial submission to filing with the U.S. Patent and Trademark Office in as little as 2 weeks. If your organization is serious about protecting its intellectual property, you should discuss how agile changes the process for patent protection with your corporate legal office.

3. http://www.extremeprogramming.org/rules/customer.html

4. Note that the Product Owner role in agile teams takes on even more importance in this environment.

competitive advantage."[5] Engaging regularly, actively, and directly with customers is the best way to ensure they're satisfied and that they're gaining the benefits your product is ostensibly designed to provide. Customers get to see the solutions to their problems as they are developed and provide valuable feedback.

Do What's Needed—And No More

"Don't build a limousine if all your customer wants is a bicycle!" This is a refrain I use over and over *and over* with teams I work with. We engineers love our own ideas about how to "improve" something, and these ideas often make it into the product. However, quite frequently, many of these "really neat ideas" wind up being just a waste. Do your customers use all those additional things that were put into the product? Do they even *want* all that additional functionality? Maybe you think it's cool, or that it's really needed, but do they? Perhaps this explains why, in a Standish Group survey, 64 percent of a typical software product's features were *rarely or never used.*[6]

Most of you will recognize the name of Jeff Sutherland. Jeff was one of the signers of the Agile Manifesto and he, too, emphasizes this point with a rather pithy quote:

> Every line of code costs money to write and more money to support. It is better for the developers to be surfing than writing code that won't be needed. If they write code that ultimately is not used, I will be paying for that code for the life of the system, which is typically longer than my professional life. If they went surfing, they would have fun, and I would have a less expensive system and fewer headaches to maintain.[7]

Given this quote, Jeff's participation in the creation of the Agile Manifesto probably helps explain how another one of the principles of the Agile Manifesto came to be: "Simplicity—the art of maximizing the amount of work *not* done—is essential" [emphasis added].[8]

I'll also put in a plug here for Mary Poppendieck's comments on the "concurrent engineering" approach versus the "plan-up-front engineering" approach. (The latter is the approach most commonly used in waterfall and which many agile teams still try to use.) Mary writes:

> A management-as-planning/adherence approach also tends to amplify, not reduce, scope-creep. In many software development projects, a majority of the features are seldom or never used. Part of the reason for this is that asking clients at the beginning of a project what features they want, and then preventing them from changing their minds later, *creates strong incentives to increase the number of features*

5. See the first and second principles at: http://agilemanifesto.org/principles.html
6. Source: Standish Group, *CHAOS Chronicles v3.0.* Referenced in: http://www.agile-itea.org/public/papers/OLIO_dooms.pdf
7. http://jeffsutherland.com/2003_03_01_archive.html
8. http://agilemanifesto.org/principles.html

requested, just in case they are needed. While limiting scope usually provides the best opportunity for reducing software development costs, fixing scope early and controlling it rigidly tends to expand, not reduce scope.[9] [emphasis added]

Replacing sequential (plan-up-front) engineering with concurrent (plan-as-you-go) engineering has been credited with reducing product development time by 30–70%, engineering changes by 65–90%, and time to market by 20–90%, while improving quality by 200–600%, and productivity by 20–110%.[10]

Finally, you should always ask, "Will adding these additional 'improvements' make the product more complex?" and "Will they result in a slipped ship-date?" Doing more than is needed is fraught with negatives, and one of the best ways to guard against it is to have crystal clear ideas of exactly what *is* needed. We believe (and we're obviously not alone) the only way to ensure that you do only what's needed—*and no more*—is to have active, on-going engagement with your stakeholders throughout a release.

Practices

Identifying Stakeholders

To begin with, we really like the way that Carl Kessler and John Sweitzer identified different categories of stakeholders in their book, *Outside-in Software Development.*[11] In the book they list four categories of stakeholders:

- **Insiders:** "These are members of the whole development team, or of the firm you work for. The insider stakeholders group includes your business, marketing, and sales teams."[12]

- **Partners:** "Partner stakeholders might be internal to the business, in which case they are usually the IT operations folks. Or they may be external business partners, who provide functions such as outsourcing, application hosting, or application development."[13]

- **End Users:** "These folks use your product, and their needs are generally to more effectively and efficiently get their tasks done."[14]

- **Principals:** "The principals are the business decision makers who ultimately buy your product or decide to put it into use. The principals, however, seldom get their hands dirty installing, configuring, deploying, or supporting your software product."[15]

9. http://www.leanessays.com/2003/01/lessons-from-planned-economies.html [used with permission]
10. Ibid.
11. Kessler, Carl and Sweitzer, John. *Outside-in Software Development.* Upper Saddle River. IBM Press, 2008. Print.
12. Ibid., p.17.
13. Ibid., p.16.
14. Ibid., p.16.
15. Ibid., p.16.

These categories are helpful in thinking about the different types and categories of customers you should consider when building your products. In addition, we also encourage teams to think in terms of their "market segments" when creating a product. Are you planning on selling your product to educational institutions? If so, at the primary level or to universities? What about the banking and insurance industry? Perhaps the Small- and Medium-sized Business market (SMB)? Perhaps all these market segments and more? The point we're making is that the better you understand your potential customer base, the better you'll understand who your stakeholders are and what they need; thus you'll be much more likely to address those needs correctly.[16] This also means that you should include potential customers as part of your stakeholder group. Do not limit your view of stakeholders to current customers, especially if you want to break into a new market segment. Get active stakeholders from new, targeted market segments as well.

The stakeholder category of "principal" may be new to you. You may have never even thought about the goals of the person responsible for buying your product. The tendency is to focus on the folks who use your products on a day-to-day basis. However, this next story makes it clear why considering the goals of principals is *very* important.

Years ago (before agile was cool) I was brought in to help manage part of an effort to create a new release of a product we had acquired when IBM bought another company. The original product had a lot of good technology, but most of the developers were systems engineers and few had any real user experience (UX) expertise. So, after the acquisition was complete, we talked with a number of customers and found that they weren't happy with the user interface (which was no surprise given the original lack of UX expertise). Given this feedback, our whole next release was dedicated to improving the user interface. We talked to numerous customers about what they liked, what they didn't like, what changes they wanted to see, and so forth. Prior to shipping the product with the updated interface, we conducted an extensive Beta program and got a lot of good feedback and a lot of positive comments. Life was good—or so we thought.

One of our senior executives went to visit the CIO of one of our major customers. During the conversation, our executive described all the hard work that had gone into the newly released version of this particular product and how well it had been received during the Beta. Unfortunately, the CIO was not overly impressed. When asked why, the CIO explained that he didn't want to buy our product to make the lives of his 12 operations-center personnel easier, he wanted to *replace* them with a "lights-out" product—something that could be put in a closet and automatically handle the work that the operations-center personnel were currently doing. In this case, the CIO was a **principal**—and we had not conferred with any principals prior to embarking on our huge effort to improve the user interface. All the customers we had talked to were

---

16. Note that if you already have some sort of a customer-interaction program in place (they go by various names such as "Design Partner Program," "Customer Action Councils," "Customer Involvement Programs," and so on), these are excellent places to begin. However, we'd still encourage you to think through the categories of stakeholders previously mentioned, as well as the different market segments you've identified, and ensure you talk to customers across the spectrum, not just those involved in your current interaction, in case they are not a good representation of the entire spectrum of customers you have.

end users. Had we understood the various stakeholder categories, and ensured we talked with representatives of each category prior to starting the new release, the release would likely have been drastically different.

Review Epics with Stakeholders

In many parts of the agile world, stakeholders are the ones who are primarily responsible for writing epics[17] and user stories. However, in the enterprise application development world, with large numbers of customers for each product, this model doesn't work. So what we suggest to our teams is that sales, marketing, product management, and even executives bring to the table their understanding of the "big features" that customers want. We then have a small group of folks from the team (generally the product owner, product architect, lead developer, lead tester, and lead writer) create epics out of the desired features. After they do this, we suggest that the epics be reviewed with a representative set of customers (whether 1-on-1 or in a group setting is up to the team to decide). The customers can either confirm that the epics capture the goals and expected business value—or not. If not, updates are made. Once there's agreement on the epics, the rest of the team is brought into the mix, and the epics are taken through the process of being broken down into iteration-sized user stories. The key point here is that epics are reviewed with an appropriate set of customers before the whole team spends any significant effort in breaking down the epics into the resultant, iteration-sized user stories.

Set Expectations

When you contact your stakeholders and ask that they participate with you during the development of your next project, they may not have a good understanding of how best to interact with you, especially because it will be different than what they are used to if they have only participated in Beta programs in the past. This means that setting expectations with your stakeholders is a necessary step. First, they need to understand that their participation will look quite different—no longer will you "disappear" for 6 months, or 9 months, or a year and then suddenly pop up, announce a Beta program, and expect them to drop everything and participate.

Second, they do not need to have test environments set up to install, configure, and deploy the product. You demonstrate completed user stories to them, so they not only understand the purpose of the functionality created, but they also get to see how that functionality serves the stated purpose. For those customers who have never been interested in participating in comprehensive Alphas and Betas, after they see that they can get significant benefit from attending

---

17. An "epic" is simply a product "theme," or "use case," "major feature," or "scenario" (in other words, whatever term you use to describe your "big-ticket" features) that is converted into the typical user story format: As a <role> I want to achieve some <goal> so that I can gain some <business value>. Epics, by definition, are too big to fit into an iteration; however, they are the starting point from which iteration-sized user stories are derived. When teaching about user stories, I use the imagery of an epic being the equivalent of a big piece of granite, and the individual, iteration-sized user stories as being smaller chunks taken out of the initial (large) piece of granite.

end-of-iteration demonstrations, chances are they'll be much more willing to participate in a regular demonstration program.

Note: If your customers *do* want to get code drops at the end of each iteration, run some scenarios in their own environments and provide feedback to your team, that would be fantastic! And if your customers are interested in participating in formal Alpha and Beta programs, that's also a great thing! We certainly don't want to dissuade you from allowing customers to put your code through its paces in their environments. In addition, if you have customers that want to "get their hands on your code," but the size of the project is too big for most customers to want to set up a Beta environment, you can consider hosting your application on an internal environment in your company and granting external access to your customers so that they can work with your code in a live setting and provide feedback to you. There are other variations to this approach, but hopefully this is enough to get you thinking about additional ways to actively engage your stakeholders.

Finally, you can tell your stakeholders that their active participation can help ensure that you build only what they actually need. You should certainly be motivated to build only the absolute minimum functionality necessary, but your customers should also understand that it's in *their* best interests for you to do so as well. Building the minimum can result in faster releases, meaning customers get relief for various problems and get to use new functionality that much faster. In addition, the product will likely be less complex if you build only the minimum, which can also benefit the customers in overall learning-curve costs and in maintenance costs. And this leads to the next practice: Encourage stakeholders to have "skin in the game."

Stakeholders Should Have *Skin in the Game*

Any customer requesting a new feature will likely tell you that the solution is needed urgently. However, we see teams that deliver capability that is not rolled out at their customer sites for months or, in worst-case scenarios, years. Delivering value that satisfies a customer need is a two-way street and, if customers are gaining real benefits by being part of the process, they should be willing to put some skin in the game. Find out how and when customers plan to roll out your new release. If customers tell you that they plan to do so at some later date, then you have negotiating room to move their requested functionality down on the rank-ordering of user stories. This also allows you to talk to customers to discover what may be delaying them in rolling out your software, and then perhaps you can help them get those problems solved.

Part of setting expectations with your customers is that, if they're telling you something is urgent, they need to commit to rolling out the software quickly. Do not accept "No" as an answer. This is where product teams get timid and, as a consequence, they do not learn much. Leslie once had a customer in Europe claim that her team did not test a new release on a new version of an operating system well enough to discover several issues that they found. Her team actually did test it quite thoroughly, but the customer's environment was so unique that her team couldn't possibly have included all the subtleties of the customer's environment in their test environment. They made an agreement with the customer to give them an early drop of the final code, one that the customer committed to testing on a short timeline. Her team told them they would respond to issues fast, and after those were resolved, they would ship the product. Getting the customer involved, and having the customer commit to work with her team, solved the problem satisfactorily for all.

If customers tell you they cannot deploy the release until they have tested it for, say, 3 months, learn about their tests and see if there is a way that you can do some residency testing with them, or find some other technique to alleviate that issue. If they say they cannot deploy the new solution because of internal problems, try to understand what those are and determine if there is anything that can be done from a product point of view to resolve their issues.

Make Stakeholder Interaction Compelling for Your Customers

Here's another story. Years ago another IBM agile consultant and I were working with an IBM team in Atlanta that was making the transition to agile. While in Atlanta for several days, we had the opportunity to join several members of the development organization on a customer visit to one of its biggest customers (who also happened to be in the metro-Atlanta area). After quite a bit of discussion about various technical issues (which I wasn't familiar with because I didn't know much about the product), I had the opportunity to talk to the customer about the team's move to agile. As part of the discussion, I asked the customer representatives if they had participated in Beta programs previously, and the answer was, "Yes." So I asked them what they thought of the Beta programs they had been involved with, and overall their impressions were positive. I then went out on a bit of a ledge and asked if they had ever made any recommendations for improvements to the product. The answer, as expected, was "Yes." I then asked if any of their recommendations for improvement had ever made it into the release that they had Beta-tested. By and large the answer was, "No." They told me that most of the time any recommendations they made for improvement to the product weren't incorporated until the next release, and sometimes not for several releases. I spent some time talking about how agile would enable customers to participate in regular demonstrations during development and provide them the opportunity to give immediate feedback, feedback that could oftentimes be incorporated into the current release. I then asked if they would be willing to participate with this particular team in such a program and I received an enthusiastic "Yes!"

Let your customers know that they will get to provide timely feedback to you. (Actually, they'll be *expected* to provide feedback—both positive and constructive.) Note that customers need to understand that the feedback they give will be considered for the current release and (typically) not for some future release. This helps to make a compelling case for their participation. As I mentioned previously, stakeholders will actually get the opportunity to put their "fingerprints" on the product *before* it goes out the door.

Doing Regular Demonstrations

After a team starts implementing user stories, the stories completed at the end of each iteration can—*and should*—be demonstrated to stakeholders. For development organizations, this is perhaps one of the greatest advantages of adopting agile—the ability to get on-going feedback from customers throughout the release. By regularly demonstrating to your stakeholders and getting their immediate feedback, you develop a high confidence that what you're building will meet your stakeholders' needs. For those times when you learn from your stakeholders that you're going down a wrong path, or that they don't particularly like something you've done, you have the ability to immediately correct it before going further down that path. Also, stakeholders don't often know exactly what they want, or what they like, until they can actually see it. Having on-going demonstrations for stakeholders lets them see the continuing progress (the *trajectory* if you will) of your project.

When you demonstrate a user story, start with a review of the user story itself: Who is this functionality directed to (in other words, what *role*)? What *goal* is in view and how does your implementation of the story ensure the goal is met and the *business value* is realized? You want to show how your implementation of the functionality meets the expected value, thus providing a compelling reason for your customers to be keenly interested in the features and the overall product.

You must also ask leading questions. Not every customer is going to be a chatter-box, so asking some pointed questions (in addition to some open-ended questions) that will engage your customers in the conversation is another good technique. For example, don't ask if they "liked it." You need more direct questions such as the following:

- How would you use this in your environment?
- Are there situations in which this would not be enough to solve your problem?
- Can you describe how this solution can save time compared to how you currently try to solve this problem?
- Is there a need to be more efficient, or more elegant, in the way that this goal is being met? (If so, offer to work together with the customer to come up with an even better solution.)

The goal is to draw your customers into the conversation by getting them to think through various issues with you.

Finally, not all customers can make every end-of-iteration demonstration. Teams need to record their demonstrations (both audio and visual) and post the recordings on some type of forum that customers have access to. This way, if customers miss a demonstration, they can download the demonstration later, watch it, and then provide feedback. Try to make it as easy as possible for your customers to give you feedback.

Reacting to Feedback Received

Interaction with your customers is a two-way street. You request their feedback actively as the product develops, and you incorporate their feedback as appropriate during development.

Because you do end-of-iteration demonstrations to your stakeholders, and because you encourage your stakeholders to give you feedback, the question often arises as to what you do with the feedback received? Again, nothing too new here: the team simply writes new user stories as necessary and the product owner places those stories on the backlog in the appropriate rank-ordered position based on risk, customer-value, market considerations, product strategy and vision, and so on. After you create new user stories based on stakeholder's feedback, it is useful to show them where on the backlog their stories are so that they know you are actively incorporating their feedback.[18] Note that if a particular item requested by stakeholders is not going to be addressed immediately due to other, higher-ranked items, this must be clearly (and diplomatically) conveyed to stakeholders so as not to thwart their interests both in attending and providing additional feedback during subsequent demonstrations as well as thwart their interest in the project altogether.

This is also a great time to ask customers about prioritization of the newly requested feature. Do they absolutely want the new feature in this release? If so, ask what other planned functionality they might be willing to give up, or perhaps have delayed to a subsequent release, to make sure that the product owner knows how to rank-order the feature on the backlog and also so that the customer understands the overall impact of the new request on the planned functionality.

If any feedback received includes a request for some new feature, the product owner should compare the requested feature with the long-term vision and strategy for the product. If a newly requested feature lies outside the desired path of the product, the customer should be told that the feature will not be considered. *However,* make sure you try to help your customer come up with an alternative solution to the problem for which the requested feature was meant to address.

When Is the Development Organization a Stakeholder?

There are times when developers, testers, writers, and so on are legitimate stakeholders, but this is mainly when they do work that can primarily benefit *their own organization.* Customers may not receive direct benefit from these efforts but efficiency and quality gains can benefit them. Typical examples include doing some build improvements and increasing test automation capabilities by significantly enhancing an automation framework. In these instances, this is work that the team needs to do—so user stories should be written for this work, sized, and placed on the backlog—but the main beneficiary of the work is the team itself.[19] The following are a couple of examples of poor user stories, and an example of an acceptable user story:

18. At IBM, some teams have moved to "transparent development," which is where product development teams place their key artifacts in the "open" for anyone to see. You can more about it here: http://www-01.ibm.com/software/tivoli/governance/action/12132012.html and here: https://www.ibm.com/developerworks/community/blogs/executivecorner/entry/the_transparent_ development_journey_tivoli_transformation_to_embrace_social_business_and_get_closer_to_its_ customers7?lang=en

19. In addition to this qualification, there's also a more subtle situation. If the project is successful in the marketplace, it means that the development organization has the ability to work on additional releases of the project, thus creating a strong and synergistic link between customers and the development organization, which, in essence, does make the development organization a stakeholder. However, for the purposes of the discussion here, we want to stick with our original assertion to avoid the problems we've seen many times, as shown in the following poor example.

Poor stories (incorrect stakeholders and *confusion* between user stories and tasks):

As a developer I want to write code so that I can implement the <xyz> feature.

As a tester I want to test the <xyz> feature so that I can find defects.

An acceptable story (legitimate stakeholder):

As the development organization we need to instrument our builds with Static Code Analysis so that we can identify defects via automated tooling instead of having to do manual code reviews to find the same problems.

Customer Support Teams as Stakeholders

In agile, customer support teams (support) now participate in the overall development process as *stakeholders* for the products they support. As such, support still works with the development organization to raise requests specific to support, but they now do so using user stories, for example:

As a customer support engineer I need the ability to automatically analyze trace dumps for error conditions so that I can respond to customers during a call instead of calling them back after a manual review.

As a customer support engineer I need the product to automatically upload a log file to the Support website when an error is detected by the product so that I don't have to ask the customer to manually do so when the customer calls in with an issue.

As a customer support engineer I need to get automatic access to the customer log file when an error is detected so that the customer does not have to find the file, collect it, and send it to me manually.

As a customer support engineer I need the application to ensure that customers understand that passwords are case-sensitive so that customers do not need to engage support services to resolve the issue of their passwords failing and, after three failed attempts, locking them out of the system.

Unless a requirements traceability framework was in place, many of the specific requests from support (or elsewhere, for that matter) would not indicate who the requestor was, or the reason for the request. Often items requested by support tend to look something like this:

Improve diagnostics

And these line items take their place among the hundreds of other line items and feature requests. Now, however, through the use of user stories, the nature of the requested item is better understood, as well as the goal of the requested functionality. This allows the product owner to appropriately rank the user stories coming from customer support with the other stories on the backlog and ensures that all stakeholder requests are balanced appropriately.

In addition, we are strong advocates of all stakeholders having access to the product backlog. In this case, support would have the ability to see where on the backlog their stories are, and thus have a good idea of when their stories will be targeted for completion based on the release burndown. If the stories are ranked low enough on the backlog that there's a question of them making it into the release, support can see this and work with the product owner to make the case for moving the support stories higher on the backlog to ensure inclusion in the upcoming release.

Working with Customers in Countries Other Than Your Own

Chances are good that if you're building enterprise-level software, you have customers in countries other than your own—and chances are good that they don't speak the same language you do. Assuming you globalize your products, here's how we suggest you interact with your foreign customers during an agile project. (For the purposes of this chapter, we'll just assume that your native language is English.)

First, if your non-English customers speak English, then no problem. You should definitely involve them in regular, active interaction with your team just like you would any other customer.

If your non-English customers don't have good facility with the English language, perhaps you can bring in someone to provide dedicated demonstrations in their native language, and allow for translation of customer comments into English and responses from English into the customers' language. What needs to be kept in mind is the *business perspective*: Is this a new market that the product is entering? If so, the cost of bringing in someone with the needed language skills may well be worth the expected ROI. Is it a market with a large, established customer base that you want to "keep happy"? If so, the additional costs of regularly using the services of translators will likely be worth it.

Also, if you do globalize your products, give strong consideration to performing all necessary globalization as part of the work completed in each iteration. For example, if your product sells not only in English-speaking countries, but also in Germany, China, and Brazil, at the end of each iteration, you would have a product that runs "natively" in English, German, Chinese, and Brazilian Portuguese so that native speakers in any of those additional countries could see demonstrations of, and even download and run, scenarios with your product, using their own language.[20]

Metrics

We suggest two simple metrics that you should track during each iteration: The first revolves around stakeholder categories and market segments, and the second focuses on the feedback received and your team's response to the feedback. Figure 2.1 shows a sample chart.

You can build a similar chart for stakeholders by market segment if this is an important metric for you to track as well.

Figure 2.2 shows sample data captured from one particular iteration (iteration #4).

---

20. Of course, working with customers in other countries requires more than just translation; it requires an understanding of cultural differences as well. If this is new territory for you, then perhaps you might be interested in the work done by Geert Hofstede and his "Hofstede Indices." You can learn more here: http://geert-hofstede.com/.

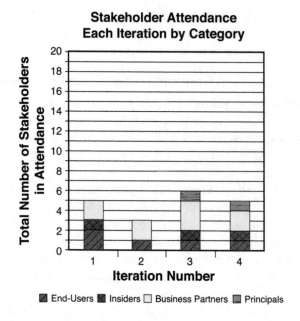

Figure 2.1   A sample chart of stakeholder attendance

				Iteration #4				
	Company	Market Segment	Stakeholder Category	Attended?	Feedback	Changes Made to This Release?	Consideration for a Future Release?	No Plans to Make Any Changes
Bob	Company A	SMB	Business Partner	X	Liked New Widget X			
Amir	Company C	Retail	End-User	X				
Susan	Company E	Oil and Gas	End-User					
Aditya	Company F	Banking	Insider	X	Wanted the option to manually change colors on the Admin Status Panel			X
Ron	Company A	SMB	Business Partner					
Hua	Company B	Banking	End-User	X	Asked that Widget A include a "notes" field	X		
Shaila	Company G	Banking	Business Partner	X	Liked New Widget X			
Steve	Company D	Insurance	Principal	X	Asked if Translation would be part of this release		X	
			Totals:	6	5	1	1	1

Figure 2.2   Sample stakeholder feedback for a specific iteration

You should track such information across all your iterations. This can help ensure that you don't lose track of any feedback received as well as ensure that you've responded to customer feedback as it is received.

Breakthrough

To get some great experience with active stakeholder interaction, try this "2, 2, 2, 2" technique: 2 customers, 2 issues, 2 iterations, and 2 weeks for feedback. Here is how it works: Assuming you already have an established customer base, you no doubt have a few customers who can be—ummm—challenging. The tendency is to shun these customers as much as possible—after all, who wants to listen to customers tell you how ugly your baby is? In this case, however, it's typically these customers who are actually trying to gain the most benefit from your product and be the most productive with it. They're stretching the use of your product to its limits. If you can make these customers both successful and happy, your other customers should also be positively affected.

First, begin by identifying two of your most challenging customers, perhaps one that continually finds quality problems and another who continually asks for new functionality, and identify the top two issues for each customer. Focus first on the customer who has quality issues. Tell this customer that you're going to fix the top two issues immediately, but that you expect them to work closely with you during the process. (Recall the previous sections about setting expectations and customers "having skin in the game.") The goal should be to solve the first issue by the end of the first 2-week iteration and the second issue by the end of the second 2-week iteration. You should demonstrate partial solutions and get feedback during each iteration. And, finally, the customer has to agree to put the fix into production within 2 weeks of receiving it. The goals are to not only solve painful customer issues, but also to also transform one of your more challenging customers into an advocate.

For the customer who asks for new functionality, commit to implementing two features for this customer over the course of two iterations (with the obvious assumption that the features are of a magnitude such that completing each one in an iteration is not unreasonable). Work closely with this customer as well during each of these two iterations—again with the goal of not only satisfying the customer, but also turning a challenging customer into an advocate.

While a couple of short iterations, *focused exclusively* on just two customers, may seem a bit constraining, don't lose sight of the fact that you'll be accomplishing multiple things by doing so. First, you can quickly learn how to work with customers and that success, in turn, can help you pave the way for continual, active stakeholder interaction on a larger scale with all your projects. Next, you can learn how to focus on one thing at a time instead of trying to work on many things in parallel. In addition, you can address some of those nagging customer issues from some of those challenging customers and, hopefully, turn them into advocates instead of detractors. I certainly can't quantify the benefits of doing this, but it should stand to reason that you can reap benefits if customers who have been vocal critics of your product in the past suddenly become advocates—all because of the attention received from you as a result of implementing this technique.

Also, with respect to the comments made earlier about ensuring customers also have some "skin in the game," make sure that your two customers agree up-front to deploy the code drops you give them within 2 weeks (of course, the preference would be *immediately*). If they're not willing, this technique is somewhat of a moot point and there are likely other issues that first need to be dealt with.

Finally, maybe you haven't tried interacting regularly with customers during an agile project—perhaps thinking that your current Beta program is sufficient. Or maybe there's just a reluctance to spend the effort needed to regularly work with customers. Or maybe you don't even think you need to interact with customers until after your product ships. Or maybe you've tried interacting with customers, but it just didn't seem to work out that well. Whatever situation you currently face, you must establish active stakeholder interaction as part of all your projects. Give this breakthrough technique a try. The value of this solution is that your interaction is focused on a particular result with a targeted customer within a specific time limit. These combined factors enable both you and your customer to make progress and quickly evaluate the benefits of the approach.

Summary

Being agile requires active stakeholder interaction because only your stakeholders can confirm that what you create actually meets their needs.

- Oftentimes customers cannot really articulate exactly what they need (or like) until they have something to "throw darts at."

- "Realize that their [stakeholder's] *real* goals may be considerably different from what any stakeholder will tell you when first asked. This is why you need to enter into a continuous collaboration with some number of stakeholders. This continues throughout the product life cycle."[21] In other words, you need to learn together!

- Read Carl Kessler's and John Sweitzer's book on stakeholder interaction referenced earlier in the chapter. It can help you gain a fuller picture of the many and varied aspects of your stakeholder's organizations and specific paradigms.

- Seek to maximize the amount of work *not* done. In other words, learn to do what's needed for your stakeholders—and no more.

- Having regular, end-of-iteration demonstrations requires that your work be focused on one feature at a time and that you achieve a level of "Done!" at the end of each iteration to have something worthwhile to demonstrate.

- Your customer support organization is not only a source of project requirements, but it is also invaluable in providing on-going feedback throughout a release. Ensure customer support engineers are invited to your end-of-iteration demonstrations as well.

- Ensure you set expectations with your customers as they become active in your stakeholder interaction efforts. It's a "win-win" situation for everyone if done correctly.

- Keep track of your stakeholder interaction each iteration to ensure you get good representation and good participation from all the various stakeholder categories and business segments. You should also track the feedback received and your responses to the feedback.

- If you forego customer interaction because you think your schedule is too tight to devote the needed time, you probably just eliminated one of your best chances to ensure success.

---

21. Kessler, Carl and Sweitzer, John. *Outside-in Software Development.* Upper Saddle River. IBM Press, 2008. 19. Print.

CHAPTER 3

Queuing Theory

Being agile requires embracing queuing theory practices because teams achieve greater effi-ciency and throughput by leveraging a steady flow of small work items.

By Scott Will

Picture this: You're at a bank and need to make a transaction. You walk into the lobby and all four tellers are available. So you pick a teller, take care of your business, and then head out the door. Life is good.

Next week you go back to the same bank, but this time it's lunch time on the last day of the month and 50 people are ahead of you, all needing to transact business. You're number 51 in line, and you know you're going to be waiting a long time before any one of the four tellers can help you. Wouldn't it have been better if the 50 people could have been "staged" throughout the day instead of all showing up at once? In that case, you might have had only a couple of people ahead of you instead of 50, and you would have gotten through much faster (not to mention everybody ahead of you as well).

The point of this illustration is that the most efficient systems are achieved when new work arrives when it can be handled, not when it has to go into a "wait-state." Systems that utilize smaller batches on an on-going basis are inherently more efficient than systems with big batches delivered just once in a while, whether it's at a bank or in software development. This is one of the tenets of queuing theory and, as its name suggests, *queuing theory* is the mathematical study of queues (or waiting lines, as we typically call them).

If big batches are less efficient than small batches, we should strive to have smaller "batches" in software development instead of the typical "big batches" that have plagued waterfall teams for decades. And this is where agile shines. Based on queuing theory, agile expects teams to produce small batches of working software throughout a release instead of having big batches of stuff drop only occasionally.[1] Think of the typical waterfall project: Big plans and designs (a "big batch") are created and then thrown over the wall to the programmers. The programmers take a lot of time to read through all the documentation; then they go off and code for several months, and they throw their code (another "big batch") over the wall to the functional testers. And the cycle repeats again when functional testing is complete and the system testers get a "big batch" of stuff to start system testing on. And don't forget about the folks who write product documentation! As you can see, waterfall is rife with big batches of stuff being dropped into the bank lobby—errr—the next phase of the project. *Waterfall is inherently inefficient.*

But why is big-batch (waterfall) thinking still so prevalent, even in agile teams? We've met with teams that have claimed to be agile but are still doing things like "waterations" where code, test, and product documentation are three distinct phases within an iteration. Other teams are still reporting project status based on each discipline. (That is, coders report on how much code they've written; testers report separately on how many test cases they've executed and how many defects they've found; and writers report status based on how many pages of product documentation have been completed—no one reports status based on how much working software has been completed.) Recall from the Introduction that one of things this book addresses is the "reflexive nature" of software engineers trained in waterfall methodologies—the tendency to respond to issues with ingrained habits instead of from an informed, agile perspective. Those ingrained habits are invariably waterfall-oriented, given both the history of waterfall in the industry and the personal history and experiences of the engineers themselves. Agile is still relatively new to the scene, and truly successful agile projects are probably rarer than most people think.

Principles

Why Does Waterfall Thinking Still Linger?

Here are a couple of quick reasons why waterfall thinking still lingers. First, it can be difficult trying to break work down into smaller chunks so that something of value can be coded, tested, and have the associated product documentation completed within an iteration. We've been conditioned for years to think in terms of completing big chunks of stuff. ("I can't start on the GUI until the back-end code is complete!") In addition, because the various disciplines don't have a history of actually working together on an on-going basis, it can be tough to break the mindset of completing just your stuff. ("I got my code done; time to move on to something else while Test

---

1. "Working software is the primary measure of progress." (See http://agilemanifesto.org/principles.html.) By the way, "working software" doesn't just mean that the code compiles...

does their thing.") We tend to think of the efficiency of our particular discipline instead of the overall efficiency of the project team.[2]

So now let's move on to a brief description of the principles of queuing theory as they apply to agile.

Small Batches of Coordinated Work

What do we mean when we advocate "smaller batches" in agile projects? What we have in mind is a pattern of completing design, coding, testing, automation, and product documentation tasks in tight integration with each other on an on-going basis. Think in terms of hours—up to a day or two at most—to complete one of these tasks. We tend to get pushback on this concept, especially from developers, because they feel more efficient when they stay heads-down writing code for weeks or even months at a time. However, working in isolation this way produces bigger batches of code that need to be tested and documented. The more code that is completed before testing begins, the slower the overall process. This is equivalent to having more and more customers line up in the bank lobby to wait for a teller to become available. Agile teams must work together—on a small scale—to ensure timely feedback and to help each other get the work done. And this is exactly why getting to "Done!" each iteration may be one of the biggest challenges for teams moving to agile. They are not used to working in this tightly coordinated fashion, and it may not seem intuitively evident that it will work, so teams resist and remain isolated in their respective disciplines, even when the work size is reduced.

Queuing theory shows that organizations actually suffer when bigger and bigger batches of stuff are built up only to be dropped into some other "phase" at a later point in time. On the other hand, working with small batches of coding, testing, product documentation, automation, defect fixing, code reviews, designs, and so on in a tightly integrated fashion is what keeps the project at the "working software" level throughout a release.[3]

---

2. The Poppendiecks do a great job of discussing optimization versus suboptimization as part of their discussion of Lean principles: "Optimizing a part of a system will always, over time, suboptimize the overall system." (See: http://www.poppendieck.com/, reference the "Principles" section and specifically the "Optimize the Whole" subsection. See also, *Lean Software Development: An Agile Toolkit* by Mary and Tom Poppendieck, specifically pages 157ff under "Local Optimization.")

   In addition, Tom Poppendieck points out that when engineers work in their own disciplines, and don't actually participate in the whole project, they're basically just doing what they are told to do, whether it's by the manager, the product manager, or whomever. Part of focusing on working software is shifting the mindset of engineers involved in a project so that they think in terms of learning and problem solving. "The question then is, '[W]hat is the most effective way to discover a good solution to the problem you are currently tackling?' [E]ffective feedback, as rapid as can be achieved, is key. But feedback is useless unless it produces learning that is acted upon. It is very unlikely that people will take pride in doing what they are told. It is likely that they are very proud and motivated by having discovered together a really good solution to a problem they care about." (From private correspondence with Tom Poppendieck. Used with permission.)

3. Read the chapter entitled "Batch" in Eric Ries' excellent book entitled *Lean Startup*.

To drive the point home a little bit more, this idea of small batches did not originate with agile, or even in software engineering. Lean's roots in manufacturing provide an interesting way to understand the value of small batch sizes. American car manufacturers were successful early because they could build a car fast and inexpensively on an assembly line in which each step in the assembly was well tuned to perform its job. Toyota had different constraints so it used an approach such that the machines used to build its vehicles could be retooled to perform different work. The net benefit to Toyota was that it could find and fix problems sooner, thus ensuring higher quality, efficiency, and productivity. An additional benefit to Toyota was that it could use the same machines to build a different design. With U.S. car manufacturers, a design change would typically require adding a new assembly line. What this equates to in agile software engineering is that small teams of engineers with different skills can work together and leverage their combined skills to produce small but complete amounts of work that can be changed as needed. Agile teams are the equivalent of the multipurpose machines, and as teams become more cross-skilled, they become more productive and able to respond to change.[4]

Frequent Feedback

Having "working software" on an almost daily basis enables frequent feedback (virtually continuous feedback if wanted). Any feedback received that requires rework should keep the amount of rework small and manageable and, thus, more likely to actually be acted upon. Conversely, if overwhelming feedback is received late in the project, teams may delay responding to the feedback until a subsequent release—or even ignore it altogether. Working software, with frequent feedback, aligns with another agile principle: "Our highest priority is to satisfy the customer through early and continuous delivery of valuable software."[5]

Ensure Sufficient Capacity

"The best way to ensure we get everything we want in this release is to overload the team. This way, they won't have any possibility of 'down time'—every single minute of every day has to be booked solid—and we'll stand a good chance of getting everything we want!"

Have you ever heard comments such as these? It tends to be a common sentiment among the "beat the team until morale improves" crowd. The sad truth is such an approach almost guarantees that the team will actually get *less* done in the same period of time than if it had what Tom DeMarco calls "slack."[6] The reality is that things are going to happen that you didn't anticipate, and if you don't have sufficient capacity to absorb the unexpected, you will get derailed. Period.

4. Eric Ries also drives home this point in *Lean Startup* on p.192 where he states, "...reducing batch size, we can get through the Build-Measure-Learn feedback loop more quickly than our competitors can."

5. Taken from the "Principles Behind the Agile Manifesto": http://agilemanifesto.org/principles.html. See also the book *Continuous Delivery* by Jez Humble and David Farley.

6. DeMarco, Tom. *Slack: Getting Past Burnout, Busywork, and the Myth of Total Efficiency*. New York: Crown Business, 2002.

Because the idea of ensuring sufficient capacity is derived directly from queuing theory, it makes sense to talk about it here. When I talk to teams about capacity, I like to use an illustration of a major highway. Interstate I-40 runs through Research Triangle Park (RTP), North Carolina. RTP is home to hundreds of companies, and thousands upon thousands of people commute to RTP every day from nearby Raleigh, Durham, Chapel Hill, and surrounding areas. Since I-40 is the main thoroughfare through RTP, it bears the brunt of the traffic. Around 5 p.m. on weekdays, traffic is so heavy that cars are hardly moving. Yet, if you believe the sentiment expressed in the previous quote, you'd somehow have to think that I-40, being at 100 percent capacity, was the most efficient way imaginable for traffic to move into and out of RTP. Needless to say, such thinking does not stand up to reality. When would you rather be on the interstate—at 5 p.m. with thousands of other cars, all at a practical standstill, or at 11 p.m. when there's hardly any traffic and you can just set the cruise control? The answer is obvious, although perhaps initially counter-intuitive.

The best way for teams to avoid over-commitments is to have an established velocity.[7] Velocity is an indicator of the team's actual capacity for completing work. Having a clear understanding of velocity prevents "wishful thinking," which is what organizations engage in when they think that "this time it will be different" in an attempt to do more in a given timeframe than they're really capable of doing.[8] Having an established velocity also prevents teams from being forced to try to do more than they've shown they're capable of doing.

In addition, the best way to handle the unexpected is to work on one thing at a time. This way, when something unexpected does happen, it's relatively easy to finish off what's currently in progress (assuming you use small batches, of course) and then switch the team's focus to the new, unexpected item (assuming it takes precedence over the next item currently on the rank-ordered backlog of work). Chapter 4, "No Multitasking," discusses the importance of doing "one thing at a time."

Practices

Small Task Sizes: 4 Hours, 8 Hours, 16 Hours

It's time for some specific recommendations for putting these principles into action. First, when you and your team create tasks for user stories at the beginning of each iteration, limit your task sizes to 4 hours, 8 hours, or no more than 16 hours in size. And do not bother trying to get any "finer grained" than just those sizes. The goal of breaking work down into these small sizes is not to be exact with the sizes, nor to make you really good at estimating to the minute exactly how

---

7. If you're unfamiliar with the concept of velocity, please refer to Mike Cohn's book, *Agile Estimating and Planning*, pp. 38–41.

8. This concept is directly linked with one of the principles of the Agile Manifesto: "Agile processes promote sustainable development. The sponsors, developers, and users should be able to maintain a constant pace indefinitely." See http://agilemanifesto.org/principles.html

long you expect a task to take, but it is to ensure that the team can more easily function in a tightly integrated fashion. (Yes, we're engineers and we love numbers and precision, but trying to use a micrometer to measure task sizes is a wasted effort—"ballpark it" and move on.) The goal is to get a handle on all the work that does need to be accomplished to complete a user story so that the team members know when they are done. When teams get used to doing this, it gets easier and more reliable.

An additional recommendation is that this task-creation activity be done at the outset of each iteration. The whole team, after it has the list of stories it's going to target for completion during the iteration, meets together to create the tasks. Developers will obviously discuss the development tasks, testers their testing tasks, and likewise the writers. We've seen two benefits to having the team participate together during the task creation. First, when developers, for example, describe their development tasks, testers and writers will listen intently (because those development tasks can help define the testing that needs to be done and the product documentation that needs to be written). Testers and writers can ask questions as applicable, thus ensuring everyone on the team has a shared understanding of the work to be done. Secondly, because of this shared understanding, it's much easier for team members to help each other when and where necessary. For example, if a developer on the team finishes the last of the required development tasks, he doesn't immediately start working on the development tasks for the next user story. Instead, the developer should see if there are any test tasks or documentation tasks that need to be completed on the current user story, or defects that need to be fixed, or automation that needs to be completed, or even if there are any code reviews and/or inspections that need to be done. This is how the whole team works together, continuing to build the synergy discussed in Chapter 1, "Whole Teams," and it's also how the whole team works together on one user story at a time, which is covered next.

One User Story at a Time

Next—and this intersects both with Chapters 1 and 4—limit the team to working on one release at a time. Even within a release, try to focus the team on one user story at a time. If you have small tasks, you can increase "parallelization" of the work being done. The developers on the team can all work on development tasks that implement a given user story, and testers can immediately start testing code as coding tasks are completed. The same holds true for writers—as coding tasks are completed, things such as necessary error messages, help screens, and associated product documentation can also be done. While the developer writes the code, the tester writes the associated test cases and sets up the test environment so that when the build finishes, the tester can immediately start testing. Tight integration between design, coding, testing, and documentation yields constantly working software. And even if defects or architectural problems are found, they can be addressed quickly (because the batch sizes are small!), thus ensuring that the highest quality levels of working software are always maintained. It's much easier and more efficient to keep code quality high than it is trying to resurrect code quality just prior to release.

Short Iterations[9]

Finally, in keeping with the idea of small batches, agile recommends short iterations.[10] We encourage teams to adopt 2-week iterations to begin with—for multiple reasons. For the purposes of this chapter, short iterations support the tenets of queuing theory. However, short iterations are helpful in breaking old waterfall habits. For example, it's harder to do a wateration in 2 weeks than it is in 4 or 6 weeks. With longer iterations it's just too easy for teams to maintain waterfall thinking—separate, distinct phases for each discipline within an iteration. And such waterations mean that working software is not achieved until the end of the iteration, which, as you can see, runs counter to always striving to have "working software."

The following are quotes from a team we worked with several years ago when helping them make the transition from waterfall to agile. These quotes come from a follow-up I did with the team after they had been on the "agile road" for about a year, and I think you'll see how the comments support the practices previously discussed:

> "Also, the scrums help keep us all on track and informed of our story progress. We quickly know when a story is in trouble and everyone on the team is more than willing to help get blocks resolved and get our stories closed. It has really been a beautiful transition for us. You would be proud."

> "It has been a difficult journey but I sincerely believe that we are better off and that our team has grown stronger as a result of agile. We will ultimately deliver a higher quality product, meeting more customer-focused requirements than we have with past releases."

> "Every 10-day sprint our stories include design, code, test execution (including data validation), automation, and performance testing (including design, code, test case, and ID [product documentation, ed.] inspections). If you recall, when we first started our agile journey, we did not think that this would be possible but with improvements from our reflections and a team dedicated to implementing solid agile practices, we do exactly this. I'm not sure what other managers are talking about when they say that 10-day sprints are 'inefficient;' I think we are living proof that they are extremely efficient!"[11]

When you and your team achieve some solid success with 2-week iterations, you should consider shortening your iterations to 1 week. Beyond that, experienced agile teams are now moving to "continuous development" in which there aren't actually any iteration boundaries at all—but that's a topic for a different day.

---

9. We use the terms iterations and sprints interchangeably.
10. "Deliver working software frequently, from a couple of weeks to a couple of months, with a preference to the shorter timescale." See: http://agilemanifesto.org/principles.html
11. These comments were sent to me from Yvonne Matute. Leslie and I appreciate Yvonne having granted permission to include these quotes here.

Metrics Should Support the Focus on Working Software

We suggest you stop reporting status on individual disciplines. When each individual discipline reports status, the emphasis is shifted away from working software, which runs counter to agile. For example, 6,000 lines of code written in a big batch, without any testing or associated product documentation, is of zero value to customers—therefore, taken by itself, it is of zero value to the organization. On the other hand, 50 lines of code that implement a user story and that have been written, tested, documented, and reviewed, and where all the known defects have been fixed is of value to customers and to the project. And that code can also be demonstrated to customers and feedback obtained. Thus, in agile, there is no such thing as "partial credit"—some small batch of functionality is either "Done!" or it is not.[12] This can be a bit of "shock therapy" when folks find that they don't get any credit for any of the work they've done until a user story is "Done!" because *the whole team* is now being measured based on *working software*—not the lines of code written, the test cases executed, not the number of pages of product documentation written. The *team* gets credit only when a user story is "Done!" Another way this concept can be explained is by removing the focus on individual throughput and focusing instead on team throughput.

Metrics

Here are two rather simple metrics that you can use to see how well the team is doing with respect to embracing the principles and practices of queuing theory. The first is to track how many user stories the team has open at the end of each iteration. If the average is much greater than one, chances are the team is trying to work on multiple user stories in parallel and only occasionally getting any stories actually done. If you see this happening, recall that the best way for the team to complete its work efficiently is to try to work together on one user story at a time. Thus, in a typical team, there will be at most one incomplete user story at the end of an iteration. An incomplete story is then simply rolled into the next iteration and completed as part of the work for that iteration.

The second metric is also quite simple to track: What percentage of user stories take more than an iteration to complete? If the team regularly has user stories that take two, three, and four iterations to complete, the team is not breaking their work down into small-enough chunks. The goal is to write user stories that can reasonably be expected to be completed within an iteration. Having the occasional story take more than an iteration to complete is OK—actually it is to be expected because teams shouldn't try to be super-precise with their estimates. (Again, it's just a waste trying to be precise with estimates.) But if having stories that span multiple iterations is a regular occurrence, recall the principles of queuing theory described in this chapter and focus on breaking the work into smaller, iteration-sized user stories.

12. Remember, "Working software is the primary measure of progress." See: http://agilemanifesto.org/principles.html

Breakthrough

If you're struggling with how to get a whole team working together on one story at time, we recommend the following: Have the team identify *four* small features (or four small aspects of a larger feature) that need to be done, and then have the team work together on one feature at a time, with the goal (or perhaps more strongly, the *edict*) of working on and completing one feature together by the end of each week.

This approach requires that the team create small user stories that will fit into a 1-week iteration. Completing each story within a week requires that the team creates small tasks and adopts the parallelization approach previously described. When the iteration story and the associated small tasks are in place, the team needs to learn how to work together to get the story completed. Remember, no partial credit. All team members will likely have to get out of their typical comfort zones and learn enough to help someone else. Everyone is needed to make it happen.

Finally, do not pre-assign tasks to team members. Highly productive agile teams can move faster because each person on the team "pulls" a task when he becomes free to do new work. In other words, team members look at the remaining list of tasks and self-assign a task. If there are no remaining tasks to complete, pair up with another team member to help him finish his task. This is how team members start to expand their skills and become more valuable team members.

The reason we recommend doing this for 4 straight weeks is to ensure the team has ample opportunity to fail a few times while knowing that it can continue to try to make it work. If the team tries this just once and fails, then it may give up. Learning to work this way may not be an easy transformation, so iterate and learn. Conversely, if the team succeeds in the first week, doing it for 3 more weeks helps everyone understand it wasn't a fluke, and it gives them even more confidence going forward.

Learning how to leverage each person's collective skills to create a strong operating team is one of the reasons that teams moving to agile have become more productive. They do not work longer hours to increase productivity—they work together more productively. This behavior is so critical to agile success that it is hard to imagine how teams can ever have working software every iteration without it. And it is easy to tell when teams do figure this out: They work in a highly focused fashion every iteration, they make progress quickly, and there is no more "us" vs. "them." Try this breakthrough technique—learn how to succeed *together*.

Summary

Being agile requires embracing queuing theory practices because teams achieve greater efficiency and throughput by leveraging a steady flow of small work items.

- Completing small amounts of work regularly is more efficient than piling up big batches of work to be done later.
- Small tasks (4 hours, 8 hours, and no more than 16 hours in size) are what enable teams to work together on one user story at a time.

- The goal of individuals on the team is to start and finish tasks one at a time. Do not, as individuals, attempt to work on many tasks at once. Having small tasks should NOT be confused with multitasking.

- Do not measure each discipline separately—doing so only encourages each discipline to work separately. Encourage whole team ownership, as well as tracking working software as *the* measure of progress.

- Stop trying to get your teams to over-commit—you'll get higher productivity when teams have sufficient capacity.

- Think of what the term agile means. An 18-wheeler is not agile, but a race car is very agile by comparison because it is smaller and more nimble than the big truck.

- Read the article titled "The Acceleration Trap" by Heike Bruch and Jochen I. Menges in the April 2010 edition of the *Harvard Business Review* to get a good idea of how pushing teams beyond their capacity actually slows things down.[13]

- Here's a quote from Mark Twain, the renowned 19th-century American novelist:

  "The secret of getting started is breaking your complex, overwhelming tasks into small, manageable tasks, and then starting on that first one."[14]

13. From the introduction: "Faced with intense market pressures, corporations often take on more than they can handle: They increase the number and speed of their activities, raise performance goals, shorten innovation cycles, and introduce new management technologies or organizational systems. For a while, they succeed brilliantly, but too often the CEO tries to make this furious pace the new normal. What began as an exceptional burst of achievement becomes chronic overloading, with dire consequences." You can find the full article here: http://hbr.org/2010/04/the-acceleration-trap/ar/1.

14. Who knew that Mark Twain was "agile" before "agile was cool"?

CHAPTER 4

No Multitasking

Being agile requires teams to avoid multitasking because they are more productive when they focus.

By Scott Will

"I'm burning the candles at both ends with a blowtorch!"

Is this quote just the latest variation of the old expression about being too busy? Or is it a symptom of an increasingly greater problem? My concern is that it is symptomatic of a much greater problem: More and more people are expected to do more and more—and all at the *same time*. And the way that this manifests itself is by trying to juggle multiple tasks at once.

No matter what teams I work with—internal or external—I can just about guarantee the answers I'll get when I ask questions about whether individuals are tasked with working on multiple projects at once (for example, "Is Bob expected to work 20 percent of his time on this project, 50 percent on that project, and 30 percent on yet some other project?"). The answers are almost invariably "Yes!" followed up with, "How did you know?"

As you've no doubt gathered from the chapter title, Leslie and I are dead-set against the idea of multitasking—the idea of trying to work on more than one thing at a time. Multitasking has repeatedly been shown to be an inefficient way to get work done, and yet it is extremely prevalent. Why is this?

Let me start by giving a quick, real-life example as to why multitasking is inefficient. Let's say we're at a restaurant, having a nice conversation, when the server walks up to take our orders. We spend a couple of minutes talking with her, looking over the menu, and giving her our orders. When she heads back to the kitchen to turn our orders in, we look back at each other—and what's the first thing we say? "Ummmm, what were we just talking about?" It takes us 30 seconds to maybe a minute to get back to our previous conversation. (And sometimes we never get back to that conversation because we can't remember what it was we were talking about just a few minutes earlier!) That little bit of time, the 30 seconds to a minute needed to recall our previous conversation, is a *waste*. Had we not been interrupted during our conversation, we wouldn't have had to spend the time getting back to it. With this in mind, it should not be surprising that multitasking incurs a 25 to 30 percent hit to productivity because of the time needed to re-acquaint oneself with a previously started, but incomplete, task.[1]

Because I am a consultant, I spend a lot of time providing education to teams who are just starting down the agile path. When I first started teaching classes, it was quite common for people to be sitting in the class with their laptops open, typing away. When I asked what they were doing, they responded with answers along the lines of, "I'm trying to finish my code before the end of the day" or "I'm getting pinged by my manager about progress on a customer issue." Not surprisingly, these same people were the ones who would invariably ask a question about something that I had covered already. Clearly they weren't paying attention to both their laptop and to the class.

After a while, I made it a policy to ask those people to leave the class—if what they were doing was so important that they had to do it in the middle of a class, then they needed to leave the class and focus exclusively on the higher-priority item. This also had the positive side effect of minimizing the distractions for the rest of the attendees. I finally made it a point to start each class with a "no laptops open" rule. The attendees were there to take a class, and I expected them to pay attention and not waste their time and mine. If they didn't think the class was as important as other things, I simply asked that they leave.

With such obvious, day-to-day examples abounding concerning how inefficient multitasking is, why is multitasking so acceptable—and even encouraged? I think it boils down to two main reasons:

- Productivity misperceptions
- Fear of not getting something done

---

1. For the purposes of this discussion, we use 25 percent because it was used in a recent *Harvard Business Review* blog article at http://blogs.hbr.org/schwartz/2012/03/the-magic-of-doing-one-thing-a.html
Quote from the article: "...because when you switch away from a primary task to do something else, you're *increasing the time* it takes to finish that task by an average of 25 per cent." [Emphasis added]

When I ask people why they engage in multitasking, the primary response I get is that people actually think they are being more efficient. And why wouldn't they think so? There is no "down time" when you're trying to juggle multiple things at once—you're constantly switching from one thing to another, trying to keep all the balls in the air at once. Obviously people think that "busyness" somehow equates to productivity. Research has shown that people who engage in multitasking actually spend as much or more time focusing on *switching between tasks* than they actually do on the tasks themselves.[2]

The other reason that multitasking is so prevalent is because of fear on the part of project leadership. And what do I mean by that? Well, say you're working on a project that has five major features, and you cannot ship the product until all five features are complete. At your weekly project reviews, what does management want to see? Exactly—it wants to see the progress the team has made *on all five features*. If progress hasn't been made on some particular feature, panic sets in, recovery plans are imposed, and sometimes even careers are put in jeopardy. Thus, there's a powerful incentive for teams to engage in multitasking to "feed the beast" because the fear is that if progress on some feature isn't made, the feature will never be completed.

Principles

One Thing at a Time Is More Efficient

Now we'll spend some time exploring why multitasking is fraught with peril, starting with Figure 4.1.

---

2. Comments from an article by Walter Kirn's in the November 2007 of the *Atlantic Monthly*:

  Multitasking messes with the brain in several ways. At the most basic level, the mental balancing acts that it requires—the constant switching and pivoting—energize regions of the brain that specialize in visual processing and physical coordination and simultaneously appear to shortchange some of the higher areas related to memory and learning. *We concentrate on the act of concentration at the expense of whatever it is that we're supposed to be concentrating on.* [Emphasis added]

  Quoted from: http://www.theatlantic.com/magazine/archive/2007/11/
  the-autumn-of-the-multitaskers/306342/?single_page=true

  Some additional, relevant comments from Clifford Nass, a researcher at Stanford University:

  One would think that if people were bad at multitasking, they would stop. However, when we talk with the multitaskers, they seem to think they're great at it and seem totally unfazed and totally able to do more and more and more. We worry about it, because as people become more and more multitaskers, as more and more people—not just young kids, which we're seeing a great deal of, but even in the workplace, people being forced to multitask, *we worry that it may be creating people who are unable to think well and clearly.* [Emphasis added]

  Quoted from an online interview which can be found here: http://www.pbs.org/wgbh/pages/frontline/
  digitalnation/interviews/nass.html

  See also: http://news.stanford.edu/news/2009/august24/multitask-research-study-082409.html, and:
  http://www.pnas.org/content/106/37/15583.full.pdf+html?sid=276660da-a767-45fb-b897-5a9dd653171b

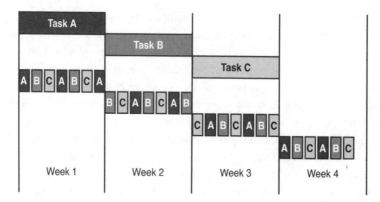

Figure 4.1   One Task at a Time Versus Multitasking (used and modified with permission from Tom and Mary Poppendieck)

Say you have three tasks, and each one is nominally expected to take a week to complete. If you refer to the top bars in Figure 4.1, focusing on the first task exclusively during the first week means that you have that task completed at the end of the first week. It's done—it's off your plate. And then you pick up the second task and complete it by the end of the second week, and likewise the third task. At the end of three weeks, you have all three tasks complete—right on schedule.

Now refer to the bottom bars in the figure. In this case you're in an organization that demands you show progress on all three tasks right from the beginning. So you do a little of Task A, then a little of Task B, and then a little of Task C. Then it's back to Task A again, then to Task B, and so on. At the end of the first week you *can* show that you've made progress on all three tasks, but at what cost? If you follow the graphic you'll note that the first task isn't complete until the middle of the fourth week, and you're not completely done with all three tasks until nearly the end of the fourth week. It took almost 4 weeks to complete 3 weeks' worth of work—which obviously isn't efficient.

In addition, if you had to stop work at the end of 2 weeks, at least by working on one task at a time, you'd have two tasks completely done. If you were to adopt the multitasking approach, you couldn't stop at the end of 2 weeks because you wouldn't have anything that was actually completed. Sure, you'd have some partially complete work, but what value does that have? The point is that there is extra effort to switch between tasks, and that results in a less effecient outcome.

Flow

I wrote code for years before moving into operations, support, test, management, quality, and finally consulting. I recall well those days when I would close the door to my office and write code for hours at a time. Fairly often I would have an experience of looking at the clock prior to sitting down at my computer (way before the days of laptops), starting to write code in earnest, and then looking up at the clock and noting that *hours* had passed—and I was *totally unaware of it*. It always seemed like just a short period of time that I had been writing code, and yet 4, 5, even 6 hours had actually passed. This is the idea of flow. Basically, *flow* means that you get so focused on something (in a "groove" as it were) that you completely lose track of time. The only time your "flow" is broken is when you get an interruption. Having the opportunity to get into flow is a great benefit to being highly productive—but flow won't happen unless you eliminate distractions and interruptions. Thus, multitasking runs counter to flow, as do the continual interruptions of instant messaging, cellphones, text messages, and so on.

If you've ever experienced flow, recall the feeling you had—you've been extremely productive, so there's a really good feeling. Compare that to those times when you're sitting in meetings, trying to pay attention while trying to instant message with two or three other people and while constantly checking your email. At the end of that meeting you're exhausted, and you're not sure you got much out of the meeting. Your body is telling you what should be obvious to your mind; the exhaustion you're feeling doesn't match with any good level of productivity.

Stop Starting; Start Finishing

Multitasking is inherently inefficient; jettison the idea that it is somehow an efficient way to work. Instead, adopt the agile mentality of "Stop starting; start finishing!" Starting tasks is only useful in telling you what you have ahead of you. The example I like is when I'm on a plane working through my email inbox. There are practically no interruptions, so not only do I pay attention to what I read, but also I respond to and delete messages quickly so that I empty my inbox. It feels good to get to that point, and it typically happens only when I can spend uninterrupted time focusing on my email.

Practices

Team Members Are Dedicated to a Project 100% of the Time

So how does a team move away from multitasking? The first practice is establishing a firm commitment to dedicating people to a team 100 percent of the time. It makes much more sense to dedicate *two* people with a particular, needed skill to a team 100 percent of the time than it does having, say, *five* people available only 50 percent of the time (assuming you're convinced of our reasoning, that is). And this also means that you should not regularly be moving people around from team to team during a release cycle. Keeping teams intact throughout a release helps build desired team synergy. You can read more about the benefits of "whole teams" in Chapter 1.

One point that I'll reiterate here (because it seems to be a common occurrence) concerns what happens if, for example, you have only one user-experience (UX) professional for three teams. There are two approaches we've used successfully—and no doubt you can come up with others also—but the main point is that you should not try to split the UX person's time across three teams (for example, making him attend three daily meetings each day, three separate iteration-planning meetings, and so on—what a waste). The two options we've seen work follow:

- The first option is that others on the team have to step in to help out however they can. As pointed out in Chapter 1, just because you don't have, for example, performance testers available doesn't mean you get to skip performance testing. Obviously, this is not ideal, so hopefully the skills imbalance will be addressed. Either that, or others on the team have to gain practical knowledge on UX in order to fill the gap.

- Another option is to dedicate the UX person's time to one team for an entire iteration, and then have her move to a different team for the next iteration. There are some significant drawbacks to this approach as well, but it's still better than trying to split the time among all three teams every iteration. And, again, hopefully the skills imbalance will be addressed.

One Project at a Time

Now that you have whole, dedicated teams, you need to focus them on one project at a time and not disrupt them until the project is done.[3] This means you need to prioritize your work. What's the most important project? Is it the new release? Or is it the maintenance release? Or is it something else? Whatever the list of projects is, prioritize the list and put the team on the highest-priority project. When done, have them move to the next project on the list. If multitasking is wasteful at an individual level, then it's also wasteful at an organizational level. One thing at a time, one thing at a time, one thing at a time....

Be a "Firewall" and Stop Being a "Fast-Forward" Button

At an organizational level, things are a little bit different. Oftentimes, pressures to multitask are externally applied to teams and individuals. Managers and other leaders need to become a "firewall" for your team and stop being what I euphemistically call a "fast-forward button." The goal for leadership is to prevent any and all disruptions to your team to allow it to focus on its work. Learn to differentiate between what's "important" and the "tyranny of the urgent." Just because something is *urgent* doesn't make it *important*.[4]

Try this out: Tell the team that you will ensure that it will not be interrupted for an entire week if it, in turn, will commit to completing an entire user story in that week. (This obviously complements our Breakthrough technique in Chapter 3, "Queuing Theory.") The hard part about acting as a firewall is that you *will* be pressured to interrupt the team because there's always something that someone wants from the team. ("Can't Bob provide a presentation to the vice-president?" "Can't Sally help this other team brainstorm on its new GUI? She always has some

---

3. Of course, common sense applies here. If you discover partway through a project that it is no longer needed, then obviously stop the project and move on to a new one. The goal is still that teams should work on just one project at a time.

4. Please note that "urgent" and "important" are not mutually exclusive. A fire alarm is both urgent and important.

neat ideas.") So steel yourself; it will be hard, and you will be tested, but when the message gets out, and you have some initial successes, the benefits should start to accrue quickly, and it will get easier to start doing *one thing at a time*. Needless to say, this practice is much easier to achieve when the iterations are short. The longer the iterations, the easier it is to sidetrack a team because they have "time to recover." But if its runway is short, then it will be obvious that an interruption *will* prevent the team from finishing its current work in the iteration.

Pair Programming; Pair Testing

Pair programming[5] has been around for a long time even though it's come into its own with the advent of extreme programming (XP).[6] I used pair programming when I first started with IBM more than 20 years ago—and it was a fantastic way to program. The code we wrote was some of the highest-quality code produced for the project. And although I am certainly an advocate of pair programming and pair testing, and even pairing programmers and testers together, the reason I mention it here is that when two people work together on the same thing at the same time on the same machine, it helps to "jointly enforce" the motivation to work on one thing at time.

Calendar Ruthlessness

One last practice is calendar ruthlessness. We all need to become much better managers of our calendars instead of being taken captive by them. Apart from the standard agile meetings (daily standups, iteration planning meetings, customer demonstrations, and reflections), are you going to a lot of other meetings? If so, do you need to go to them? Or are you going just out of curiosity or because you're looking for some "face time?" Do you need to invite 36 people to your meeting, or can you get by with just a small subset of folks? Does the meeting have to be scheduled for an hour, or can you time-box it to 20 minutes?[7] (Poorly run meetings are a bane to productivity.) Constantly running from meeting to meeting is a symptom of *busyness*, not *productivity*. Writing code, executing test cases, preparing user documentation, fixing defects, and creating automation are signs of productivity—and maximizing the amount of time for team members to focus on these activities can help ensure high levels of productivity.

In addition, you may want to consider starting the day by doing the thing you are avoiding, or even dreading. After you address it and get it off your plate, everything else will seem like a pleasure.

5. In case you're unfamiliar with pair programming, see the work by Dr. Laurie Williams. Dr. Williams is a former IBMer and is now a professor of software engineering at North Carolina State University. You can read a short overview of pair programming, with links to more information including her book on pair programming (*Pair Programming Illuminated*), at http://collaboration.csc.ncsu.edu/laurie/pair.html

6. "All production code is pair programmed." This quote comes from "The Rules of Extreme Programming" found here: http://www.extremeprogramming.org/rules.html. See also the attendant link on pair programming at http://www.extremeprogramming.org/rules/pair.html

7. Ever notice how meetings tend to fill up the entire allotted time, even though the purpose of the meeting could probably have been covered in much less time?

Metrics

If multitasking is prevalent in your organization, and you're convinced that you need to take steps to eliminate it, we can suggest a couple of simple metrics to track.

The first is to note how many people on a team are "multi-allocated." By this we mean note the number of people who are partially dedicated to more than one team. Having one or two people that fall into this category is probably not a big deal (but, even here, we would ask, "Why?"); however, if you have a fairly high percentage of your team members that are multi-allocated, then you are most likely being inefficient with these people's time.

As a side note, review your "people allocation" as a part of your reflection meetings. That is the time to understand how significant the problem is and agree on ways to tackle the problem if it is significant.

The second metric that we can suggest is, admittedly, a little off-the-wall. Take a look at the number of emails you have in your in-box. Of those, how many of them have you looked at (or maybe just glanced at) and said to yourself, "I'll get back to this one later"? If this describes your habits, you're actually multitasking. The time you spent looking at the email initially, only to come back and deal with it later, is a waste of time. Yes, we fully get that this is simply your way of trying to address the important stuff first. Wouldn't it be easier (and more efficient) for you to just set aside a time during the day to work on your email? Then there's no need to spend time trying to figure out if something is important or not—you just handle the email when you first read it.[8]

A third metric we can suggest, but only for extreme cases (such as when management hasn't learned that it needs to *protect* the team from unnecessary interruptions), would be to track the number of interruptions that occur during the iteration as well as how much time was spent dealing with each of the interruptions. One team that we worked with years ago did this very thing. Management had regularly interrupted the team to add something unrelated to the current work to the list of things the team was trying to get done. Management was repeatedly heard saying things like, "Oh, this is only a small item—you can handle it." Well, when the team started tracking how much time it actually spent on these numerous "small" items, it turned out that those additional items had nearly doubled its work load. Individuals on the team were regularly putting in 80-hour work weeks to get everything done that they were being told to do. Team members knew it—and they kept telling management that this was the case—but it wasn't until the team put up a graph with all the data showing exactly how many interruptions occurred and how long each one actually took that management finally "got the message" and started protecting the team.

---

8. You might find the following interesting if you struggle with keeping your email under control—it's called "Inbox 0" and there's a link to a video as well as several articles that provide helpful ideas on handling email: http://inboxzero.com/articles/

Breakthrough

How do you tame the multitasking beast? You may be convinced of everything we've previously written, and you may have even tried to limit multitasking, but without much success. So the question is, "Why is it so *hard* to stop multitasking?" Simply put, almost all our technology today *encourages* multitasking. It is hard to even recognize how prevalent it is and even harder to stop it. There's also the misperception that multitasking is a more efficient way to work. And one other thing, there's a latent fear that you might "miss something." Ask yourself, is it really that important that you find out *right now* that your best friend is going to take his girlfriend to see the new movie tonight? To ask the question is to answer it—you need a breakthrough.

The breakthrough comes from adopting what Leslie and I call *the nuclear option*. As a team, turn off your smartphones, pagers, office phones, instant messaging, email, and other items that serve to distract you when you need to focus on productive work. Why do we call this the nuclear option? It's because people today are utterly addicted to these devices. To begin with, turn off all the devices for just 1 hour, and you'll see how hard it is to "kick the habit." You'll probably be unable to avoid checking your email several times, or checking your "smart phone" to see if you've received any new text messages as well as seeing what new posts your friends have just added to their social media sites. Just doing this for an hour is probably going to be tough—but do it anyway. And here's how to approach it: As a team, set aside an hour in which no one can be distracted. The goal of the team is to work exclusively on the project (without interruptions) during this time. After you conquer doing this for 1 hour, then move to 2 hours, and then to 4 hours. If you really, absolutely, positively have to be responsive to outside interruptions, perhaps designate one person on the team as the interface to the "outside world" during the time when the rest of the team focuses on the project. This might require that one person field any crises that arise while the rest of the team is focused, but it will still be worth it. You can even rotate this responsibility from day to day if necessary.

With this breakthrough thought in mind, you can see that this is one of the reasons that pair programming works so well. A common rule in pair programming is to set a time limit and eliminate all distractions. And you can also see how this thinking supports the adoption of bullpens discussed in Chapter 1 because with bullpens the team establishes a set time every day that it works together.

One final note: As a team, try to set aside this time at the beginning of the day every day. If you try to make it happen later in the day, it's too easy to succumb to the pressures that start accumulating from the moment you walk in the door, and you wind up never getting around to dedicating the time to focus.

If you can get to the point in which the team sets aside "focus time" at the beginning of every day, you'll be well on your way to taming the multitasking beast.[9]

---

9. As one aside, I know people who allocate 1 hour a day to responding to email, and that's it. And it's at the same time every day. They let people know how to get hold of them if something is extremely important and needs their immediate attention, but otherwise, email can generally wait.

Summary

Being agile requires teams to avoid multitasking because they are more productive when they focus.

- Multitasking is inherently inefficient. Agile encourages—and even expects—teams and individuals to be quite productive, so why continue with a practice that demonstrably runs counter to agile?

- There is a widespread perception (misperception, actually) that multitasking is an efficient and productive way to work. This is based primarily on confusing *busyness* with *productivity*.

- Organizations should focus their teams on one project at a time. As a result, individual team members should be dedicated to one team and work on only one project at a time.

- Learn to control your calendar instead of letting it control you. Learn to control your interruptions instead of letting them control you.

- Leave your laptop in your office if you find it difficult to not focus on other things during meetings. If everyone does this, you'll find meetings tend to be much more efficient.

- Breaking the multitasking habit will likely be quite difficult, both at the individual level and at the organizational level, but it must be done.

- Stop starting; start finishing!

CHAPTER 5

Eliminate Waste

Being agile requires eliminating waste to realize significant efficiency, productivity, and quality gains.

By Leslie Ekas

Agile teams should embrace the concept of eliminating waste. It is crucial for achieving many of the benefits of agile as well as the goals outlined in the Agile Manifesto.[1] Waste is defined broadly to mean anything that does not provide value to the customer. Any complex discipline, such as software development, is bound to suffer from accumulation of waste as teams handle ever-increasing product complexity while meeting aggressive product schedules. Teams must apply the concept of eliminating waste to their day-to-day activities to increase their ability to be productive.

Years ago, before Scott was even in high school, he was one of the first employees of a small furniture manufacturing company. Over the years, as the company grew, it moved from the owner's basement in Scott's neighborhood to an actual business location. From the time the company first started until Scott left to go to college (and even afterward), there was an intense focus in the company on eliminating waste. And waste was easy to see: Examples included left-over scraps of wood, scraps of fabric, and excess use of seating foam that needed to be trimmed off. The owners and employees were always on the lookout for ways to avoid waste because any waste negatively affected the company's bottom line.

In manufacturing, waste is often easy to see. In software development it can be much harder. Here is one example of waste that may not seem obvious but does, in fact, show how a development team allowed waste to accumulate while delivering no value to the customer. A product team got complaints from its customers that, as the usage of the product at customer sites increased, the customers needed to monitor the resource usage to adjust to the growing

---

1. http://www.agilemanifesto.org/.

demand on system resources. The development organization responded by integrating an existing resource monitoring product with its product.

Several of the customers tried to set up the monitoring product and use it to address their needs but found it difficult to set up and cumbersome to use. The monitoring product was a good product but was designed to manage larger and more complex systems. Tuning the product to work better in this environment was not a high priority for either the monitoring product team or the other product team.

After a few years it became apparent that this product integration was not providing enough additional value to customers as demonstrated by low adoption. The team continued to test the product integration as its software was updated, but as new product needs put demands on the team, it had to take a hard look at focusing its efforts on what was actually providing business value. After much consideration, the teams decided to deprecate the product integration and recommend to the remaining interested customers that they should not pursue this functionality further.

Teams may hesitate over deprecating unused functionality because it feels like a defeat. However, not all product solutions work—and teams are better off discovering that quickly and reapplying their resources to higher value solutions for their customers. Teams may not want to characterize an unsuccessful product feature as waste, but if it is not delivering value, then it *is* waste—especially as in this case in which the teams continued to test the integration functionality even though they knew it was not used by customers, which was only compounding the waste. Deprecating the functionality (read: eliminating this waste) freed the teams to do higher value work.

Principles

What Is Eliminating Waste?

Mary and Tom Poppendieck applied the lean concept of eliminating waste to software development as part of their seminal work on lean software development.[2] They describe waste as "building the wrong thing," "building the thing wrong," and "a batch and queue mentality."[3] If not remedied, the costs of such waste will impact the team's overall efficiency and likely product quality as well.

There are two elements to eliminating waste: identifying it and removing it. Identifying waste may take some practice because waste can occur in many forms. Removing it is often hard—and this why it tends to accumulate in the first place. However, eliminating waste is critical for agile teams that want to be successful with regularly having working software, releasing often, and delivering value. Teams need mechanisms to keep their focus on identifying and eliminating it.

---

2. See Chapter 1, "Eliminate Waste," in their book, *Lean Software Development: An Agile Toolkit*.
3. Quoted from the Poppendieck's website: "Principles: Eliminate Waste" http://www.poppendieck.com.

Why the Focus on Eliminating Waste?

It is obvious that waste can be costly, but why emphasize eliminating waste as such a critical practice? Developing the discipline of regularly looking for and eliminating waste enables teams to remove nonvalue-adding work before it becomes a problem (as in the opening story). And this is the key: Find waste proactively and eliminate it before it becomes a visible problem. In almost all cases the costs associated with eliminating waste are lower the earlier it is addressed—and the gains from eliminating waste are likewise obtained earlier.

Traditional waterfall thinking tended to rely on process tuning and better resources to improve productivity. And tuning tended to happen in response to a problem, like *manual testing takes too long for us to release on time*. There is no agile practice that *ensures* teams will look for and eliminate waste, but the requirement for teams to always have working software will help to reinforce the imperative of eliminating waste. Teams that capitalize on the practice of eliminating waste do not limit where or when they look for waste; rather it becomes just part of how they work.

Furthermore, eliminating waste gets teams into the habit of building high value and high quality software with a mind toward efficiency. An Agile Manifesto principle captures this benefit well, "Simplicity—the art of maximizing the amount of work not done—is essential."[4] Teams that struggle with their agile transformation often come face to face with their accrued waste when they try to get to "Done!" every iteration. They may be working on code that already has design limitations; they may be limited in what they can finish due to a pattern of faulty builds that they have to work around; or they may be handing off code to a team of testers who are only available for part of the iteration. If teams do not remove this kind of waste, they will continually struggle to succeed with agile.

Technical Debt

Technical debt is a type of waste that has garnered a lot of press because the metaphor of "debt" succinctly calls attention to the fact that there are costs associated with it (as there are with all forms of debt). Technical debt is the term Ward Cunningham used to describe the situation occurring when short-term software design solutions are used at the cost of the longer-term viability of the code. There can be good reasons to take shortcuts to release code sooner—even knowing that the team is taking on debt as the result of the decision. In fact, Eric Ries introduced the concept of the Minimum Viable Product[5] that encourages teams to get a product out quickly to provide rapid learning about whether the product will succeed in the marketplace. However, the point that Cunningham impressed on the software industry is that this technical debt needs to be paid back—or the associated interest on the debt will continue to increase the longer the team takes to

4. http://www.agilemanifesto.org/.
5. Ries, Eric (2011). *The Lean Startup: How Today's Entrepreneurs Use Continuous Innovation to Create Radically Successful Businesses*. New York: Crown Business, p. 93ff.

resolve it. Ward Cunningham's technical debt metaphor is such a concise way of describing an engineering problem that avoiding technical debt has been adopted as a critical concept by many software teams.

Technical debt is a common and understandable occurrence in software development because design compromises may be used to hit a deadline. In addition, teams learn more after the product is used "in the real world" and what they learn should then be factored back into the product. The problem is, in both cases, it is often hard to sell the value of doing rework to non-technical stakeholders. Putting a value on doing rework is much harder than defining the value of paying back financial debt. And this is precisely why Cunningham's metaphor is effective in explaining the merits of paying down debt or, even better, avoiding the debt in the first place. It has been easy to ignore such debt in software development, but the costs of neglecting debt have impacted the viability of software products in the long term.[6]

As an example of technical debt, the following is an account of a team that was assigned to build an API for its product that client software could access remotely. The team needed to get something to its customers quickly, but it was a new team and therefore lacked necessary domain knowledge. As a result, the code was fairly buggy and lacked some critical functionality to make it completely worthwhile. However, customers used it because they did not have an alternative solution and needed immediate relief for their problems, no matter how buggy and incomplete the solution was. Because customers were using the functionality and gaining some benefit, and because of significant business pressures elsewhere, the team was moved to another project while the first project languished. This was a situation in which the design was in need of improvement and the customers needed to be given a better solution. In fact, some customers were adamant that having this capability fully implemented was more critical than anything else. But business pressures elsewhere kept the team from returning to this project and providing a better solution for several years. The code was eventually rebuilt to the long-delayed delight of many customers. Had the team taken a little extra time at the outset and not accrued technical debt as the result of making hasty design decisions, the initial solution provided to customers would have been better. And even when the team finally did return to the project after a couple of years, the team's ability to provide the more comprehensive solution customers had been asking for would have been easier. The costs of redoing the initial work were significant.

There are many more examples of technical debt that do not have this level of business visibility, and this is part of the problem. When technical debt is accrued during a project, it is often forgotten by the time the next version is underway and thus doesn't get addressed. If teams do not avoid accruing debt to begin with, or if they don't pay back their debt quickly, there will be increasing "interest costs" on the debt for the life of the product.

---

6. Highsmith, Jim, October 2010, "The Financial Implications of Technical Debt," http://jimhighsmith.com/the-financial-implications-of-technical-debt/.

Project Debt

To ensure that the original meaning of the term *technical debt* is not lost, we will use the term *project debt* throughout this chapter as an umbrella term to cover typical wastes that occur in software development (including technical debt). Project debt describes a broad range of compromises that teams make to ship a product sooner. Examples include defect backlogs that carry over from release to release; performing manual testing instead of pursuing automation; automation that is in place but is broken; having hard-coded strings (especially if globalization is required); code duplication and code complexity; faulty builds; an out-of-date version of a compiler; and incomplete cross-functional criteria (for example, accessibility, security, performance, scalability, and so on not being at the required levels). These are but a few examples—there are many more. If not remedied, these shortcuts can hinder the long-term viability of any product, and the costs to remove the debt will likely increase the longer it is delayed.

As with technical debt, project debt needs to be paid back quickly to minimize project costs and maximize the viability of the product. The concept of *debt intolerance* should drive home the point that teams need to avoid debt to begin with and also recognize areas in which they have debt and remove it as part of their normal practice. Debt intolerance is a way to enforce waste elimination. It is an essential behavior.

Why Is It Hard to Eliminate Waste?

The first reason it is hard is because teams have grown accustomed to living with it. And if a team can justify allowing it in the first place, then it can often justify living with it "a little longer." Some teams do track their waste but almost always as work that needs to get done "as soon as there is time." (And when does that ever happen?) The connection between the decision to delay doing necessary work and the negative consequences of not doing the work (which typically occur much later) is hard to see and especially hard to quantify—and this is one of the fundamental reasons why waste tends to accumulate and, even if identified and tracked, is never actually eliminated.

Here is a well-worn example, but one that is so universal that it is easy to understand. Many teams regularly allow defect backlogs to accrue; however, studies have shown that the cost of fixing defects increases the further from inception they are fixed. Think about it this way: Say that 4 months have elapsed since a defect was first found. The developer has moved on to other code and has no doubt forgotten many of the subtleties of the code where the defect was found—and will require time to re-acquaint himself with the code before even attempting to fix the defect. Time is also required to set up the scenario with which to re-create the defect and validate the fix. If automated unit tests are not available to validate that the surrounding code is not impacted by the fix, additional regression testing may be required. We would bet that most developers would agree with this understanding based on their experiences. Adopting a debt intolerant behavior— meaning that defects are fixed when they are found—will improve the quality of the code, reduce the cost of fixing the code, and reduce the overhead costs of managing defect backlogs. It could easily be argued that each benefit by itself is worth the effort, but getting all three benefits should seal the deal.

The same thinking can be applied to many other examples of project waste like code refactoring, unmaintained automation, faulty builds, and so forth. Addressing problems when encountered is usually cheaper and increases efficiency when handled. This is why getting to "Done!" each iteration is critical!

The second reason why it is difficult to eliminate waste, and perhaps the essence of the issue, is that eliminating waste requires significant discipline, takes critical time, and, frankly, is hard work. Software development is complex, and as a code base increases, the demands on managing the code increase right along with it, generally faster than teams anticipate. Starting with high quality—and maintaining high quality throughout a project—is not easy. Even so, it is better than allowing waste to build up and then trying to resurrect quality at a later point in time. Waste accrual usually starts out as something small that is easy to deprioritize.

Here's a story of waste that may well resonate with you. A highly skilled software team I know of built a framework to automatically execute tests that made system level API calls to test server functionality. It did this because, at the time, there were no commercial frameworks to do the equivalent work. This team was progressive in both its innovation and its attention to quality—each time the team added server functionality, it added corresponding tests to the automation framework that could validate the new functionality. This framework was well tuned to its specific product and had the added benefit of running against a wide variety of platforms. The team estimated that approximately 90 percent of the core code was qualified by the tests executing in this framework, so its value was obvious. A subset of these tests was executed as part of the build verification testing accomplished for each "delta build." The entire automated suite was executed after a complete build.

The product was certified for a wide range of hardware and software platforms. Any automation test failures tended to be the result of either new or changing functionality in the server, or the result of a software update in a particular platform. The automation framework and the automated tests both required regular upkeep to maintain pace with the new code and the platform changes.

Over time, the team size decreased, and the domain expertise on the automation framework dwindled as a result. Consequently, the team let the automation framework fall into disrepair, and failing tests started to accumulate. The team kept trying to set aside time to fix the problems but it did not make doing so a priority. There was just too much pressure to do other things. The core code base had not changed substantially, so the problems never seemed that urgent in spite of the failing tests.

As time went on, additional problems surfaced, but these were not addressed either. The team got behind on both the maintenance of the test framework and the tests. One day, a consistent set of tests associated with the build verification that had been working all along began to fail. An analysis was unable to show whether the problem was due to new code that was failing or due to the out-of-date automation framework. To add to the growing number of problems, the framework was no longer enabling debug on some of the platforms where problems were encountered—making eventual resolution of the failing tests even more difficult. Many of the test environments took time to reproduce so that they could be debugged, and few developers had the knowledge to determine whether the problems were in the framework, the automated tests, or the software being tested. The developers who did have some familiarity with the framework suspected that the main problem was with the framework, but they couldn't tell for sure without spending a lot of time investigating.

The previous example is a typical scenario regarding project waste; it tends to grow, steadily and almost imperceptibly, until one day it comes back to bite the team in a big way. To avoid such scenarios, when problems arise, they should be fixed, and fixing them must be a high priority. In situations in which project waste is allowed to accumulate, the team usually does the rest of the work required to release the software, claims victory, and moves on. It tracks these nagging issues as problems to fix "when it gets time." As time passes, the problems often compound and related problems surface. What's even worse is that the issues not addressed might well be masking problems that customers will find. And whenever customers find problems, the problems almost always cost more to fix than if the problems had been fixed before the product was released. This is the proverbial frog-in-the-kettle scenario. The heat keeps building—slowly— and the frog isn't aware of it until it's too late. Eventually the team is *forced* by circumstances to fix the problems at great cost or, even worse, to scrap the project altogether.

When Scott and I started working with the team previously mentioned to help it transition to agile, having it fix its automation framework was a top priority. This was waste that the team had accumulated, and it was costing time every time the tests were run. It may seem obvious in reading the story that the team needed to stop and fix the problems, but justifying additional time on a short-term project schedule is not always an easy sell.

Consequently, teams often believe that tracking project debt is an acceptable alternative because they *might* someday need that information *if* they get more time and resources, which would allow them to get rid of the debt. If your team does have a track record of tackling debt and eliminating it, then you are in good shape. However, if lists of wastes have survived for multiple releases without being eliminated, you should make the decision to either address the debt and get rid of it now, or just stop tracking it altogether with no plans to ever eliminate it. If teams do not believe the value of tackling the debt is high enough to prioritize it, they should stop tracking it. If it ultimately turns out that you were wrong about not addressing something, and it actually was important enough to finally warrant your attention, it will come back and make itself known. Put simply, if it is in your near-term plans to address it, address it; otherwise, do not track it. Tracking outstanding work that is never going to be done is also a waste.

Practices

Get Rid of Waste... One Way or Another

Software projects and teams that have been in place for some time have likely accumulated waste that they need to address. One of the reasons that waste does hang around is that removing it is hard to prioritize over adding new features that customers request, as well as other business priorities. And yes, there are scenarios in which it does not make business sense to remove waste. But a choice should be made instead of just letting it continue to hang around.

To evaluate whether it makes sense to remove the waste, track the debt in the backlog as a user story that defines the value of solving the problem. For instance, refactoring some part of the code may reduce customer incidents by 25 percent. Or perhaps fixing automation defects would increase test efficiency by 30 percent, thereby ensuring release deadlines succeed 90 percent of the time. If you cannot define the value of removing some debt that you are tracking, the debt may not be worth resolving.

However, what is best for the customer as well as what is best for the business both need to be considered. The following example from several years ago shows both perspectives in play. A server team was in place to maintain the current server technology while another team was developing a new server technology. The existing software was in production at thousands of customer sites, and it would be several years before many of those customers would upgrade to the new technology. The team working on the existing software found scenarios in which it made a lot of sense to refactor parts of the code to better support the customer base. However, it hit a big problem with the code that only a couple of customers encountered. In essence the code updated an inherited property of all items in a hierarchy recursively. It was an elegant solution for a small hierarchy; however, a handful of customers had created huge hierarchies. For those customers, the updates took the server days and essentially ground performance to a halt. The team looked at ways to fix the problem but concluded that refactoring would take months of work because it would impact the rest of the system. After investigating this issue for weeks, the team devised ways to help the affected customers work around the problem. The proposed solution still impacted the team and the customers, but after much review, everyone decided this was a better resolution to the problem than undertaking a major rewrite of the code, especially because the new server project was underway. The other team, the one working on the new server technology, was made aware of this problem and they took this into consideration and avoided similar problems.

There are many examples of project debt and, therefore, how teams resolve their particular types of debt will vary as well. In the cases in which debt needs to be removed, the act of removing debt is often liberating and tends to result in better habits going forward. Removing debt is also often critical to getting to working software constantly.

Small Tasks

Many agile practices are built on the adoption of queuing theory, which involves using small tasks to accomplish work. Within an iteration, it is easier to complete a steady stream of small work items, or tasks, than it is to complete one or two big tasks. When tasks are small, their boundaries are easier to define and contain. Using small tasks limits the scope of the work so that project debt is more readily noticed and, therefore, harder to accumulate. Other wasteful practices are also more readily apparent.

The idea is to break the work down into tasks that can be completed in several hours, or 1 or 2 days at most. Small user stories, small tasks, in short iterations, make it easier to define the boundaries of completion. When teams implement small user stories and actually get to "Done!" they develop a different attitude about accumulating waste in the process. The team has to get to "Done!" and accumulating waste prevents this, so the impetus to eliminate waste when it is first noticed is increased. Before moving on to a new user story, the team has to first confirm that the story completion criteria for the current story is satisfied, and only then does the team move on to the next story. This means that stories have to be something that can actually be completed within an iteration—and this is a key point. If more code is written in an iteration than can be tested, there will be leftover defects at a minimum, and quite possibly other debt as well. When teams start employing user stories and learn how to work together on a story and get to "Done!," accumulating waste slows them down, giving them incentive to avoid it. See Chapter 3, "Queuing Theory," for a more thorough discussion of the importance of using small tasks to accomplish work.

Build Quality In

To get ahead of the waste accrual predicament, establish a mindset that encourages problem *prevention*. When I learned about lean and agile in a class led by Tom and Mary Poppendieck, Mary said that teams have to learn how to avoid problems. Instead of just getting into the habit of testing thoroughly and fixing problems quickly, start developing in a way that avoids problems altogether. Preventing defects is far less costly than the process of finding and fixing defects.

One of the significant benefits to following an agile methodology is the focus on "building quality in." Many options are available to teams to build quality in, including test-driven development, automated unit testing, static code analysis, automatic deployment of the code when a build completes, and follow-on automated testing. Using these practices allows a team to deliver working software in short, time-boxed iterations where success is measured by delivering code that is "Done!" at the end of an iteration (that is, working and bug-free).

Test-driven development is one of the most popular ways to build quality in. The obvious advantage to test-driven development is that developers test *first*. In other words, developers must "technically describe how to evaluate the solution" before code is written. One of the non-obvious advantages to a test-driven development approach is that writing code to satisfy the tests ensures that developers write only the code required to pass the test. This way, no *extra* code gets written, code "that *might* make the functionality more complete" (or so the thinking goes...). The less code that is written, the less code needs to be tested, automated, and supported. Test-driven development often results in leaner code that does "just enough" and thus eliminates a lot of typical wastes.

Another useful approach for defect avoidance is *pair programming*. Two sets of eyes expand the view of the software as it is written. *Pair design* is another avenue to explore. Before writing code, try working together with someone on a design, for the same reasons that you would pair program. Chances are you will each look at the task at hand differently and will come up with different problems to avoid and ultimately discover an overall better solution.

Finally, build quality into the product by actively avoiding and removing complexity. Avoiding complexity in code is as hard as writing prose clearly and with brevity. For instance, if I want to write a useful email, a clear, short message is more effective than a long-winded one, but I might have to start with a long message that I then prune. I have to go through a process of refining the points I need to make, writing those well, and eliminating the rest.[7] Reducing code complexity may require a similar effort; that is, if you start with complexity, then refactor the code to define and limit the critical code paths, improve those code paths, and eliminate the rest. Static code analysis tools that evaluate the conditional complexity (that is, things like the number of code paths and the amount of nesting) can help identify areas in the code that can be improved by reducing complexity. Reducing complexity can reduce test requirements and potential maintenance headaches.

There are more ways to build quality into the code than previously mentioned. Teams need to continue to try new ways to build quality in. See Chapter 11, "Continuous Improvement," for more ideas in this area.

Focus on Customer Value

The first agile principle says, "Our highest priority is to satisfy the customer...."[8] This thinking helps teams focus their efforts on delivering customer value and avoiding other activities that have resulted in waste in the past. In traditional software projects, teams created a set of product requirements based on what customers said they wanted. The requirements were described thoroughly, and typically features were fully designed and test cases were written to test every code path. What years of using this approach have taught us is that many of the features did not get used or, at best, only a few code paths of those features were used. Testing was comprehensive and often revealed many obscure issues that may or may not ever have been discovered in real deployments by customers. Furthermore, it was hard to do an adequate job documenting the myriad of features in case customers did want to use them. This approach invariably resulted in unused code, tests that tested unused code paths, documentation that covered the breadth of the product but often missed on the depth, and defect backlogs. In other words, this was nothing more than a pattern of creating waste.

Agile thinking gives us a way to operate that enables teams to deliver customer value and avoid debt creation. User stories enable teams to limit their focus to solving the problem described by customers instead of creating a lot of general functionality. The focus is on satisfying the most critical usage scenarios instead of offering functionality that *might* be useful.

User stories define the goal of a user or, more specifically, what problem a user is trying to solve. For example,

> As an IT Administrator, I need to ensure that contents of folders marked as proprietary are only accessible to need-to-know users so that our company's intellectual property is only accessible to authorized personnel.

---

7. The 17th-century French philosopher and mathematician Blaise Pascal famously said, "I have made this letter longer than usual, only because I have not had time to make it shorter."

8. http://www.agilemanifesto.org/.

To mark the story as "Done!" the team needs to make sure that only authorized users can access items in a proprietary folder. The team may want to give the user different access options, but if this is the only mandate for user differentiation, make this scenario work and expand only on the feature if customers indicate that it makes sense. As the code is implemented and tested during an iteration, developers and testers stay in lock step so that defects are fixed as they are found. Working this closely together ensures that the team completes the critical work and gets to "Done!" User stories define the essence of what problem needs to be solved and, therefore, what needs to be tested. Doing more than necessary will likely result in waste.

To provide an example, think of an application you use regularly that does not work well in some way. My favorite example is of an email application that can sort only email message subjects alphabetically. An email thread cannot be grouped together because email replies prefixed with "Re:" (Reply) do not align with email messages from the same thread prefixed with "Fw:" (Forward), or for that matter with the original email message that has no prefix. This behavior drives me *nuts!* It is an annoyance that I have to work around. As an email user, I need to manage related email threads so that I can respond within the appropriate context and with an understanding of the history of a given thread. In this case, the product's implementation of sorting works alphabetically—but that is not the way I use the product. Chances are, sorting this way was not considered a design defect. However, from my perspective as a customer, the software does not work well for one of my most common usage patterns. I do not care about all the features I do not use nor whether defects were fixed in those unused features. My point is that focusing on customer value ensures teams make the critical features work well, they avoid doing unnecessary work, and they also avoid creating unnecessary debt.

Expand "Done!" Criteria

Iteration "Done!" criteria should be used as a vehicle to prevent the buildup of project waste. Putting it another way, expand "Done!" criteria to foster debt intolerance. As teams progress through a project and discover that there are particular kinds of project debt building up, they should consider adding those additional items to your "Done!" criteria to prevent any further accumulation of those particular kinds of debt.

For example, say that teams notice that they are falling behind in maintaining the expected levels of security enforcement in the code. In this case, they should add security enforcement to their "Done!" criteria. Teams may resist this because they think it is slowing them down. But, as they build the security enforcement into the code as part of their day-to-day work, as well as learn how to keep their testing current to validate the security compliance, they will get more efficient than if they were to pile up their security enforcement work until late in the project. After the initial slow down to learn how to add the new security enforcement work efficiently, they will avoid the long-term drag it would have on the project if it were delayed.

Handling Latent Defects

How do you handle pre-existing defects that are discovered in the code when you work on it again? We suggest treating all newly found defects in the same way. No matter whether the defect has existed for years or whether it was just injected this morning, the approach is to "fix it now." Do not wait until later to fix a defect just because it has existed in the code for a long time.

Of course, the caveat here is that if the defect has been lying dormant in the code for a long time—and customers have not found it yet—then it may not make sense to fix it. In this case, professional judgment needs to be used to ascertain whether the new code being written will likely surface the latent defect. If it does, fix it as part of the work of the iteration in which it was found. Otherwise, cancel the defect without fixing it.

Stop Writing Defect Records

There is a case for not writing up defects at all. I had a team that adopted continuous integration aggressively. After 6 months of effort, it went from two or three multihour builds a week to multiple builds daily, each build taking less than 30 minutes. (Even 30 minutes may seem long to some, but for many large enterprise code bases, this is relatively fast.) Builds were made continually as new code was checked into the source control system. If the build, the automated unit testing, and the static code analysis were completed without error, the build verification tests ran. Upon successful completion of that testing, the build was deployed to test servers where longer running test suites were started. At the same time the team was notified by email that the build was completed and deployed. In this way developers and testers could both be on the same build. In fact, the process became so tidy and predictable that testers would validate that defects were fixed the same day the updated code was checked in.

As the team got used to this predictable turnaround, their process evolved. When a defect was discovered, the tester notified the developer. They often discovered the defect together, as they stayed tightly connected while doing their work. The developer would evaluate how soon he could target a fix. If he thought it could be turned around within a day or two, the testers started to experiment with not writing up a defect record. They decided that the process of recording the defect, updating it, and closing it, was slowing them down. So they established a new practice: If a defect could be targeted for resolution within 2 days, they would not write up the defect. Communication between developers and testers was all that was needed.

When I tell other teams this story, they generally react with horror. "How can they *not* track defects?" "If they don't track their defects, how do they know how many defects were actually found?" "They won't have a history of defects to determine where the code might be vulnerable." "They cannot validate how good their test efforts were!"

At the risk of further alarming those of you who may harbor similar sentiments, consider the following: Do defect counts tell you anything about product quality? If 300 defects were found and fixed in the last release, and the total was 350 in this release, does that information tell you *anything at all* about the relative quality of the two releases? If you find 10 defects in this release, and you found 100 in the last release, did you write better software? Or test less? Or both? Or something else? How often do you go back and review the defects that you found and use that analysis to write better code? Much of the response we get to this suggestion reflects waterfall thinking: "We have to do it because we've always done it this way!"

We would argue that, in keeping with the lean and agile practices touched on throughout this book, the supposed benefits of tracking all defects are rarely (if ever) realized, and thus it is clearly a waste. Reconsider the value of creating defect records for every defect. We suggest focusing your energies instead on what produces the best software with the time and resource constraints that you have (that is, focus on defect *prevention* instead).

Teams with a robust continuous integration practice tend to adopt this "no tracking" strategy on short-turnaround defects. The real, critical difference here is that everyone in a "no-tracking" environment is working on the same build, which is enabled only by a continuous integration build practice. This point may sound minor, but it actually is key: *Everyone is on the same build*. This single practice can significantly change the way teams work together. The entire team can achieve higher productivity because it is working on the same build. It eliminates the wastes of task switching that occurs when team members are all working on different builds and trying to coordinate their efforts.

Teams that work on the same build become more comfortable not tracking short-turnaround defects because this strategy enables them to work closely together to regularly complete small slices of functionality. Problems are discovered and fixed close to when they are created, so the combined team has a much better handle on quality and can agree together when it is "good enough." By not recording defects (for example, by using a "2-day turn around rule"), a team can minimize waste and thus stay focused on more critical work.

Metrics

An easy way to validate whether you are accumulating project debt in terms of defect backlogs is to track how many open defects there are at the end of every iteration. If the team is working closely together on small user stories, defects may be found throughout the iteration, but the number that remain open should trend toward zero by the end of the iteration. A handful of defects—at most—should remain if the team is completing stories and counting them as "Done!" Ideally, teams should strive to get to zero known defects but, as many teams experience, defects may be discovered during live demos of the code at the end of an iteration. The goal, however, still remains: Stay as close to zero known defects on your backlog as possible at all times.

Any remaining defects must be closed at the beginning of the next iteration. This should be considered a hard-and-fast practice because it ensures that a defect backlog will not accumulate. It will also encourage teams to push harder at the end of an iteration to close everything out because starting an iteration with unfinished work is a drag.

Look at the defect backlog at iteration boundaries and use that as a guide to determine if you are kicking the project debt habit. The backlog of defects should be low at the end of each iteration and should not increase over the project life cycle. It should be at zero when you ship your product.

I have repeatedly challenged teams to ship with zero known defects. Some people who read this might say, "Well, of course!" But many teams are used to having a remaining backlog that they carry from release to release and think that having *no* backlog is an unrealistic goal. When I first started with agile I, too, thought that this was an unrealistic goal—and I could argue into submission anyone who disagreed. But I now think that it is both a realistic *and critical* goal. Fix the problems that you know need to be fixed, and delete the problems that it does not make sense to fix. Do not give yourself a buffer at the end of a release to drive the backlog to zero; rather, start with zero and keep it as close to that as possible throughout the release. Learn how to get to "Done!" every iteration and drive toward high-quality consistently. Shipping with no known defects is liberating—and it *is* achievable.

Note that we've discussed defects a lot in this section because they tend to be a fairly large component of teams' project debt. Do not forget, however, that waste is more than just defect backlogs: Lack of code automation, code that needs refactoring due to complexity, code duplication, and so on are also forms of waste. Design decisions of the "chewing gum, bailing wire, and duct-tape" variety, resulting in "spaghetti code," is technical debt, which is a *big* form of waste—just ask any team whose responsibility it is to maintain code that resembles a labyrinth instead of something created in a disciplined fashion! When you kick the defect debt habit, apply the same approach to other types of waste—and keep getting better.

Breakthrough

If you want to get into the habit of not accumulating waste, try this technique: Limit defect priorities to *just one classification*: *"Fix it now!"*

It is a common practice in waterfall (and even with many agile teams) to assign severities to defects when encountered, store them in backlogs, and then review the backlog periodically with an eye toward deciding which ones need to be fixed and which can be put off until later. If teams are willing to spend the time to find, document, and track defects, why are they not willing to spend the time to actually *fix* the defects—and preferably at the point in time when the defects are found because it's a much less wasteful approach?

Prioritizing defects is an old software development practice. Most software teams have developed their own strategy to characterize defects by priority, severity, impact, and various other criteria. The highest priority defects usually define issues that make a system inoperable. The lowest priority defects are generally annoyances that do not affect the software's capability to operate. (However, they're still *annoyances*—think of your customers!)

The sequence usually follows a pattern like this: Test engineers are responsible for testing some aspect of the code, identifying problems, and recording them. As defects are identified, team leaders are assigned to triage incoming defects, prioritize them, and assign them to developers. Defect triage sessions can be arduous because they require that the defect description be decipherable, they require an understanding of how critical the defect is, and who has the skills to fix it. After a defect assignment is complete, developers typically tackle the highest priority defects first. As they work through their queue of assigned defects, they may start by trying to understand all of them so that they can group them and tackle defects in the same area of the code at the same time. When developers start working on a defect (or on a set of defects) they usually have to set up a system to re-create the defects and, to do this, they may need to go back to the defect author for help. After they can re-create a given defect, they look for a solution. If the solution entails code fixes, they submit these and notify the test group that the defect fix can be verified in the next build. This is a linear process and is, therefore, typically slow and often disjointed. Managing defect lists is a logical consequence of developing lots of code and then testing via a linear process. And shipping with defects violates the mandate to ship high-quality software.

A Value Stream Map[9] of the defect resolution process often reveals hours spent simply reviewing and triaging defect backlogs. If teams were to make efforts to fix defects when they are discovered, the defect lists would be short. If the goal is to fix all defects before moving on, teams should not spend time prioritizing them—what's the point? If the team agrees that a defect needs to be fixed, it agrees as a team to fix it before moving on. But how can this be "enforced?"

Agile's time-boxed iterations provide the solution. One of the benefits of the agile methodology is that it enables teams to deliver working software in short, time-boxed iterations where success criteria is delivering code that is "Done!" at the end of an iteration. This strategy improves a team's motivation both to prevent defects as well as find them as soon as possible after the code is written. Fixing defects while developers are working in the code is cheaper than finding and fixing them later in the project. Teams that follow this end-of-iteration "Done!" behavior get into the habit of closing out all defects during the iteration in which the code was developed. If there are a few stragglers, they get front-loaded in the next iteration. If all defects are managed within iterations, why bother prioritizing them?

Although this breakthrough targets only defects, you can apply the same thinking to other types of project waste that you track. Minimize the process of managing the waste. Decide that you're going to address the waste—and then do it. Or decide that you are not going to address it and forget about it. Do not revisit the decision unless the problem returns.

Summary

Being agile requires eliminating waste to realize significant efficiency, productivity, and quality gains.

- Eliminating waste means removing anything that does not deliver value to the customer, as well as removing all forms of project debt.
- Eliminating waste as a practice enables teams to handle problems when they are the cheapest to handle. Addressing waste later always costs more.

9. See the discussion of Value Stream Maps in the Chapter 11, "Continuous Improvement."

- Ward Cunningham's *technical debt* metaphor is a concise way of describing the costs incurred due to compromises in software design. Project debt is a term that applies more generally to various wastes that can occur in an overall project. Trying to be "debt intolerant" can help teams inject the habit of eliminating waste into their day-to-day activities.

- Avoiding project debt is hard because teams have gotten used to living with it and still think they deliver "successful" software. It is also hard because "no project debt" behavior requires discipline that can be hard to establish and maintain.

- Start to establish a debt intolerant culture by removing any accumulated debt. When done, strive mightily to keep it from accumulating again.

- Teams can use small tasks to limit the scope of the work so that project debt is both easier to see and harder to accumulate. Small user stories help teams learn how to work together on small tasks to get to "Done!," thus leaving no project debt.

- Adopt mechanisms to build quality in and reduce complexity to avoid project debt, including unit testing, test driven development, pair programming, static code analysis, and automated testing and deployment.

- Prioritize customer value, as defined in user stories, by focusing on qualifying critical customer usage scenarios over creating unused functionality that can result in project waste.

- Expand your "Done!" criteria to include items that start to accumulate as project debt to ensure that they are no longer allowed to accumulate.

- Breakthrough your project debt habits by challenging your team with one defect priority: *fix it now!*

CHAPTER 6

Working Software

Being agile requires always having working software because it validates progress, ensures the highest levels of quality, and enables regular feedback.

By Leslie Ekas

Working software is the heartbeat of a project. It is the key to understanding status, viability, and risk. Even for software that does not ship every iteration, always having working software (release-ready, shippable software) is critical to project success. One of the benefits of having working software when working at the enterprise level is the ability to deploy and use the product continuously—the code undergoes constant validation in more realistic environments. However, some teams still wait for their code to be "all done" before they are willing to use it in a real deployment scenario.

I know of a team of engineers who refactored their kernel-level code and who held off deploying it in a live environment. They wanted to have all the code done and fully tested before even considering putting it into such an environment. The stakes were high because newly found defects in this code often felt random, resulted in "blue screens," and, in rare cases, lost data. When a user encountered a problem with the product, the team needed to work with the user at his workstation to isolate the situation that resulted in the failure. This process could take hours, or even days, and thus prevented the user from continuing to do other work. And problem resolution could be just as time-consuming. With these challenges in mind, the team did not want to use the updated product "live" until it had run all its tests and fixed all the known problems. The team did not want to negatively impact an organization by going live before it thought the code was ready. The problem with this approach, however, was that the team was unable to test all the usage patterns that active users typically employed, and thus there were always problems that would arise when the product was deployed live. By delaying any deployments the team actually compounded its problems instead of avoiding them—the team never knew for sure whether it had working software.

Given the team's reluctance to deploy its newly redesigned software until it had "hardened," it wasn't finally deployed live until late in the release cycle. When the new version finally was deployed, it was readily apparent that the code was not ready for release. Of course, the team was disappointed. The code worked in the team's testing scenarios—but live deployment quickly revealed several problems. Worse, after evaluating the problems discovered, it was apparent that the design approach used was not going to work. Had the software been exercised in a live environment earlier, it is likely critical time would have been saved because the problems would have been identified much earlier and needed changes would have been more manageable. Ultimately, resolution of the problems uncovered was going to require a large amount of time to redo much of what had already been done. Although the team did not want to impact the productivity of the greater team by avoiding live deployments until late in the project, it didn't know until the end of the project that it did not have working software and had to pull that functionality from the release. To make things even worse, not having that functionality ultimately did impact the success of the release.

Teams should do everything they can to find defects as early as possible so that they can be fixed as quickly—and easily—as possible. If big defects are found early, the team should *celebrate*, not be "hung out to dry." Demonstrating working software throughout a project helps teams have high levels of confidence regarding the quality and viability of their project.

Principles

What Is Working Software?

Essentially, working software is software that is "release-ready." The notion of working software is so fundamental to agile thinking that it is included in the Agile Manifesto: "Working software over comprehensive documentation." The point is also included as a principle of the Agile Manifesto: "Working software is the primary measure of progress."[1]

Many teams use the term *working code* interchangeably with the term *working software*. Developers think in terms of code because that is the level at which they are working, but Scott and I want to push hard for thinking in terms of working *software* because working software is what customers want and thus it defines real project progress.

Agile thinking requires teams to have working software every iteration. For many teams this means shipping or deploying the product into production at the end of each iteration. Releasing this frequently may be an unrealistic goal for teams developing enterprise application software—in enterprise application software development, the breadth of some new functionality being developed is often significant. A small slice of some larger feature (that is, the amount completed as part of a single iteration) is likely not enough to warrant a full release of the product. However, as enterprise products start to embrace newer delivery models like PaaS[2] (Platform

---

1. http://agilemanifesto.org/ and http://agilemanifesto.org/principles.html
2. See: http://en.wikipedia.org/wiki/PaaS

as a Service) and SaaS,[3] (Software as a Service) having release-ready, shippable software every iteration will become more critical.

In any case, having working software as a goal is important, and teams need to think in terms of "shippable software" having the necessary level of quality so that it *could* be deployed by a customer. The software should be from a production-level build; defects should be fixed and verified; all necessary testing should be complete; and any required product documentation should be written and reviewed. Having shippable software every iteration does not mean that it has to make business sense to actually release a new version of the product each iteration, but should such a decision actually be made, it should be easily manageable.

Many enterprise products require multiple iterations to create the needed level of business-relevant functionality. Because of this, teams often feel OK with dropping the goal of having working software for those intermediate iterations. Consequently, these teams lose the value that having working software brings, the value that makes agile so effective. The ability to have shippable software every iteration requires that teams focus on the most critical work, do just enough of it, and finish. Doing just enough in this context means that teams provide the functionality critical to customer success—and no more—and that the functionality is tested in the way that a customer will use it. This way, teams do what is necessary in the shortest amount of time. Doing just enough does not mean that you skip critical work, but it does mean that you limit the work to the most critical work.

Waterfall thinking has repeatedly lulled teams into believing there will be time at the end of a project, or time after the release ships, to tidy up and address loose ends. This almost never happens because engineers tend to be eternal optimists and almost always underestimate how long a project will take. Teams that achieve shippable software each iteration are required to make hard choices about what to do and what not to do. They have to develop enough, test enough, document enough, and decide when to move on to the next user story. Always having working software enforces this discipline and keeps teams from practicing wasteful habits. That is why it is critical that teams never stop trying to produce working software every iteration.

In addition, keeping this goal in place motivates teams to continually improve their practices, their software, their technology, and their enablement. For example, no matter how good you are at testing, technology changes, test methods improve, and hardware gets better—meaning that testing can always get better. On the other hand, complacency results in an open invitation to the competition. The software industry is competitive and getting more competitive all the time. Doing just enough with high quality is a requirement to "stay in the game."

Being agile requires having working software because it validates project progress. It confirms that what is being created actually works. It allows testing of the architecture early—and continually—as the code evolves. It provides short feedback loops so that teams can ensure that the product meets customers' needs and continues to do so throughout the project. Working software enables software to be deployed early, in real environments, using real usage patterns, and it enables teams to build confidence in product quality by constant live usage.

---

3. See: http://en.wikipedia.org/wiki/SaaS

Why Is It Hard to Regularly Have Working Software?

Teams transforming to agile may have a variety of hurdles to overcome to get into the pattern of having working software every iteration. First, teams need to have both a continuous integration system and a continuous integration practice in place to enable rapid software builds, test validation, and deployment. This constant cycle is essential for teams to get to "Done!" each iteration. If it takes more than a few hours to successfully build code and validate the build, then it is hard to regularly get to "Done!" in a short iteration. As code is developed during the iteration, the continuous build/test/deployment cycle must be short enough to "harden" the code. Teams must make continuous integration a top priority. With a well-functioning continuous integration cycle, teams will find it much easier to get to "Done!" each iteration. When teams get good at continuous integration, they need to expand their practices to include continuous deployment. Implementing a continuous integration environment takes effort to establish and continual effort to update and evolve, which helps explain why teams may not prioritize it, which in turns helps explain why teams struggle with always having working software.

Second, waterfall teams often build their product components separately, making it impossible to have working software until they successfully merge the components together. Having teams made up only of members who all share the same skills reinforces this poor practice. The software practice of teams working individually on specific components precludes meeting the goal of regularly having working software. See Chapter 1, "Whole Teams," for a discussion of the importance of creating cross-component teams.

A third hurdle for teams is learning how to get to "Done!" every iteration. How does a team finish—really finish—developing, documenting, and testing code each iteration? Shippable software means the code is developed, tested, and documented, that defects are fixed, and that it is now usable. The key to getting to "Done!" is that teams have to learn how to do "just enough," and they have to do this as a team. Together, they must limit the amount of functionality targeted for an iteration so that not only can the code be written, but necessary testing, documentation, defect fixing, automation, and deployment can all be accomplished as well. Because team members succeed or fail together, they have to make the hard choices together. The more discipline teams apply to getting to "Done!" the more it enables them to have working software continuously, and the more it enables them move on to new work sooner.

Working Software Extends Test Suites

You could argue that an adequate test suite should satisfy quality validation required for shippable software. However, real users have varied usage patterns and often find alternative ways of doing work. For example, every user station might have a slightly different configuration and different versions of software and hardware. These are subtle variations that typical testing suites are not likely to cover. When new usage patterns uncover problems with the code, these new patterns need to be factored into the test strategy.

Having working software enables the team to discover new usage patterns that may not have otherwise surfaced if its customers were unable to use the product. And the constant validation of working software by users in their environments vastly improves the team's confidence that what it has completed up to that point works.

Practices

Short Iterations

Short iterations help teams learn quickly how to get to "Done!" every iteration. We believe that iterations should never exceed 2 weeks in length, no matter the circumstances. This assertion causes alarm bells to go off for many teams. Team members know how to break down their own work into small chunks, but the trick is understanding how to break down functionality in such a way that the whole team can focus on completing all aspects of development for a given user story within an iteration. For waterfall teams, this is always a tough concept to put into practice: Developers have historically worried only about coding, testers only about testing, and writers only about writing. Getting all disciplines working together to achieve the shared goal of working software at the end of an iteration is typically a big, big change.

As coaches, Scott and I insist that teams use 1- or 2-week iterations. I think we have heard every reason why such seemingly short iterations will not work. "There is no way to break down user stories to be that small," "We cannot get enough implemented to test," "Team members have too many distractions to complete their work in that amount of time," "Our tests take too long to run," and on and on and on. In one case we worked with two organizations that each had more than 100 engineers worldwide. Both teams *knew* that 2-week iterations would never work—and they were adamant. We gave them a litany of reasons why shorter iterations were a better approach, none of which was able to convince them completely. We eventually settled on a compromise. They would try shorter iterations for just a few months to see if they could make them work. (The great thing about short iterations is that it doesn't take long to try them, and realizing good results doesn't take long either.) One year later I listened to these teams tell their customers (in person) that they would never give up two-week iterations. They laughed at how hard they had initially resisted, but they ultimately ended up firmly on the side of "shorter is better."

With another very large team, one of the chief architects admitted to the greater team that he *hated* short iterations. He also said that he would *not* give them up. Because he used short iterations and was always striving to have working software, he could identify problems extremely early. For him and for his team, short iterations were worth the initial pain of becoming more disciplined.

Our belief in the merits of shorter iterations strengthened as we worked with more teams. We have a long list of reasons why short iterations are better, but let me focus on just a few. First, your estimates are better when you are planning for a shorter amount of time. Two weeks seems to be about the limit to how well many teams are able to forecast. It is just hard to know exactly how the work will proceed, so the further out you plan, the more prone to error the plans will be.

The next reason why short iterations work is that success requires that teams break their work down into smaller pieces. We encourage teams to develop small user stories—stories that can be completed in an iteration. Small user stories result in a closer connection between development and testing and documentation. The continuous feedback cycles while working on a user story enable teams to make continual progress towards having working software and getting to "Done!," thus ensuring teams always have working software.

Creating small user stories is not easy for teams building enterprise software. When you're thinking in terms of large amounts of functionality, it can be hard to imagine how to break work down into pieces that can be completed within two weeks. It obviously can be done, but only with practice. Here is a story of how one team achieved this goal: they had to migrate their large installer to a new platform, which seemed like a simple enough process because the installer code already existed for another platform. The team spent several hours together and came up with the following user stories:

- As a product administrator I need a user-guided installation process for the new environment that does not require manual inputs so that I have a baseline system that works without tuning.

- As a product administrator I need a non-interactive installation process that leverages my IT infrastructure deployment tools so that systems can be automatically installed.

- As a product administrator I need the installer to provide all necessary prerequisite components required to run the core system so that the installation can be executed without requiring additional manual software installations.

- As a product administrator I need the installer to provide the typical default parameters for each of the supporting components that require parameterization so that a baseline system can be created without needing knowledge of the system.

Once they completed breaking these high-level stories down into iteration-sized stories, they realized that these stories adequately defined how much work they really had to do. They knew at the outset that there was a lot of work, but had struggled to demonstrate it. This methodology not only outlined the real work required but also gave them the opportunity to have working software each iteration since some small, definitive chunk of the installer migration was able to be completed each iteration.

As a side note, if you truly want to learn fast, try 1-week iterations. Whether you stick with 1-week iterations is not important, but you can quickly learn what is required to get to "Done!" We've found that 1-week iterations are useful for maintenance software. Teams that manage maintenance releases and critical short-term product problems often deal with rapidly changing priorities, for example, a critical customer problem always trumps any other work that is underway. One-week iterations give teams a better chance to complete their work without interruption. Highly productive agile teams can work in 1-day iterations entirely, but that generally requires a robust continuous deployment environment and a disciplined team.

Continuous Integration and Automation

When one of my former teams first started implementing a few of the agile practices, the team leader learned about continuous integration and asked me to support its adoption. In our case, adopting continuous integration required moving to a new source code management tool, a new build tool, and a continuous integration server. It sounded great, but the team got tremendous resistance from the build team because the build team would have to support new tools and it was already stretched thin. Furthermore, new tools meant more costs to the company—so the uphill battle was significant.

My team solved both problems by developing the system using free, open-source software, and some of its existing hardware. It took the team many months to develop the new system, and then more effort was required to migrate all the code over to the new system. But the end result was amazing. Builds that regularly took 4 to 8 hours now took less than 30 minutes. In addition, the team automated the build generation, validation, and notification, and the team continually added capabilities from there on.

The outcome was so compelling that I became convinced that continuous integration was a critical component of agile success. When I started coaching agile teams in IBM, one of the first recommendations that I typically made was for teams to move to continuous integration. Unless the build and test cycle is very short, it is difficult to have constantly working software. This book does not attempt to define what is required to build a good continuous integration system, but it does reinforce that such a continuous integration system is critical for agile success, particularly in getting to "Done!" each iteration.

Continuous integration and automation go hand in hand. I use the term *automation* generally because it can be applied to more than just testing—it also applies to all work related to continuous integration. Successful continuous integration requires automatic code check-in notification, automatic build on check-in, automatic "successful" or "failed" build notification, automatic unit test and build verification test execution, and automatic deployment. Automation should be used anywhere repetitive tasks can be automated. When you start automating work, it becomes habit-forming.

There are many reasons why automation is critical. It is much cheaper in the long run than manual testing, it can be performed anytime, it can be run continuously, and it can be used by other teams reusing the same code. It is amazing to think that some teams still have to be convinced to automate, considering that computers are more powerful than ever before and teams are stretched to their limits. There are upfront costs to getting automation in place for build, test, and deployment, but the payoffs have been shown time and time again to be well worth the effort.

Automation requires maintenance—and this becomes the next challenge for teams. When teams start to invest in automation, the automation itself has to be maintained. Changes in code will often require corresponding changes to automated tests. When teams invest in automation, necessary maintenance must become part of the work completed each iteration and included in the definition of "Done!"

Vertically Sliced Stories

Vertically sliced user stories (vertical stories) are another critical tool to delivering working software every iteration. After I learned about and tried user stories, I was hooked. But it took me a while to realize the full value of user stories. It wasn't until I caught on to *vertically sliced user stories* that their value really became apparent. Vertical stories deliver a very thin slice of functionality that requires code that works across a product's architecture stack. Completing such a story in an iteration requires that the team deliver incremental functionality.

Teams used to a waterfall style of developing are less comfortable with vertical stories because this mechanism forces them to integrate different architectural components before they have been independently "hardened." And that is exactly why vertical stories are valuable: The goal is to validate the architecture before it is "hardened" so that it can be adjusted much more easily than it can when it is hardened. (An apropos analogy here is working with cement—it's easy to make changes when it's still wet, and almost impossible after it has hardened.) Adopting vertical stories promotes the integration of components as a critical test of product quality and thus a crucial part of getting to "Done!"

One team I worked with tried vertical stories. It started by scoping out a small story: connectivity from the user to the server and nothing else. Before trying vertical stories, the team was convinced that it would not have working software for multiple iterations because it felt it had to get many components of the code completed first and then get them to work together. To adopt vertical stories, it had to stop thinking about completing all the desired functionality for each component before trying to get an end-to-end scenario working. That was a big change in thinking. But having a thin slice of functionality as a goal each iteration kept the team focused. In the first iteration the team completed the work to get connectivity from the user to the server. This thin slice of functionality cut across the architecture stack, although it produced no marketable functionality. However, just because it was not marketable functionality did not mean that it was somehow not valuable. Quite the opposite—this functionality was valuable—customers were going to do it all the time. It is just that this was not all the team wanted to do. But having this initial slice of vertical functionality enabled the team to not only accomplish unit testing and function testing, it also did some initial performance testing ("How long does the connection take?") as well as finishing the product documentation associated with how to log on to the server.

The result in the first iteration was not user-friendly, it was not fast, nor was it "sellable" as a final product. However, it *worked*. And, what was even better, the team was excited because it was sure that it discovered problems in the first iteration that would have taken weeks or months to find using a traditional approach. The results of this initial foray into using short iterations and vertical user stories astounded everyone because they actually got something to work end-to-end, and it was actually fun because, *as a team*, they were all involved in getting it to work. The team continued with this approach throughout the project and ended up confident in the resulting architecture because it had working software throughout the entire project.

Evolutionary Architecture and Emergent Design

Evolutionary architecture is an important practice that enables teams to maintain working software as it progresses through a project. As teams write code and evaluate what works well, the best design patterns "emerge." When architecture, design, or redesign is part of the work needed in an agile project, the concepts of evolutionary architecture and emergent design should be considered. Contrary to popular mythology, evolutionary architecture *does* start with an architectural model, just not a *finished* model. So, if you've heard that evolutionary architecture is nothing more than an architectural "wild-west show," I ask you to set such thoughts aside and read on.

The idea behind evolutionary architecture is to start with whatever architecture is needed to get started, but to leave out as much as possible. The more settled the architecture is in the beginning, the harder it is to change. The architecture describes what components are required and how they work together at a high level. Coding, testing, and actual usage are required to evaluate and validate the architecture. After a general architecture is defined, the coding patterns established to make the software work actually describe the design. Design is a vague term, but think of it as the patterns in the code that work well. When the best design patterns are identified, repeat them as the project progresses. It is hard to know what is going to work well until teams actually have working software.

Vertically sliced user stories, as previously described, are a critical element in evolutionary architecture. Starting with a high-level architecture, teams create vertical stories that deliver thin slices of functionality that cut across the architecture. In the first iteration, the team develops just enough of each component to complete the first user story. In the next iteration, the team adds another thin slice of functionality. They continue in this manner until the design has been proven or needed changes are identified and made. The most significant advantage to this evolutionary style of architecture and emergent design is that it tests the architecture early in the development cycle and repeatedly throughout. Adjustments to the architecture are easier to make if it is not locked into place from the outset. Risks should be handled early: Focus on the highest-risk areas until the architecture is well tested. Nonfunctional requirements like performance, scalability, and so forth, can be tested and confirmed earlier as well. The ability to identify design patterns early is also critical. These advantages are all achieved because this approach capitalizes on the practice of teams creating working software each iteration.

This evolutionary architecture and design approach was adopted years ago in an interesting way by a team that converted a large web client application to adopt the then-new Web 2.0 capabilities (such as the elimination of unnecessary page updates and better usability through application messaging). The work needed to do the conversion was both significant and costly because the application was quite large. The team settled on a new architecture approach and estimated the work to complete the entire conversion. It was no surprise that the estimates well exceeded the targeted time frame that was believed critical for customer success. Furthermore the team's approach was to develop the overall architecture for the entire application first, which, unfortunately, was going to ensure that none of the application would work for a long time.

Because of these issues, the team adopted an evolutionary architecture approach. They decided to convert the architecture incrementally, meaning that they had to leave the existing architecture in place so that the remainder of the application continued to function. The team's rule was that the application had to continue to work, even as the team was incrementally changing the framework upon which the product was built. The team started with a small slice of functionality as an experiment, and after it figured out how to isolate the changes, it determined that applying this technique to the rest of the code would work. The team started with a set of vertical user stories to convert a critical part of the application where the usability gains would be the most desirable for customers. The team started small and validated the initial approach at a high level over the course of several iterations.

As the team progressed, and converted more of the application, it discovered both problems and new design options. This resulted in an iterative improvement of the new architectural approach. The team also worked closely with usability experts and with customers to test the interface. When the primary interface started to work differently, and the team received customer affirmation of the new direction, it continued converting the rest of the highest priority interfaces. Not too long after this work was underway, the team asked the customers if the progress was sufficient to release the code. Surprisingly the customers said, "Yes! Ship the product now so that we can start to take advantage of the improvements." And that is what the team did. In the end, the team never completed the entire conversion. The software shipped with both architectures in place, and the team moved on to build a new product, basking in all the lessons it had learned from this project and from the fact that it shipped the updated product earlier than anticipated and with the customer's support.

I thought this project was a tremendous success because the team improved upon the application at a pace that made its customers successful far earlier than the original plan anticipated. The team learned as it progressed and incrementally improved upon the architecture. The only way these results were possible was to have working software throughout the project. This example also reinforces the concept that active stakeholder interaction is *critical*. In this case, such interaction allowed the team to release much earlier than anticipated and with less functionality than originally planned while still delivering real value to customers. It also proved the idea that you sometimes do not have to do *everything* to satisfy customers: Do what is needed and no more. (See Chapters 2, "Active Stakeholder Interaction," 7, "Deliver Value," and 8 "Release Often.")

I am not trying to describe evolutionary architecture and emergent design in detail, but these concepts are extremely valuable to any style of development. Neal Ford has a great series of articles that provide a starting place for further research.[4]

In-House Deploys

A particularly beneficial practice that can help you gain confidence with working software is to deploy your software in-house (that is, inside your own company) and *use* it. When you figure out how to deploy in-house, it is critical that you get into the habit of doing this every iteration or, even better, every build. I have been fortunate enough to work on software that can be used by employees in the company to do their day-to-day jobs—it made in-house deployments easy. If, however, your software has no application inside your own company, be innovative and invent a way to use it.

---

4. Ford, Neal, *Evolutionary architecture and emergent design: Emergent design through metrics. Using metrics and visualizations to find and harvest hidden design in your code.* (Published 30 Jun 2009). Web. http://www.ibm.com/developerworks/java/library/j-eaed6/index.html

Repeated use of your own software by others in the company not only helps you discover new problems through new usage patterns that may not be covered by your test suites, but continual usage also gives you information on how well it works for extended time periods, how well it performs, how well it scales, how user-friendly it is, and other real-world factors that take time to discover. And, typically, your colleagues won't be bashful about quickly telling you where you messed up.

As my opening story shows, teams resist deploying their own software internally because it may involve risk if the software has defects that negatively affect users. But, if in-house usage can help you discover problems faster, it is better that you take such risks and plan for what needs to happen should a problem arise. Furthermore, frequent in-house deploys may be time-consuming and require additional hardware and enablement, but the rewards are so great that it is worth overcoming any skepticism and any obstacles to do it.

Metrics

Because "working software is the measure of progress," it should be a fairly straightforward metric to track. We especially like the Advanced Release Burndown Chart[5] in IBM's Rational Team Concert™ (RTC) for tracking completed user stories ("completed user stories" equates to "working software"—we encourage the use of a strong definition of "Done!").

Apart from release burndown charts, we suggest that teams also count how many times they deployed their software in-house and compare that to how many iterations there were. Target at least one in-house deployment for every iteration. Even better, use continuous deployment methodologies to continually update your in-house deployments.

In addition, teams can measure how many defects were discovered during in-house deploys. If significant numbers of defects were discovered, an analysis of the types of defects can help teams understand how testing should be improved.

Breakthrough

A good way to make sure you always have working software is to develop "stop the line" behavior with your builds by applying the "Fix It Now!" rule to build breaks. Successful builds are critical to maintaining the rhythm of the team by enabling constantly working software, early discovery of defects, and keeping everyone on a new build every day. The "Fix It Now!" concept drives home the point that the goal of always having working software takes precedence over all other work.

Here is how this breakthrough works: As a team, establish a definition for what constitutes build success. Keep it simple, but *tough*. For instance, *anything* that keeps the build from reporting success is a build break. Build success is reported in binary fashion: It was either completely successful or it's a broken build—no "partial" success. Next, the team needs a "build status

---

5. See some additional discussion of Release Burndown Charts in the "Breakthrough" section of Chapter 8, "Release Often."

notification" capability, preferably an automatic notification from a continuous integration build platform. When the team gets a notification that a build is broken, follow these rules:

1. Everyone stops working.

2. No one checks in code when the build is broken (unless it is specifically for fixing the build).

3. Every team member reviews the build break notification.

4. A team member with the appropriate skills self-assigns build break ownership and notifies the team that she is taking ownership.

5. The new build break owner drops all other work and focuses on fixing the build. The owner gets help from anyone on team as necessary, and perhaps even creates a short-lived build break team if the work required is significant.

6. The build break problem is identified at its root cause.

7. The person (or team) responsible for fixing the problem works on solving the problem.

8. The build break owner notifies the team when the fix is in place and the build is working again.

If the team determines that the root cause of the build break requires an iteration or more to fix, it can add this problem to its backlog as a user story and start to address it the next iteration. This is the least desirable option because it does not get the team into the habit of using "stop the line" thinking. It can become just another excuse to delay.

The first time I saw a team try this breakthrough it was actually fun because when a build break notification went out, the team energy level rose because everyone immediately worked together to find the problem and get it fixed. Furthermore, some friendly peer pressure within the team occurred because no one wanted to be the one to break the build—they knew that the whole team would be visibly affected. They also quickly realized the advantages that this technique afforded them. From that point forward, the team gave working builds its utmost attention and looked for ways to improve its continuous integration system. When a build break was fixed, it was always a big success story, and the team felt excited about its collective achievements.

At this point I should compare this success with another team Scott and I worked with that had not adopted the "Fix It Now!" approach to build breaks. This team had an automated build break notification system, and everyone on the team received a notice when a build break occurred. But no one even stopped to look at the build break notification. They often did not fix a build break for days on end because no one took ownership. They had just grown accustomed to living with pain and ignoring the notifications (probably because the build break notifications happened frequently). We ultimately convinced them to adopt the "Fix it Now!" approach.

The real value of this "Fix it Now!" technique is that it reinforces the goal of having working software all the time. Team members will be encouraged to help with getting a build break problem solved because they cannot check in code until the problem *is* solved. Broken builds slow down team progress by breaking up the rhythm of producing working software.

In addition to having working software all the time, using this "stop the line" technique helps teams learn the value of fixing a problem at its core instead of just dealing with symptoms. To improve upon this technique, expand your definition of a successful build to include having all unit tests pass, no problems discovered by static code analysis, successful deployment to test machines, successfully running build verification test suites after the code has been deployed to the test machines, and so forth. As the gauntlet of build validation checkpoints strengthens, so will your confidence that you have working software.

Summary

Being agile requires always having working software because it validates progress, ensures the highest levels of quality, and enables regular feedback.

- Demonstrating that you have working software each iteration provides the best indication of project status. Working software is software that has high enough quality to ship; however, achieving shippable software each iteration does not imply that a team *must* ship what has been completed.

- Achieving working software requires teams to identify the most critical work, do just enough of it, and finish. Teams learn to make hard choices about what to do and what not to do.

- The primary barriers to getting to working software each iteration include not having a sufficient continuous integration system to enable rapid feedback loops, being organized by product components, and not having the discipline to regularly get to "Done!"

- Short iterations, not to exceed 2 weeks, give teams the best chance to get to "Done!" each iteration and successfully produce working software. Small user stories that can be completed within a short iteration enable teams to get to working software because the code/test/feedback cycles are short enough to do useful work and finish.

- Continuous integration and automation together enable automatic code check-in, successful or failed build notification, automatic build on check-in, automatic unit test and build verification test execution, automatic deployment, and more. Use automation anywhere there is repetitive, manual work.

- Vertically sliced user stories deliver a slice of functionality that works across the architecture stack. This results in working software. The goal of vertical stories is to complete just enough work across each component to complete some thin, vertical slice of functionality.

- Evolutionary architecture leverages vertical stories to test the architecture and develop design patterns iteratively. As the architecture evolves, design patterns "emerge" so that adding additional code moves faster and with less risk. This approach enables teams to produce working software while validating the architecture.

- In-house or live deploys of working software help uncover quality problems that may surface via unique usage patterns.
- A breakthrough technique to get teams into the habit of prioritizing working software is to apply a "Fix It Now!" rule to build breaks. When a build breaks, the entire team stops its work and focuses on fixing the build problem at its root before any other work continues. Solving the root problem may be hard, but doing so is what provides the most value.

CHAPTER 7

Deliver Value

Being agile requires delivering real value so that customers succeed with your product.

By Scott Will

Years ago, Leslie and I were working with a team, helping them to write its first-ever set of user stories. (The team was in the earliest stages of adopting agile, and user stories were a brand-new concept for the team members). It took a little while, but the team started to get the hang of it and soon it was doing a good job writing stories without our help. After the project had been under-way for a while, the project executive contacted the lead architect to say that a customer had just requested some new feature and wanted to know if the team could include the additional work in the project—and still maintain the scheduled ship date (of course...). The architect briefly considered how much work the new request would entail and, thinking it wouldn't be too much, told the executive that the team could handle it.

Well, as soon as Leslie and I heard about this, we contacted the architect and gently chided him for agreeing to do the work. From an agile perspective, there were two reasons why what he did was wrong: First, he had violated the agile *whole team* concept by not involving the team in the decision. (He was used to acting unilaterally in his former waterfall projects, so acting on his own here was almost second nature.) Second, he didn't go through the process of creating user stories for the requested feature. After a little bit of urging on our part, he agreed to call a team meeting where we would help them write user stories for the newly requested feature. This turned out to be an extremely enlightening experience for all involved—especially the project architect. By the time the team finished writing user stories for the requested feature, it had become apparent that neither the architect, nor the executive, nor anyone on the team *initially* had any real understanding of the requested feature. (This is one of the biggest reasons why Leslie and I are such strong advocates of user stories—the use of user stories continually reinforces to the team that what it creates needs to be understood from the customer's perspective.)

When the feature was better understood, it became apparent that the requested feature was more complex than first imagined, and that the team could not complete the additional work without either dropping some other feature from the project or extending the targeted ship date. Because dropping another feature was out of the question, as was delaying the ship date, the architect had to go back to the executive and explain that the newly requested feature could not be accommodated in the release. This was ultimately the right decision, but had the architect used the recommended agile processes (that is, whole teams, ensuring a good understanding of a requested feature from the customer's viewpoint, writing and sizing user stories, and so on), he would have saved himself some embarrassment.

So, what does this story have to do with delivering value? Had the feature just been "squeezed in," the team would likely have failed to deliver real value to the customer because it didn't know exactly what the customer actually wanted. The root of the problem came from the fact that the architect did not know what was going to provide actual value to the customer—his initial interpretation of the requested feature was colored by his presuppositions. There wasn't a lot of information to go on initially, so the architect mentally filled in the gaps with his own knowledge and assumptions. Had we not "encouraged" the team to go through the agile process of writing user stories, the team would likely have delivered something that did not match the customer's needs and expectations. Not only would this outcome have been embarrassing, but there might also have been worse outcomes, such as the customer pursuing alternative solutions from a different company. The team would also have put in a lot of overtime, or missed its ship date, or both, in an attempt to squeeze this additional feature in—all of which would have been a waste because what would have been delivered would likely not have met the customer's needs.

The key point behind "delivering value" is to deliver what your customers will actually use—not what *you* think they need. Sometimes, what customers actually need may even differ from what they originally tell you they need (hence our emphasis in Chapter 2 on active stakeholder interaction). This chapter can help you move away from the waterfall tendency of thinking you know what customers need based on some one-line requirement that you get handed. It is critical that you understand what problem you are trying to solve and, with that in mind, this chapter will help you move toward actually delivering real value to your customers.

Principles

Why User Stories?

Agile teams tend to be familiar with user stories. Mike Cohn[1] introduced them as a way to concisely describe functionality that would be valuable to a user, and they are a key agile practice. User stories emphasize feature essentials from the stakeholder's view, helping to ensure that *only what is needed* is developed—and no more.

---

1. Cohn, Mike, 2010. *User Stories Applied: For Agile Software Development.* Pearson Education, Inc.

A user story takes the following format:

As a <role> I can <goal> so that <business value>

- The role is a specific stakeholder role that the story is targeted for.
- The *goal* is what the story will accomplish (not the "how").[2]
- The *business value* is a description of how the feature will benefit the *role* when the feature is made available.

Here is an example of a user story:

As an application administrator I need to be notified when a monitored item of the middleware infrastructure has exceeded its expected value so that I can use the diagnostic tool to determine the root cause.

As you can see in this example, it is clear who wants a particular capability and why. In the past, a line item for this feature may have looked something like this:

Display the health indicators of the middleware.

In this example of a line item, no one on the team knows who wants to see the health indicators or why. By adopting user stories, the team has to figure this out to determine the correct role for the user story. Discussing this with the product owner and/or the customers then allows the team to learn that it is the application administrator who needs to see the health indicators. With this understanding the team can integrate this new capability into the other capabilities the administrator regularly uses, thus strengthening the value of the product for the application administrator. Also, because the team now knows that the administrator is primarily interested in those situations in which an indicator exceeds an expected value and, thus, needs to use diagnostic tooling to determine the root cause, the team can come up with ways to seamlessly integrate a connection to the diagnostic tooling when an indicator's value exceeds a threshold.

---

2. A necessary comment here—one of the biggest problems we see with teams when they first transition from waterfall to agile is the desire to put implementation details into their user stories. This is a tough nut to crack for most teams. Waterfall has encouraged (often *required*) teams to create all sorts of detailed implementation plans at the beginning of a project, so it's no surprise that teams carry this thinking forward into writing user stories. Stakeholders care only that you solve their problems and deliver real value; how the team goes about implementing the value is typically of little concern to the stakeholders.

For example, when I teach classes on writing user stories, I use the situation in which someone wants to go to an ATM machine and get money from his bank account to go buy a meal at a restaurant. Think of the typical user of an ATM. Is he worried about the specific security protocol in use? Or how the ATM communicates with the main bank? Or what technology is used to display his account information on the screen? Most likely not; all he wants is his money and assurance that his account will properly reflect the transaction.

When writing stories, keep the stakeholder's perspective in mind and you'll avoid getting into tangential discussions on implementation. The implementation discussions can wait until the story is targeted to be worked on in an iteration. (This approach intersects with the Evolutionary Architecture and Emerging Design practice that agile advocates and which is discussed in Chapter 6, "Working Software.")

User stories differ from traditional requirements in many ways. As previously pointed out, in waterfall projects teams typically get short, brief, or even one-line requirements that they wind up having to further elaborate. Unfortunately, this often results in a solution that differs significantly from what the customers need. Because user stories target specific stakeholder roles, identify the specific stakeholder needs, and finally ensure that business value is identified from the stakeholder's viewpoint, agile teams do a better job of creating features that deliver value.

Here's another example of the differences between requirements and user stories:

A typical requirement: "Support AIX®"

A good user story: "As a remote user I need the client to run on AIX v6.1 so that I can connect to the server from my remote machine, which has the new POWER6® processor."

Note the differences between the requirement and the user story. Imagine how much additional (and unnecessary) work a team might do by trying to figure out on its own how to satisfy the Support AIX requirement. By having a good user story instead, you can see how the total effort can be drastically reduced: the team will focus specifically on version 6.1 and it will focus its testing on the client on a remote machine running the new POWER6 processor—and that's it. This is where the real value of this particular feature lies.

Finally, requirements differ from user stories in that requirements use specifications and design documentation to predict the effort or the duration of the project for planning purposes. In contrast, user stories are sized using "story points" before the "how" is determined. This approach to sizing works if user stories are small and if the entire team is involved in the sizing process. In waterfall, project estimates were always difficult to make and prone to error because teams provided estimates based on the individual work in each discipline. Sizing user stories with story points takes a different approach in that it bases estimates on relative sizing between stories and incorporates a whole-team perspective. This process of sizing stories further leverages *the conversation* to ensure that all aspects of the story have been considered in the estimates. These conversations often lead to interactions with the stakeholders, further driving the focus on delivering value.[3]

As a side note, another valuable aspect of user stories is that the entire team is involved in writing them. Developers, testers, writers, business analysts, and stakeholder proxies (such as product management, sales, marketing, and even customer support) all work together, discussing each user story that the team will be working on. We refer to this as *the conversation*. It really is meant to be a true conversation among all the participants—a conversation that draws out the

---

3. Jeff Sutherland wrote a short, but informative article on why sizing stories with story points is much better than trying to predict how many hours, or days, or "person-months" (or whatever time measurement you're used to using in waterfall) a project will take. You can read his article here: http://scrum.jeffsutherland. com/2010/04/story-points-why-are-they-better-than.html

key parts of each story and clarifies the stakeholder's perspective for everyone on the team.[4] This also differs from line items where typically just one person, far removed from the development organization, is responsible for writing them.

Practices

The "So That" Clause

In some of the earliest examples of user stories, the "role" and the "goal" were the only parts of a typical user story. After many years of helping teams with writing stories, Leslie and I have found that including the "so that" clause as part of the story definition (which focuses on the actual business value wanted by stakeholders) is invaluable. Ensuring teams include a so that clause as part of every user story in turn ensures that the teams understand *why* a customer wants some feature. It's one thing to understand *that* a customer wants some feature, and even to know exactly what that feature is, but it's a whole different ballgame when teams understand *why* a customer wants some feature and how, specifically, that feature is going to be beneficial to a customer.

Not only does having a so that clause help the team come to a better overall and shared understanding of the feature, but it is especially helpful in at least two additional ways: First, having an understanding of the business value often minimizes what the team actually produces (in keeping with the agile and lean principles of doing what's needed and no more). Second, it can help with understanding the best way to test the feature prior to shipping the product. Testing a feature in the way that corresponds to the way the customers are expected to use the feature is quite valuable to agile teams—and it's something that waterfall teams rarely achieve. In agile, it's now an expected part of developing software.

Here's an example of how the so that clause enabled a team to gain a better understanding of why a customer wanted a particular feature. Initially, the team knew only that customers had requested that the product's content management GUI mimic the Windows Explorer interface. Without the so that clause, here's what the initial user story looked like:

> As an IT manager I want my content management system to be represented as a library in the Windows Explorer interface.

But the why of the desired functionality was an unknown. Why did customers want the GUI to look like something from Windows? Was it

---

4. You may be thinking that user stories should be written by stakeholders—and we agree that this is the best way. However, recall that our focus is typically on enterprise-level software, and so it's pretty much a given that we won't involve hundreds and even thousands of customers in writing user stories. So we typically use "proxies." Even here, however, we advocate that teams review their high-level stories (which we typically call "epics") with stakeholders before breaking their epics down into iteration-sized stories. Also, if there are any questions that arise that the stakeholder proxies cannot provide answers to, then it is incumbent upon them to contact the stakeholders for clarification and additional insights to ensure a proper understanding of the requested item is achieved.

- So that it works with existing Windows applications on users' desktops?
- So that users would not have to be trained to use a new interface?
- So that it looks like just another repository in the Explorer interface reminding users to save their files to the content management system?
- Or something else?

The reason in this instance was the second one: The customers requesting the feature did not have a training budget. If the team had made the Explorer dialog look and feel differently from what the users were used to in Windows, then users would have required training—which was a showstopper.

The more we work with user stories, the more we believe that the so that clause is the most critical aspect of a user story. But it tends to be the one part of a story that gets left out most often. Teams sometimes struggle with distinguishing the so that clause as the story size gets smaller and smaller during the process of breaking stories down. Yes, it can get harder as the scope gets smaller, but be careful not to give up at this point: The differentiation between small stories based on the so that clause may allow you to eliminate a story where the value anticipated is not of interest to customers.

Vertically Sliced Stories

The phrase *vertically sliced user stories* (also known as *vertical stories*) were discussed in Chapter 6, "Working Software." They are also critical to delivering value. As a reminder, what vertically sliced stories signify is the idea that your user stories should encompass a thin slice of functionality across multiple components. Stories written on a component basis should be avoided (for example, a separate GUI story and a separate database story—your customers don't think in terms of components; they think in terms of goals and business value). With vertically sliced stories, the idea is to write user stories in such a way that the envisioned functionality encompasses the GUI, the database, and any intermediate layers such that, for example, with each user story a single database command (starting at the GUI, going through the API layer, to the database, and returning to the GUI) can actually be completed and demonstrated to customers at the end of an iteration. In addition to demonstrating real functionality, vertically sliced stories enable the validation of the architecture. How many times in waterfall projects have you seen teams build out the entire database layer, then build out some sort of middle-layer API or analytics engine, and then start working on the GUI—only to discover quite late that the architecture isn't right because end-to-end testing wasn't started until some of the GUI was in place? By validating the architecture early with vertically sliced user stories, teams have confidence that what they build is actually working and, if there are problems, they can discover them and fix them while the problems are still small.

As one simple example, imagine a client-server product: If the team were to build out the entire server component first, that would not be valuable to a customer because there's none of the necessary client functionality. And it's of little value to the team because no one can confirm that the server is doing what it needs to because there's no client functionality to exercise the server. Similarly, if the team builds only the client, that's of little value because there's no server to connect to. Obviously, having a little bit of the client built, and a corresponding portion of the server built at the same time, can allow for some early testing and validation of the functionality from the client to the server and back. Even if the team can complete only one, simple client-server transaction at the end of its first iteration, this is demonstrable value.[5] Vertical stories help ensure that the in-progress code will deliver the value intended.

Acceptance Criteria

Another practice that Leslie and I have found helpful for writing good user stories is to create acceptance criteria at the time a user story is written. In essence, *acceptance criteria* is what helps the team confirm that what is created actually satisfies the so that clause of the story. In other words, if you can meet the defined acceptance criteria, chances are good that you've delivered the expected value of the user story. Of course, you won't know for sure that you've provided the anticipated value until you get feedback from actual customers, but defining acceptance criteria is a great way to help minimize any gaps between what is built and what stakeholders expect. Said another way, defining good acceptance criteria, and showing that you've met them at the completion of a user story, should be a strong indicator that no surprises await you when you demonstrate the story to your customers.

Each story will have its own unique acceptance criteria. We encourage teams to discuss and agree to the acceptance criteria for a given user story at the same time the story is written. Don't wait to write acceptance criteria until some later time—we've found that questions that arise during the discussion of acceptance criteria often cause teams to go back and refine the story. One fascinating technique that one of our teams came up with was to discuss, as part of defining acceptance criteria, how it was going to demonstrate the completed functionality. This helped the team focus principally on the value proposition of each user story because the discussion around demonstrating the functionality to customers meant that the team not only had to *really understand* the intended value of the story but also to communicate value to its customers during a demonstration. After seeing this technique and seeing its benefits, we now recommend it to all our teams (and now to you as well!).

A quick note in passing: The folks on your team whose primary responsibilities involve testing should be the ones most keenly interested in ensuring good acceptance criteria is created for each user story because the acceptance criteria will be used to drive the testing. Acceptance criteria are not meant to be a list of test cases, but acceptance criteria will directly influence the test cases that get created and executed. This is not to say that developers can gloss over

---

5. Writing vertically sliced user stories is a key agile practice. Refer to Chapter 2 of Mike Cohn's book, *User Stories Applied: For Agile Software Development*, titled "Writing Stories."

acceptance criteria; they need to understand the acceptance criteria as well because it can help define the code they write.

Acceptance criteria are different from "Done!" criteria, and we strongly urge teams to create both. Acceptance criteria are unique to each user story. As previously mentioned, they're how a team tries to ensure that the value of a given user story has been achieved. "Done!" criteria is more general and applies equally to all user stories. "Done!" criteria typically includes things such as the following:

- Needed automated unit tests have been written and are executing as part of the build.
- Unit test coverage and function test coverage goals are met.
- Unit test pass rate is 100 percent.
- Automated function tests have been written and are executing as part of the automation framework.
- Function test pass rate is 100 percent.
- Performance testing measurements remain within acceptable parameters.
- Any needed code reviews or inspections have been completed.
- All defects that were found and that need to be fixed have actually been fixed.
- Regression testing is complete and passing at 100 percent.
- Any required product documentation has been written and is at least in a draft state.

"Done!" criteria should be robust because the goal is always to have working software. With minimalistic "Done!" criteria, the likelihood of teams building up project debt is high.

Using Velocity Effectively

In Chapter 8, "Release Often," the breakthrough recommendation is that your team should write the bulk of its user stories at the beginning of the release prior to the start of the first iteration. There are many reasons for doing so, not the least of which touches on the topic of this chapter: delivering value. Effectively using velocity helps deliver value because it enables you to work with your stakeholders to prioritize user stories to best meet their needs. To illustrate, I'll use a well-worn example: the frequent-flyer program.

Say that you and your team are creating a frequent-flyer program and there are five major features that are targeted for completion. You've completed the first one (the ability to book a flight using frequent-flyer points) and demonstrate it to your customers. During the demonstration, the customers ask about the other features, and you explain that the ability to upgrade to first-class using frequent-flyer points is next, followed by the ability to buy a ticket for a spouse using frequent-flyer points. Figure 7.1 shows what your backlog of user stories might look like at this time.

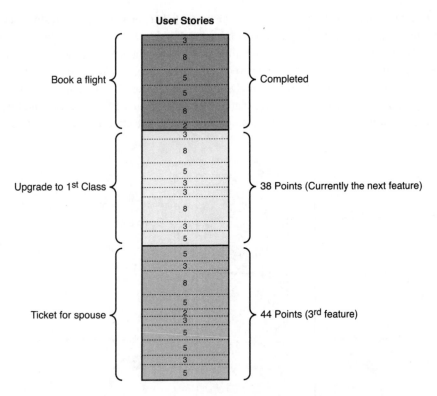

Figure 7.1 Current backlog of user stories with their respective story-point sizings

The customers show a particular interest in the ability to buy a ticket for a spouse and want to know how long it would be before they could begin to see any implementation of the feature. So, you look at your backlog of user stories and notice that there is 38 story points' worth of user stories associated with the upgrade feature. Assuming the team's velocity is 12 points an iteration (as just a made-up example), you tell the customers that it will likely be approximately 6 weeks before the team starts working on the buy-a-ticket-for-your-spouse feature because that's how long you expect it to take to complete the upgrade feature (which is next). At 12 points an iteration, it will likely take three, 2-week iterations to complete the 38 points for the upgrade feature (and perhaps a little more because 12 goes into 38 just over three times). Your customers then ask if there is any way that they could see the buy-a-ticket-for-your-spouse feature any earlier. So, you look at the stories for that feature and note that the total story points associated with those stories is 44. So, you tell your customers that you can move that feature ahead of the upgrade feature, and you'll start working on the buy-a-ticket-for-your-spouse feature next. And you also tell them that it will likely take approximately 8 weeks (which is four, 2-week iterations, calculated by taking 44 story points and dividing by 12 story points per iteration) to complete the feature. Given the intense interest on the part of numerous customers in the third feature, moving the associated user stories for the feature higher on the rank-ordered backlog makes sense; you're delivering value to your customers, value that they have told you they're interested in. Figure 7.2 shows what your updated backlog of user stories might look like after making the switch.

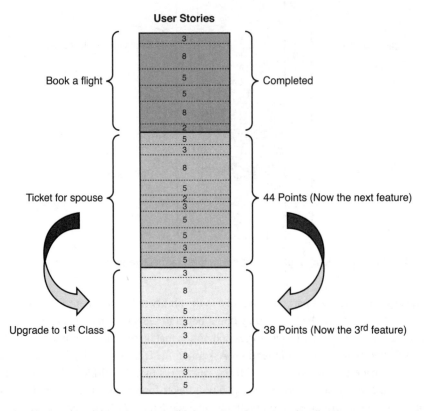

Figure 7.2   Updated backlog of user stories based on customer feedback

In addition, you may make the decision to ship the release once the buy-a-ticket-for-your-spouse feature is completed and not wait until the remaining three features are complete as originally planned. If the customers show that much interest in the buy-a-ticket-for-your-spouse feature, making it available as soon as it is complete could very well be the best business decision, even if the remaining features have not yet even been started. Those features could roll over into a subsequent release.

Using velocity in conjunction with a backlog of user stories is what allows these kinds of decisions—decisions that ensure you to deliver value to your customers.

Metrics

We have three fairly simple metrics to suggest regarding delivering value. The first is to analyze the feedback you get from the demonstrations you give to your customers. Also try to read between the lines and see if you can figure out what their impressions of the product are thus far. Yes, such feedback is obviously subjective, and you can't actually measure it in the typical sense, but understanding what kind of feedback your customers are giving you is valuable. Knowing whether they are actually seeing functionality that they believe is of value to them is key, so don't overlook it. You may also want to use this suggestion along with the metrics covered in Chapter 2, "Active Stakeholder Interaction"—noting not only who attended your demos, what stakeholder categories and markets were represented, but add to it this suggestion about analyzing the feedback received. The combination of these should provide some good insight into whether the team is delivering value. If not, "stop the line" and figure out where the problems are.

The second is so obvious that it's almost not worth mentioning it—but we'll mention it here anyway. Are your sales going up? Is your revenue increasing? Is your market share growing? These, and other similar financial measurements can help you determine whether the market believes there is value to your product.

The third is to track when customers plan to roll out the latest release into their environments. They will likely roll it out quickly if you are delivering real value.

Breakthrough

Struggling with the so that clause of your user stories? Is your team discovering problems with stories during the middle of an iteration, even though the team thought it had done a good job writing the stories? Has your team worked together for such a long time that it forgets to mention the assumptions on which it may or may not be agreed? One of the best techniques Leslie and I have used to help teams overcome such problems, and write better user stories, is to include a zero-gravity thinker in user story writing sessions.

What Exactly Is a Zero-Gravity Thinker?

A zero-gravity thinker (ZGTer from here on) is a credible outsider brought in to help address the following situations (at a minimum):

- Catch instances in which GroupThink[6] and ExpertThink[7] are occurring.
- Ensure that unstated assumptions are being surfaced.
- Raise questions to ensure that the final version of any given user story has clarity to all who read it—including (especially) the stakeholders.

The notion of zero gravity thinking came from a book authored by Cynthia Barton Rabe titled, *The Innovation Killer: How 'What We Know' Limits What We Can Imagine*.[8] The following quote appears in a review of her book:

> Basically, this meant that Rabe...was placed onto teams where she had related but not identical expertise and didn't report to anyone on the team. She was able to ask questions that forced the team to question their most basic assumptions and brought a fresh perspective and new insights to their work.[9]

From this quote you can see that the requirements of a ZGTer are relatively straightforward. First, (for our purposes) a ZGTer should be adept at writing user stories. Next, a ZGTer should be someone who has both technical expertise and who is comfortable having technical conversations, but *not* someone who is familiar with the specific technology or domain your product focuses on. In addition, ZGTers should not be expected to contribute to a user story but

6. "Groupthink is a psychological phenomenon that occurs within a group of people, in which the desire for harmony or conformity in the group results in an incorrect or deviant decision-making outcome. Group members try to minimize conflict and reach a consensus decision without critical evaluation of alternative ideas or viewpoints, and by isolating themselves from outside influences. Loyalty to the group requires individuals to avoid raising controversial issues or alternative solutions, and there is loss of individual creativity, uniqueness and independent thinking" (see: http://en.wikipedia.org/wiki/Groupthink). ZGTers combat GroupThink because they are not part of the group and have been brought in specifically to prevent such things as GroupThink from occurring.

7. ExpertThink is "GroupThink on steroids" (according to Cynthia Barton Rabe – quoted from the online article entitled, "Seeking to Innovate?" at the http://www.ideaconnection.com website. This article recounts an interview with Ms. Rabe which can be found here: http://www.ideaconnection.com/open-innovation-articles/00028-Zero-Gravity-Thinkers.html). ExpertThink is the situation in which every decision made is made by one person—generally the identified domain expert. Other team members are often afraid to question the expert for fear of looking stupid (echoes of the tale of the "Emperor's New Clothes"). ZGTers combat ExpertThink by continually asking questions to ensure that other viewpoints, aspects, impacts, and so on are considered.

8. Rabe, Cynthia Barton. *The Innovation Killer: How 'What We Know' Limits What We Can Imagine*. New York: AMACOM, 2006.

9. Quoted from the article entitled, "Get Creative" found on the Entrepreneur.com website at: http://www.entrepreneur.com/article/194390

should be expected to make a number of "I don't understand" comments and ask a lot of associated questions, such as

- "Why does the product need to perform better? Don't tell me *that* it needs to perform better—tell me *why* it needs to perform better."
- "Why is that particular feature beneficial to the customer?"
- "Is *this* what's really important to a stakeholder, or is it <*something else*> instead?"
- "What do you mean by 'decrease the footprint'? Is this something customers have asked for? If so, by how much should the footprint be decreased? Is 10 percent enough? 20 percent? How about 50 percent? How do you know?"
- "'Easier to use' is an ambiguous phrase. What specifically is in view with the request to make the product 'easier to use'?"

The answers to these types of questions help expose unstated assumptions that team members often have, especially as a ZGTer helps teams to think in terms of stakeholders and not in the "techno-speak" that engineers use. Furthermore a ZGTer may help you get to a new perspective and shake you out of entrenched thinking patterns.

In spite of the emphasis on *the conversation*, teams often miss important details when creating user stories. Team members can be too close to the product—especially when stakeholder proxies are involved—thus preventing them from raising the right questions about business value and technological assumptions from a stakeholder-perspective. If teams are not careful, they can fall into bad habits such as using ambiguous terminology (for example, "faster" and "more easily"), not getting the right role (for example, stating "administrator" when "application developer" was intended), and especially omitting the so that clause of a user story. ZGTers have an advantage in that they do not know why you are building new functionality; they get to figure it out and will ask lots of questions and raise lots of issues while doing so.

ZGTers can help with all these situations and others as well. They have the advantage of being *technically competent* but having *domain ignorance*. Including them in your user story writing sessions helps teams break out of their waterfall thinking patterns and create better stories.

Finally, ZGTers cannot be afraid to appear ignorant. ZGTers need to be "tough," that is, the ZGTer cannot let the team box him out of the conversation. Sometimes teams don't want to deal with the questions ZGTers raise, even though they're good and necessary questions. When this happens, it's usually with a team that hasn't yet seen the value of writing good user stories—the old waterfall mentality that "one-line requirements" are sufficient is hard to break. A good ZGTer can help break this mindset quickly.

As a coach I fill the role of a ZGTer all the time. I've participated in many sessions during which I've asked questions that produce different responses from among the team, usually followed by a lot of raised eyebrows as the team realizes that an assumed consensus wasn't actually there. The ultimate goal of the ZGTer in story writing sessions should be to get the team to say something like, "If we can get the story to make sense to Scott, then it can make sense to anyone."

A Real Example

The following is an example of zero gravity thinking in action. Leslie and I were involved in helping a team during a user story writing session. Although we were not specifically identified as ZGTers, we were participating to help a team create better user stories—and we simply brought zero gravity thinking to the task.

In this example, the following user story had been written by the team:

"As a customer, I want to use the IBM cache instead of the default, open-source cache so that I have improved performance."[10]

The initial assumption behind the story was that the IBM cache had better performance than the default, open-source cache. And to prove this, the team was going to have to do performance testing on all its platforms and in all environments.

As ZGTers, we asked the team how the IBM cache is different from the default cache and how it would demonstrate the improved performance. We also asked what the team meant by "improved performance." The resulting conversation surfaced an unstated assumption that proved to be incorrect. It turned out that the IBM cache could operate in *distributed* environments, whereas the default, open-source cache did not work in a distributed environment. The default cache actually performed on par with the IBM cache, but it could not handle distributed environments. Thus, the real benefits would come from the distributed environments in which the IBM cache would be used. In the end, the team rewrote the story:

"As a customer, I want a cache that works in all supported environments (local and distributed) so that I can obtain the benefits of a distributed environment when I complete the move to a distributed environment in my lab."

An additional benefit was that testing needed to focus only on distributed environments—no longer was all the performance testing needed that was originally envisioned.

Zero Gravity Thinking in Sum...

Teams are often not aware of their unstated assumptions. When these assumptions are exposed, this drives the team to discuss and clarify the business value, the scope, and the impact of any given user story. Unless exposed during the story writing sessions, these unstated (and often differing) assumptions among the team are not discovered until the development, test, and product documentation work is well underway when implementing a story. The varying assumptions can be minor, but many times their impacts are significant and can derail a story.

---

10. You've probably noted the use of ambiguous terminology in this story—what is meant by "improved performance?" This is something the team should not have let happen to begin with. However, a good ZGTer should pick up on this immediately and force the team to eliminate the ambiguousness of the story.

ZGTers make excellent participants in story creation meetings because they compel teams to articulate user stories in understandable terms, they combat both GroupThink and Expert-Think, and they help teams surface unstated assumptions. They also help teams focus on why a given story is critical to stakeholders, thereby ensuring (enforcing) team agreement on the business value. And they also ensure that user stories have clarity.

So don't wait—invite a ZGTer to your next user story writing session!

Summary

Being agile requires delivering real value so that your customers can succeed with your product.

- Agile focuses on delivering what customers will use—not on what people in the development organization think customers want.

- If you get handed a line item, or an incomplete requirement, don't just immediately assume you have to fill in the gaps—write user stories. If you can't write good user stories due to the lack of detail, work with your product owner, your stakeholders, and your stakeholder proxies to get the right understanding before going further.

- User stories with "so that" clauses can help teams focus on delivering customer value instead of focusing on implementation details to the detriment of the customer's perspective.

- Defining acceptance criteria for each user story can also help focus the team on providing value to the customer as well as ensuring testing focuses on expected customer usage patterns.

- Implementing vertically sliced stories allows for real value to be realized faster, which also allows customers to provide feedback earlier.

- Implementing vertically sliced stories also allows the team to validate the product architecture earlier.

- Having a backlog of rank-ordered user stories, as well as an established velocity, can help teams determine the time it will take to deliver a particular feature (that is, deliver value) to the customer.

- Using a zero gravity thinker, someone who has a good command of the practice of writing user stories and who also has technical competence (preferably *not* in the same technical domain as the team) is a proven way to ensure the team focuses on the right things when writing user stories.

CHAPTER 8

Release Often

Being agile requires releasing software often so that teams learn fast and customers succeed sooner.

By Leslie Ekas

Unfortunately, for many enterprise software products, upgrades can take hours, days, or even weeks; they can be labor-intensive and often error-prone. The harder it is to update software, the more likely it is that customers will delay upgrading and insist on one-off enhancements and fixes as a stopgap. This is the worst possible scenario for customers because these one-offs are likely to experience the lowest amount of testing. They are also detrimental to product development organizations because these one-offs leave numerous customers each with their own particular version of the product, which is costly to manage. As customers slow down their update cycles, product teams often correspondingly lengthen their release cycles, resulting in larger software updates, which customers view as more risky, thus actually amplifying the problem. This is a hard pattern from which to break free.

Years ago I managed an organization that produced a rather large, enterprise-level software application. It had fallen into the pattern described above regarding the release of software fix-packs. The fix-packs were only available a couple of times a year and had become thick with bug fixes, padded with minor new features, and were time-consuming to test. Because these fix-pack releases were so large, customers tested them as well before putting them into production. When a customer needed an urgent fix, the organization had to send yet another one-off build with the bug fix in it.

This was costly for both our customers and for our team, but we didn't know how to break out of this pattern. So putting our new agile training to the test, we created a value stream map of the entire fix-pack process, from the time when a customer first reported a problem until the problem was fixed and in production. The resulting value stream map was not a surprise—but it was still enlightening to see on paper. This was early in our agile adoption, so it was no surprise that our value stream map showed a serial development process in which domain and functional

109

experts came and went throughout the process based on when their particular expertise was needed. It was *extremely* inefficient, as shown in Figure 8.1. We then drew up the *desired* value stream map, showing paralleling of work to achieve better coordination and efficiency as shown in Figure 8.2. Putting the desired changes in place was both hard and time-consuming because it required that each discipline work differently. Comparing the "as-is" and the "desired" value stream maps was the critical element that sold us on making the changes necessary to get to the "desired" state.

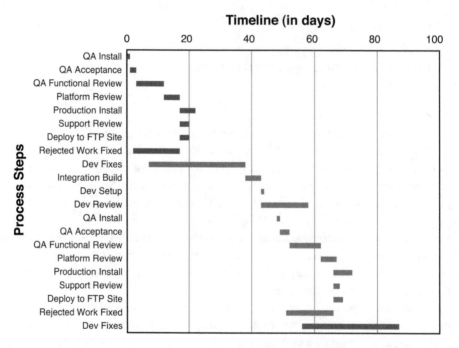

Figure 8.1   This graph shows each process step on the y-axis against the number of days to complete it on the x-axis. The lighter bars show the steps to complete 1 fix-pack cycle. This view shows that the work was mostly serial. This variation of the layout of a value stream map shows waste where there is little to no work being done in parallel.

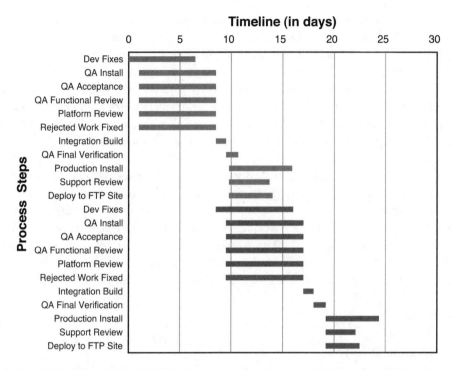

Figure 8.2 This is the "desired" value stream map that the team derived, showing how it wanted its processes to work along with some changes in task. One complete fix-pack process is shown lighter. It obviously shows much more paralleling of activity and, consequently, less waste. Note also that the timeline has shrunk significantly—from nearly 70 days to approximately 20 days. This still looks rather waterfall-ish, but it was quite early in our attempts to adopting agile.

After a value stream map is created, the goal is to look for waste and to try to eliminate it. The creation of our "desired" (or "to be") value stream map pointed out the significant improvements that we wanted to undertake:

- Work completed in parallel
- Short bug-fix, unit test, and build and verification cycles
- An average of 10 defect fixes per fix-pack
- A reduction from 2- to 3-month release cycles to a 3-week cycle

Our goals were challenging but we believed they would result in much higher value to our customers, not to mention the positive impact of improved efficiency for our organization. Our intention was to offer fix-packs every 3 weeks—reliably—and with critical fixes only. We described our new release plans to our customers and asked them to try this approach with us. It required that they prioritize critical bugs and also apply the fix-packs into production on this 3-week cycle instead of requesting one-off fixes. They agreed.

To achieve these goals, the team overhauled its build process and put continuous integration in place. System-level testing occurred throughout the process instead of at the end. From an agile point of view, all these changes may seem like rather obvious steps, but getting teams to actually change how they work can be hard. It took the team more than six months to work all the kinks out of this new process, and our customers had to adjust their behavior as well. Customers were not *required* to install every fix-pack (because the fix-packs were cumulative) but we asked them to limit (if not completely eliminate) their retesting with each fix-pack they did install. When this new process was in place, we no longer got requests for one-off fixes. Our customers were happier and so were we.

This is *release often* thinking applied to maintenance releases. The sooner the customer gets a needed fix, the better. The need to keep software updated is more pressing now because software is widely used to safeguard intellectual property, manage daily operations, and more. Software solutions are applied to solve continually harder problems and the complexity of software increases to meet the demand. Many software applications used today need to be updated monthly or even more frequently. With these demands in mind, teams need to develop good mechanisms for customers to get fixes and other updates both fast and easily.

Principles

Why Release Often?

The first principle in the Agile Manifesto highlights that "Our highest priority is to satisfy the customer through early and continuous delivery of valuable software."[1] Releasing often ensures short feedback loops from customers to the development team to ensure the team is building the right product and getting it to the stakeholders on time. Release often behavior gets teams in the habit of discovering what is "just enough" to be successful.

However, teams that build enterprise software do not often see the value of short release cycles because their customers typically do not update their software frequently. Furthermore, enterprise software upgrades are often slow, require IT downtime, a lot of hands-on management and troubleshooting during the process, and involve coordination of hardware, software, and Human Resources. In a word, upgrades tend to be expensive and, as a result, are done infrequently. Databases are notoriously hard to update, so customers tend to avoid upgrading to a new release of a product that requires a corresponding database upgrade. For large database installations, performing backups may be slow and costly. And the list goes on.

If these kinds of arguments are used to justify your lengthy release cycles, you may be giving up-start competitors an invitation to ace you out of your market hold. For teams moving to a SaaS or PaaS delivery model that requires very regular upgrades, overcoming these challenges is even more important.

---

1.   http://www.agilemanifesto.org/principles.html

It is critical for agile teams to get in the habit of releasing often, to learn and adjust quickly, and to give customers what they need on a regular basis. This applies to releases with new functionality as well as maintenance updates. In addition to helping customers stay more current and get more value with planned updates, short release cycles also provide the vehicle to add product capabilities that can secure new customers. As the software industry becomes more competitive, it is critical that products rapidly adapt to changes in the market.

Do Just Enough

When I started practicing agile, I found the notion of "do just enough" not only liberating but also a subtle, yet fundamentally different way to think about delivering customer value. The basic idea is that just enough functionality is created to meet the needs of stakeholders—*but nothing more*. Do not include extra capabilities that may or may not be used. Applying "do just enough" thinking solves several problems: Noncritical features will not be developed, value is delivered to stakeholders sooner, and teams get early validation that their product is actually solving customer problems. The Agile Manifesto principle, "Simplicity—the art of maximizing the amount of work not done—is essential"[2] reinforces do just enough thinking.

It is critical that product users be closely involved with the software development process so that everyone realizes when "just enough" has been achieved. When I started working in short iterations and demonstrating to customers at the end of each iteration, I discovered something wonderful: On several occasions, customers told us that what we developed up to that point had solved their problems; they told us *not* to add anymore functionality. The first time it happened, it was a liberating experience and we were hooked! In fact, in one particular instance, my team was demonstrating some early code, and another customer on the phone spoke up and said, "Hey— this is how we use the existing code to solve that problem." Voilà! It was not the perfect solution to the problem, but it worked—it was *just enough*, so we quit adding more to the feature.

How does "doing just enough" enable teams to release often? The answer is probably pretty obvious. As a general rule, by developing just enough to solve a problem, the team can ship earlier because it is doing less. Customers get what they want sooner, and the team is free to move on to providing solutions to other requests sooner as well.

Apply release often thinking to internal software deployments, alphas, and betas also. The sooner you get code into your users' hands (whether external or internal), the faster you can discover if it solves their problems and whether it is ready to formally release. Teams need to get away from waiting for code to be "finished;" by that time, any feedback received is likely too late to be considered for the current release. It is just as critical to discover if you are building the right software as it is to find software defects early.

2. http://www.agilemanifesto.org/principles.html

Although the idea of "doing just enough" is generally applied to feature development and architecture, it can also be applied elsewhere. For instance, test-driven development encourages developers to write just enough code to make the tests work. The tests should cover just enough to determine if the user problem is solved. One of the less obvious benefits of test-driven development is that software designs tend to be less heavy-weight because the software is designed to make the tests work—it's not designed to handle all potential contingencies. Software built to handle large numbers of potential contingencies means that more code will be written and more testing will be required. In many cases, a lot of code will be written, tested, and maintained for the product lifetime but never actually get used by customers. The same notion can be applied to evolutionary architecture that enables a similar "development-driven design" approach to defining the product architecture: Do enough development to establish the design, but allow the development problems you are solving dictate how much design is required.

"Do just enough" can also apply to "user help." Traditionally, software help provides step-by-step instructions on how to use the software. With all the software I've purchased over the years, I don't think that I've ever looked at this kind of documentation. I generally try to figure out how to use the software to accomplish some goal and look for help only if I run into trouble. If I do run into a problem, much of the help documentation isn't helpful, and I wind up having to find my answers using a web search. How about trying a different approach with documentation? I suggest taking an outside-in approach to providing user help: For example, sit with some new folks in your organization who are learning the software and find out what questions they have. Provide answers to all their questions, and then sit with another group of people learning the software to see what questions they have. Use this interaction to discover the two or three primary issues and describe how to succeed in those scenarios. Do just enough—do not create documentation that will not be read.

"Do just enough" can be applied to much of what is done in software development. It is not an excuse to be sloppy, but it helps motivate teams to look for the highest value functionality and prioritize that.

Defer Commitment

Deferring commitment is another practice used by agile teams that comes from Lean.[3] Deferring commitment means waiting until the last responsible moment to make a decision. It might be easier if we rephrase it this way: *Defer critical decisions*. Deferring all decisions is not practical or useful. So how in the world can deferring critical decisions help you release often? These two ideas might not seem to have much in common.

Deferring critical decisions is the practice of delaying decisions (such as a specific design point) until you have learned enough to make a good decision. It may also mean that the time has come (the last responsible moment) to make the decision. Even if you delay and are not sure of

---

3. Poppendieck, Mary and Tom Poppendieck. *Implementing Lean Software Development: From Concept to Cash*. Boston: Addison-Wesley Professional, 2006. pp. 32–33.

the right decision when you have to make it, you should know more and, therefore, you will most likely make a more informed and better decision than you would have had you made the decision at the beginning of the project.

For example, imagine a team is adding access control lists to its document management product. Access control lists are lists of individual users and groups of users associated with some level of access to a document (like "view" and "edit" rights). In this scenario, a software architect needs to determine how to store the user and group data related to the access control lists. For simplicity, here are just two possible design options:

- The document object points to the lists of users and groups that have access to the document.
- Each user object and each group object contains a list of the documents to which each has access.

It is easy to discover all the users that have access to a document with the first option because that data can be directly accessed from the document in question. Getting the same information with the second option is more compute-intensive because it requires a query of all the user objects in the system to determine if each can see the document in question. However if you remove a user from the system, the second option allows you to simply remove one object with a single call. Removing a user with the first option, however, may require an update to all the document objects that specify access to the user being deleted. Removing users may not be a frequent usage scenario, so the costs may be tolerable. However, if you need to remove a user in the case of a security breach, timing could be critical. The point is that some of these scenarios may not be known when the objects are initially designed, so taking steps to delay such a design decision would be prudent. In this example, applying stub code to security access calls enables you to delay the decision of how they are implemented. All the surrounding code can be developed, but how the access list is actually coded can be delayed. Of course, I am over-simplifying this scenario, but the point is that you will not likely know the critical usage scenarios at the beginning of a project when you are first developing the design. Deleting a single user may be an infrequent use case, or it may be one that requires responsive software if security of the system is jeopardized. Deferring the decision allows the team to make good progress, learn more, and then make a much more informed decision.

So, back to the question: How can deferring critical decisions help to release more often? Critical decisions made too early can add a lot of rework later in the cycle if the wrong design decisions were made at the outset, and significant rework can delay a release. If you can take an educated guess at your most difficult design problems, and use stub code or some other method to delay making a final decision, then you will likely eliminate unnecessary rework. Teams should spend time determining which problems are the hardest problems to tackle and discuss ways to delay those decisions until a more informed decision can be made, which can speed up the overall project and enable the team to release earlier.

Why Can It Be Hard to Release Often?

There are many reasons why releasing often is hard. So many, in fact, that this can be one of the more difficult challenges to tackle. For starters, releasing often is hard because teams can always fill up more time with more work. I have never seen a software product that is "finished," that is, that there are no ways left to make it better. If a team commits to ship in September, but finishes the critical functionality in June, then the teams I've seen tend to use the extra time to do some less critical functionality instead of just shipping the product in June. Furthermore, for enterprise software, releasing a product requires a fair amount of legal, marketing, and sales preparation just to name a few of the activities associated with releasing a product. Releasing often impacts all parts of an organization, not just the part responsible for development.

It is also hard because it will likely mean that teams have more releases in the field to support (depending, of course, on their support policy). If software is hard to upgrade, and customers get behind on upgrades, then it is probable that development and support teams will wind up supporting many versions of the product for years. Adding even more versions to the support matrix seems counter-productive in this scenario. In such a scenario teams should look at ways to keep their customers more current because if software gets better with each release (as it should), then moving to the latest release will benefit the customers as well as the development organization.

Releasing often may be difficult for software engineers that love to "over-build" code. *Gold-plating* and *over-engineering* are old terms that describe "over-solving" engineering problems. With a release often emphasis in place, these temptations are corralled because a team will be successful in releasing often only by focusing on just the critical functionality and doing just enough. Over-engineering is detrimental to a release often approach. Avoiding over-engineering does not mean that *no engineering* is the necessary consequence. In the best of software development, well-written code has a flexible design that can easily adapt to new situations, can easily be retooled to solve different problems, is defect-resistant, and so forth; all software engineers should strive for this. But it typically takes code usage to learn how to improve the code and then refactoring to apply what you have learned to actually improve the code over time. Software should get "sturdier" with age—not more brittle.

Releasing often may also be difficult for teams that develop large and complex software. They will reasonably claim that developing relevant new functionality may take too long for short release cycles. That may or may not be the case. Sometimes the issue is that teams are often inclined to envision a big software solution without understanding the problem being addressed. In one instance I'm familiar with, a database team received repeated requests from their customers concerning the need to perform database updates without shutting the database down. The development team looked at the problem and determined that managing the database integrity while upgrading it live would require a solution that executed over the course of days or even weeks. The development costs would be enormous. After pursuing the reasons that customers requested this solution, the team discovered that its customers actually *could* incur a down time, but not one that exceeded 2 hours. That was a far different problem to solve, but one for which the solution was much easier. The team came up with a simple solution and delivered it to the customers much earlier than if it had taken on the work originally envisioned. If a requested feature seems too large to deliver in a shorter time period, re-evaluate the problem and look for easier, shorter-term ways to solve the problem that might require different but more manageable costs.

Releasing often encourages teams to use short feedback cycles to evaluate if their software is actually delivering customer value. If it is, continue. If not, then adjust, which may include canceling the project altogether. (Why continue throwing money and effort after a doomed project?) It is imperative to learn fast and, if necessary, fail fast. Developing high-end software that stands the test of time is not worth the effort if the code never gets used. Instead, the focus should be on ensuring that the software solves a problem first and then that it stands the test of time. Don't build "something" the right way—build the "right thing" the right way.

Practices

Start with Shorter Release Cycles

Shorter release cycles enable teams to get critical functionality out sooner to solve customer problems. And because getting critical functionality out the door becomes the main focus, the desire to keep adding more and more functionality—even if requested by customers—is mitigated. That functionality will simply go into the next release because it, too, will be released in a short period of time. Shorter release cycles can better enable you to add capabilities to sell to new customers, react to market conditions, as well as to keep the competition at bay. It also helps handle the impact of ever-changing requirements. Longer release cycles severely limit a team's flexibility to adapt to changing market conditions, changing technologies, and evolving customer desires.

One thing to keep in mind: As previously mentioned, with shorter release cycles may come the problem that you have more versions to support. So, with shorter release cycles, it is imperative that the upgrade capabilities are virtually effortless, thus making it easier for customers to upgrade.

The following sections cover additional practices that help make shorter release cycles possible.

Epic Stories

Scott and I are big fans of user stories because they focus on problems that users want to solve—as well as *why* they want to solve them. Epic stories are simply higher-level user stories that act as a starting point. Individual, iteration-sized user stories are derived from epics. Epic stories set the general theme of the user stories they encompass so that the primary reason for the effort is not lost. A well-written epic story should help demonstrate what the smaller user stories should accomplish for the customer and provide relative prioritization of the overall anticipated functionality.

Epics also ensure an "organic connection" between the iteration-sized stories that the team works on and the "root" story (the *epic*) from which the iteration-sized stories are derived. That is, if teams start with an epic (or root) and break the epic down into smaller stories, then the small stories connect logically with the epic story. (Think of it this way: The epic is the *root node* of the tree, and the iteration-sized stories are the *leaf-nodes*.) Conversely, teams that try to connect a disparate group of iteration-sized stories into an epic story may lose the overall value that the epic story targets because the smaller stories were not developed with a coherent, "organizing" goal in mind.

At this point you might be asking yourself, "How do epic stories enable you to release often?" Fair question. Epic stories envision the high-level theme of the functionality but not the details of behavior or implementation. Epic stories are broken into iteration-sized stories that are prioritized by highest value to the customer. As the stories are implemented and demonstrated, customers can actually see how the functionality works and they can even try the functionality in their own environments (if they want) because teams should always strive to have "working software." When users see functionality in action, they often change their minds about what they want. This is not to say that they did a poor job of describing their problem initially, but actually seeing a solution can be different from imagining how it will behave. As the team completes more and more iteration-sized stories, customers may see for the first time that their initial understanding of what was needed was incomplete, or even wrong, and thus require a change in direction. In some instances, customers may even decide that there is enough functionality that solves their problem before the team completes all the originally anticipated functionality.

Consider the following epic and iteration-sized stories:

[Epic] As an IT administrator I need to install and deploy a ready-to-use content management system so that each team that I service can securely manage its intellectual property using the same secure technology.

[User story #1] As an IT administrator I need to secure each content item in my repository so that no unauthorized users can access it.

[User story #2] As a content creator I need to add content to the system so that it is secured as company intellectual property.

[User story #3] As a content creator I need to update content that I added to the system so that new versions of the document are secured as intellectual property.

[User story #4] As a content reviewer I need to view the content of other user's content so that I can provide feedback to the owner of the content.

. . . .

[User story #13] When I am logged in as an editor I need to get access to and update documents in my group so that the updated documents are secured in the repository.

[User story #14] When I am logged in as an approver I need to get access to all the documents awaiting approval so that I can review and approve them.

The epic indicates that the content management repository must include security for each content item to avoid unauthorized access. Each iteration-sized story is derived from this epic story. The first three user stories discuss the need for user-level access. The last two stories discuss access based on the role of the user as defined when the user logs into the system. Each of the iteration-sized user stories that flow from the epic story will have to meet the high-level story requirements. It is easy to see that starting with user-level access might be more important than role-level access highlighted in the last two stories. If the team runs out of time, these last two stories can be moved to the next release. Completing the other, higher-ranked stories will deliver on the intent of the epic story.

The software teams will likely want to complete the user-level access stories first and then add role-level access as a variation of that. That is why the stories are ranked in the order shown. This is the value of the epic stories; they prioritize the critical value of the feature so that the team can focus on completing that work first. After that value has been delivered, the team and their stakeholders can jointly decide if the product can be shipped as-is before more functionality is added. After seeing the user-level security working well first, customers may decide that they need that capability right away and adding more functionality will obviously delay the solution to the customer's immediate problem. That is the value of epic stories: They define the overall goal but not how that goal will be completed.

Evolutionary Product Design

Evolutionary product design provides the opportunity to release early with less overall content *but with more valuable content*. The simple notion of evolutionary product design is to allow the design of the product functionality to evolve as the software is developed and feedback is incorporated.[4] It is common for users to describe the problem they are trying to solve by prescribing a solution. However, their ideas for a solution may not actually be the best solution.

My Enterprise Content Management team used a tree view to display the contents of the repositories to the users. The team got requests to allow users to set up their own personal view of the documents in the repository. The team looked at different ways to satisfy this request, but all options entailed too much work to fit into a release relative to the other, higher priority items. After discussions with the customers, the team concluded that the most critical problem that the customers were trying to solve with that feature request was to get easy access to the documents they accessed the most. The team implemented a Favorites folder in which all users could store links to their frequently accessed documents. This solution satisfied the customers, and they no longer asked for the much more expensive solution originally requested.

Development teams need to understand what problem needs to be solved. (In other words, focus on the "what" and the "why.") The best solution for a problem (the "how") may not be easily identifiable at the beginning of a project.

---

4. This topic is also covered from a different angle in Chapter 6, "Working Software."

Teams practicing evolutionary product design get iterative feedback as they develop vertical slices of functionality so that both the development organization and the product's users ensure that the code being built actually solves the identified problems. And, maybe more important, the process ensures that the best results evolve through constant feedback and small updates.

The story that I use to explain this thinking goes as follows: When mapping software became available on the web, I used it to find out how to get directions from one place to another. I typed in both the starting address and the destination address. The software calculated the shortest driving route and displayed a map with the route highlighted, as well as written directions and total mileage. As a runner, I was particularly interested in knowing the mileage so that I could track my runs in my training log. The next time I tried the software, I was interested in altering the route slightly, and I found that I could change the highlighted route with my mouse. The route was readjusted to include the new roads, and the resulting directions and mileage were updated. The next time I used the software, I noticed that there was a new feature that enabled me to find routes based on whether I was driving or walking. That was just what I needed for tracking my runs—using the "walking" option worked great! These additional features were not available when I first tried the software; they were added iteratively. Also, I do not know if these features had been planned for from the beginning, but I do know that as I used the software more and more, these were the features that I wanted next. Due to the nature of this type of application, it could be released frequently, and what became evident was that with each new update, new features were added that solved needs that I had or new desires that arose from having used the software. The team developing the mapping software did not wait to release the product until *all* these features were complete; it simply released often, and each release had one or two additional, *useful* features. In fact, it may have prioritized what it delivered by listening to users like me provide feedback based on how the application worked at the time they used it. I had an idea of what I wanted in the application, but my ideas changed as the application evolved.

In years past, if my team had been given the charge to develop a mapping program, we would have talked to prospective users to understand their needs. They would have likely outlined the capabilities that I just discussed, and added more—things like the best route based on traffic congestion, identification of road construction spots, a display of posted speed limits, and probably others. We would have targeted a release time frame and planned to include as much of what our customers told us were their desires as we could. Furthermore, we would have likely designed the behavior upfront. This would have resulted in a big release with lots of features, which would not actually have shipped for a long period of time. "Doing just enough," however, encourages teams to target high-level functionality at the epic story level and allow the detailed design to evolve as teams learn about what can be implemented and how well it works solving the problems at hand based on feedback provided by customers.

High Value First

Agile emphasizes delivering high-value functionality to customers. This essentially means that teams need to build the most critical functionality first and get it to their customers. Both evolutionary product design and do just enough thinking overlap and are both complementary with *high value first*. To demonstrate this, return to the notion of a backlog of prioritized user stories for a release. A backlog of user stories provides a powerful tool to deliver high value first, do just enough, and to allow the design to evolve as you progress because a rank-ordered list of user stories enables teams to complete successive functionality in order of importance to the user. Well-written user stories will each describe a small problem to be solved for a user with the anticipated benefit(s) being understood as well. In an ideal scenario, user stories are independent of each other, so they can stand alone in value. User stories should fit easily into an iteration. Writing user stories that follow this pattern allows teams to complete the most critical stories first and get feedback—feedback that may require additional work or that may result in requests for new, unforeseen functionality. If this happens, the lowest-ranked stories may get dropped to make room for the new stories. This won't cause any disruption to the project because no work has started on the lower-ranked stories.

As the list of user stories evolves based on short customer feedback cycles, teams work with their customers to determine what is just enough to release. The compelling benefit of working on high-value stories first may be subtle, but the benefits are realized because lower-value stories can be dropped if necessary to provide opportunity to expand upon higher-value stories or new, unforeseen stories. This cannot usually happen in waterfall projects because all the requirements are typically developed as a whole. Waterfall teams plan out the list of requirements upfront, develop them, test them, and only too late discover what was not necessary. By the time waterfall teams discover something is not needed, these low-priority features are already in progress, and deleting the partially done work is often costly, so teams just finish the work anyway. The end result is a lot of wasted effort producing functionality that was not needed.

Delivering high-value user stories at the beginning of the development cycle is a key practice for releasing often.

High Risk First

In agile, we obviously want to complete capabilities that are of high value to the customer first. It is also important that teams prioritize high-risk items early. If you are implementing a new technology, re-architecting some critical part of the product, making significant changes to the database, and so forth, these items should be addressed early in the project so that you discover the challenging problems while there is enough time to fix them, and can test long enough to have confidence in the solution.

This sounds obvious, but many teams do not take this approach or, if they do, they tend to complete the coding first and leave the hard testing for later. Teams should always identify any high-risk areas at the beginning of a project and prioritize working on them early to significantly mitigate the risks. In essence, to manage risk, it is better to tackle it early. At the end of each iteration, validate what was learned, what risk remains, and how to continue to address it if needed, noting also any new risks that might have come to light. Managing risks early enables the team to build confidently upon the solution in subsequent iterations, provides more time to ensure the risks have been alleviated, and increases the hardiness of the solution.

One item that can be easily missed is testing design patterns rigorously from the beginning. Teams often start with unit testing and executing small test scenarios to validate a solution. However, for many high-risk items, this level of testing does not uncover bigger, architectural problems. After unit and functional testing, teams should add more rigorous performance testing, system-level testing, scalability testing, and so forth. The names may vary but the idea is the same: Put the solution under comprehensive, heavy, longer-term, testing. This type of testing needs to start with the first iteration. It's easier said than done, but it can make a difference because it can help to uncover risk as well as to ensure that any steps taken to address risk are confirmed as having actually mitigated it.

The first time I tried this with a team convinced me that the hurdles are always worth crossing. We had a significant code rewrite project that was necessary for dramatically increasing performance. We also had a performance testing team that served all our development teams according to need and project timing. In our case, the performance testing team was unavailable to test until well after our code would be completed. I suggested that we leverage our own developers to do performance testing. The developers would have responsibilities to both write the code and do performance testing beginning with the first iteration. This required that our developers learn how to build and run performance test scenarios. After some convincing, they were willing to give it a try. We had to borrow time from the performance test team experts to get started. The work slowed down our developers, but they succeeded in building performance tests that could be run starting with the first iteration. After they got over the initial learning hurdle, they started to enjoy their ability to do performance testing, especially because significant design problems were found early. About halfway through the release, we were confident in our solutions to our performance problems and could prove it. The risk posed by not having performance testers available early in the release was mitigated. The skilled performance testing team did join later in the project and were impressed by the progress that had been made. My team believed that learning these skills enabled it to build much better code, and it continued to incorporate performance testing as part of its work in future releases.

This all looks easy in the rear-view mirror but it was a hard transition to achieve. The benefits of this approach, however, are clear. Front-loading high-risk items helps with releasing often because it enables teams to find hard problems early so that there's enough time remaining in the release to get them solved. Finding hard problems late in a project is likely to require more significant code changes, or even major design changes, that will likely delay the project. Making design changes is more manageable if less of the code is in place.

Furthermore, demonstrating high-risk solutions to customers early allows them to offer feedback regarding any choices that still have to be made. Most high-risk strategies require compromising on some capability once any limitations are uncovered. Customers can help the team with understanding the right trade-offs to make. On one of my projects there were several product teams trying to create a seamless, single sign-on capability between their products. The short-term solution required adding client code to manage the credential sharing between the applications, which incurred a user installation cost. The more elegant solution required more time to develop, but it did not incur a user installation cost. Delivering the easier solution first, followed later by the more elegant solution, created additional customer costs for migration and development costs for support. After the options were disclosed to the customer base, the customers opted to wait for the better solution and totally forego the option that would have delivered some value to them initially, but at a cost. That outcome was not what the team had expected, but by disclosing both the technical challenges and the timeline challenges, the customers were part of the solution. And as you no doubt noted, in this particular instance the customers opted to wait for the more elegant solution instead of getting something earlier that did not meet their needs.

Value-Driven Development: the Outworking of Frequent Code Drops

I mentioned earlier that shipping alphas is another way to support releasing often. Releasing often may be difficult for enterprise software products because significant functionality may take some time to develop. However, releasing often is important so that you get timely feedback on the value of the functionality currently in progress. Another way to achieve this goal is to provide frequent code drops to your customers to receive timely feedback. The old-fashioned notion of a beta was a "feature complete, test complete" snapshot of the code for customers to try. The problem with this mechanism is that customer feedback usually came too late to make any big changes in the product prior to the scheduled ship date. More often than not, doing betas this way works as a late-stage quality check, without offering significant value for the customer who engages in the beta effort.

As an alternative, consider shipping code drops before the product ships, each time with additional, interim functionality included so that customers actually have the opportunity to not only see the functionality but, more important, also evaluate whether it solves problems in their specific environments. End-of-iteration demonstrations are critical for agile success, but enabling customers to use the product themselves as it is being developed can provide additional feedback to product teams. Teams resist this option for the same reasons that they resist doing demonstrations at the end of every iteration; they worry that they won't have enough new functionality to demonstrate. What I have found from doing frequent demonstrations, and from doing frequent code drops, is that customers learn more about the solutions that teams are building and, consequently, provide more timely and valuable feedback. This ensures that teams are always working towards providing value for customers, hence the idea of "Value Driven Development."

I managed a team that was required to replace its long-standing, easy-to-use installation with a technology that would become the company-wide standard. Our team was one of the first product teams in the company to migrate to the technology, so it was not well tested with any customers. We needed to make sure that the customers would succeed with the new installer and understand its long-term benefits. We targeted three code drops to help guarantee success for our customers. Our first code drop was fairly disastrous, with few customers successfully completing an install. As a result, we formed teams of engineers and support personnel to partner with each customer to sort out their specific challenges. This gave us the opportunity to understand first-hand the installation challenges in different customer environments. We incorporated all the feedback into our product for the next code drop, which was much more successful. Feedback from the third code drop made us confident that the release would be of great value to our customers.

It is a significant request to ask enterprise customers to adopt code drops that frequently. Actually, we went a step further and requested feedback from each code drop, each with specific deadlines so that we would get critical feedback in time to include it in the product. We asked our customers to meet with us on specific dates after each code drop, thus ensuring their commitment. When they saw proof that we addressed their issues in the next code drop, they became committed to the process as well. Furthermore, our frequent conversations with them enabled us to spend more time educating them on how they could better use our product for their success.

If you cannot release as often as you want because of (for example) the high overhead and costs of actually releasing a product, try releasing code often in the form of frequent code drops so that you can still learn quickly from the short feedback cycles.

Metrics

There are some simple metrics to track your effort to release often. The most obvious is to review and map your release history. Decide what release cadence you want to establish and set a path for that pace. Your existing customers may not have urgent needs requiring them to immediately move up to your latest releases, but selling to new customers may require that you ship more frequently. If releases are costly to install, then evaluate why that is, and prioritize improvements to product installs and migrations.

To help you determine how often to release, find out how often your customers are willing to upgrade your software. Do not use that information as a limitation, as they may not be following the best plan. Use the information as a guide for improvement. The same strategy should be applied to software maintenance updates, or fix-packs. Find out how often your customers deploy these and what gets in their way, and discover ways to fix the problems. Like you, they may be stuck in their habits and not realize that more frequent updates can improve their productivity. Just think about the radical change our customers went through when we went to releasing maintenance releases every 3 weeks instead of every 2 to 3 months.

A large product team I know of was eager to have its customers install a significant new version of its product that had just been released. History suggested that customers would delay the upgrade for a long time, so the development organization put together a small team that worked with a set of targeted customers to find out when they could move to the latest release and what was in their way. One by one, this team helped get obstacles out of the customer's way and move to the latest version (helping the customer with that process if necessary). As the team successively worked with customers to achieve these upgrade goals, it learned a lot about how the customers worked, and the customers learned more about how to use the product more successfully. As an outside observer, it may seem obvious that this would work as well as it did, but the team was surprised by its level of success and used the lessons learned to make the next release even better.

In terms of using metrics to evaluate your efforts to release often, review your remaining backlog at the end of a release. Because your backlog was rank-ordered based on value and risk, the items left on the backlog are obviously low-value and low-risk by comparison to what was completed. Decide if it makes sense to drop these user stories completely instead of carrying them over to the next release. Has the "landscape" changed enough that these items are no longer important to consider at all? If so, then focus on the new, critical functionality for your next release instead of thinking you have to complete everything just because it was originally under consideration.

Finally, evaluate the design decisions that need to be made for your next release, and (for starters) pick one design decision to defer. Build your code such that you can stub out the code now, and then finalize your solution later in the process. Track the effectiveness of the defer decision approach by capturing the criteria that finally led to a decision in comparison with the time at which you discovered the criteria. At the end of the release, review how well the mechanism worked by comparing the timing of the decision relative to the knowledge of the key criteria required to make the best decision possible. If the criteria were not completely understood when the design was conceived, then deferring the decision provided value. It is hard to quantify how much value because it is hard to estimate how much code would have been adjusted, but the exercise should prove to be worthwhile and provide insights for use elsewhere.

Breakthrough

To help teams get to release often thinking, Scott and I suggest that you create the bulk of your backlog of iteration-sized user stories at the beginning of a release. We know that the typical recommendation is to write stories at the beginning of the *iteration* in which the team plans to work on them, but there are some benefits that you may not be aware of in creating the bulk of your user stories at the outset of the *release*.

The process starts with an agreement on the epic stories. Make sure your epic stories characterize and clearly prioritize the vision for the release so that the team knows what to focus on as well as what *not* to focus on as they make decisions each day. Make the initial pass at creating the epics the responsibility of a smaller team of cross-functional domain experts, which should typically include the product owner, lead developer, lead tester, and lead writer. This small team helps get the *initial* process completed faster. After this small team has taken a first pass at defining the epics and breaking them down into the next layer of smaller stories, involve the rest of the team in the process of further breaking down the stories into the resulting backlog of iteration-sized stories. Once you have the bulk of your iteration-size stories created, rank-order the backlog with the highest-value and highest-risk stories at the top. Size the stories with story points.

It is important that you time-box this process so that the work is completed and the team does not get distracted. On average, for a variety of team sizes and project sizes, we see that this process takes 1 to 2 weeks. Set an aggressive target, remove interruptions and distractions, and focus the team exclusively on this process to get it done.

When the stories are rank-ordered and sized, the team can get started and quickly establish a velocity. Most teams establish a reliable velocity in about three iterations. Using their velocity, the team can create a release burndown chart, which is a chart that tracks the burn down of total user story points against time. Figure 8.3 shows a release burndown for a backlog of more than 130 user story points. It shows the possible end dates using the team's velocity as a guide.

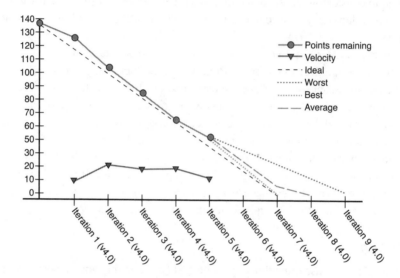

Figure 8.3   This is an example of a Release Burndown Chart showing a total of 137 user story points on the y-axis and nine iterations on the x-axis. The light "Best," dark "Worst," and long "Average" dotted lines demonstrate the "best-case," "worst-case," and "expected" scenarios respectively, based on observed velocity through the fifth iteration.

One of the greatest metrics that agile introduced is the release burndown chart. If your backlog is complete, then it is fairly easy to get a view of what functionality can be completed by any given date. The accuracy of these charts increases with time, they can be generated automatically with a spreadsheet (or, better yet, use a tool like Rational Team Concert's "Advanced Release Burndown Chart" originally developed by our coworker Mark Wainwright), and they also provide visibility to anyone regarding how the release is going.

Many agile proponents are opposed to the practice of creating an upfront backlog because they fear that it sets the tone that the backlog cannot evolve as the team learns and forces too much upfront planning. Those are valid concerns, so it is important to reinforce the purpose of a rank-ordered backlog of user stories. User stories, by definition, do not get into the "how," but rather the "what," so there's little or no focus on implementation details. The focus is on customers' goals and desired outcomes.[5] As teams get feedback each iteration, they can tweak the

5. See also Scott's discussion of user stories in the "Why User Stories" section of Chapter 7, "Deliver Value" (especially footnote 2).

remaining backlog as required, perhaps adding new stories, eliminating stories, or even updating the rank-ordering of the stories still remaining on the backlog. If the user stories are at the level suggested, tweaking the backlog will not be an issue.

Furthermore, many enterprise-level software projects have well-known requirements because there may not be a lot of "dynamic" activity in the marketplace, nor are there typically a lot of "customer unknowns." Consequently, creating an upfront backlog in these situations makes more sense than writing stories on a just-in-time basis, especially given the power that release burndown charts bring to the table.

An upfront backlog does mean some upfront planning must take place—no arguments on that. The case to be made here is that this initial, high-level planning can provide a realistic perspective on what is ahead so that teams can better judge how much time to spend on the current work. It helps with seeing at any point in time what is just enough.

Why will completing the backlog at the beginning of the release help you release often? Contrary to some myths, agile requires more rigor and discipline than traditional software practices. Agile is not the "wild west" of software development, nor is it the equivalent of "drive-by coding." Instead of heavy, upfront planning, agile requires planning every iteration. Teams that start with an upfront backlog get into the rigor of agile sooner. For the teams that Scott and I coach closely, we require this step, despite the resistance we often face. By focusing on the *user* stories that need to be included in a release rather than focusing on implementation details at the beginning of a release, teams have a better view of the value of the release in its entirety. The release backlog enables them to get a better feel for what it means to "do just enough" for the release.

Each team we've worked with that has tried this technique has found it quite useful. With one team, we broke down the epic story about the new installer mentioned earlier. Breaking the epic into iteration-sized stories was easy because the purpose of the installer was obvious. After completing the process, the team said that it always knew that it was going to have a lot of hard work to do but could never adequately describe it in a convincing way that enabled it to target a sufficient amount of time for the release. This process provided a more realistic view of what the effort would be, and an upfront agreement on the critical elements of the overall epic as well as a reasonable time-frame.

This technique also helps keep teams from waterfalling backward. Teams that struggle with getting to "Done!" each iteration, and that also try to develop their backlog as they go, get pressed for time. In the cases where we have seen teams pressed for time, they begin taking serious shortcuts when creating their stories at the beginning of an iteration. Then the worst often happens; they lose their discipline, and with that their agile practices often fall apart.

Try this breakthrough technique to help your team succeed with agile, especially for releasing often.

Summary

Being agile requires releasing software often so that teams learn fast and customers succeed sooner.

- Releasing often is a concept that uses short release cycles to deliver just enough value to customers to ensure that customers are successful. Short release cycles provide rapid feedback to the organization so that they can learn fast.

- Do use just enough thinking to deliver enough value to meet the customers' needs, but do not deliver more than that. Doing just enough is critical to releasing often because it gets teams out of the habit of developing more than is needed and more than will be used. Apply just enough thinking to other aspects of software development as well.

- Deferring critical decisions can help teams deliver often because committing to a solution early in the development cycle, when there is less information, can lead to finding difficult design problems late in the project that may force a delay in releasing. Defer critical decisions until there's enough information to decide on a solution, or until the last responsible moment to make a decision.

- Epic stories help get to shorter release cycles because they enable teams to commit to the high-level theme of the story—but not to the details of behavior or implementation. When customers have a solution to their primary problem, customers can help the team evaluate how much more is required.

- Evolutionary product design allows the product design to evolve as the software is developed through the process of discovery.

- Prioritize high-value, high-risk user stories first to meet the customer needs sooner and remove project risk early.

- If your release cycles need to stay long, plan to make multiple code drops to customers before the product ships to get valuable feedback from them. Incorporate their feedback into the code and demonstrate the value of the process.

- Issue maintenance releases often to get critical fixes to customers in a timely manner.

- Try building your entire user story backlog before you start your first iteration. This provides a view of the entire release so that a regular assessment of what is just enough is possible.

CHAPTER 9

Stop the Line

Being agile requires that teams stop the line to solve critical problems at their core so that they do not lose time by dealing with the same problem again and again.

By Leslie Ekas

Early in the days when web programming was new, one of the earlier companies I was involved with came out with products that leveraged a web server architecture. As the web development technologies advanced, we did our best to keep pace and leverage cutting edge technology to give our customers the advantages the new technologies offered. We had a strong heritage of ensuring that our software protected customer's critical intellectual property, so it came as an unhappy surprise when a customer found several ways to breach our security. The customer was concerned about what had been found and escalated the issues to our executives. Part of the problem was that we had not kept our skills sharp regarding the ever-growing ways that web interfaces could be used to break into a system. We were horrified and understood that this required immediate attention.

And, naturally, this did not happen at a good time because we were in the throes of a new release. The whole team stopped work on our current release to get a handle on the reported problems and decide what to do next. We needed to understand the nature of the problems so that we could even begin to understand how to fix them. We also needed to assure our customer that the problems would not resurface. Furthermore, we needed to develop expertise on the rapidly changing challenges of security and bake new practices into our development discipline so that we could guarantee secure products with all our future releases. (We ultimately formed a small team that was assigned the responsibility of becoming experts on how to keep our software secure, stay on top of new security challenges continually, and educate the rest of the organization.) When we understood and fixed the root cause of the problems, we could then understand how to avoid these problems moving forward.

This is what the Lean concept of "stop the line" behavior looks like. Stopping the line means that you stop what you are doing and fix a problem *by fixing the root cause of the problem so that the problem does not return.* Even though we had never heard of stop the line behavior at this time, we nevertheless modeled it perfectly. We spent the time required to educate ourselves and improve our operating discipline. Had we not addressed the root cause of the security problems, we would likely have hit the problems again—and that would have led to an even greater issue with customer trust. Another point to make concerning stop the line behavior is that we put the whole team on the problem. Too many teams today would have just assigned one person to the problem while the rest of the team was expected to continue working on the new product. In our case, such an approach would have led to a lengthy delay in fixing the problem, which would have been unacceptable. Stop the line behavior means not only fixing a problem at its root so that it doesn't occur again, but it also means focusing on the problem with *all* necessary personnel to ensure a timely resolution.

Principles

What Is Stop the Line?

The stop the line concept comes from a mechanism used on Toyota production lines that enables *any* worker to stop the production line if *any* problem is encountered. Stopping the line means that the *entire* production line is stopped until not only a problem is fixed, but that it is fixed at its *root*. As counter-intuitive as it may seem, this practice enabled Toyota's production lines to actually increase productivity.

Stop the line behavior was conceived in response to efforts to improve the efficiency of manufacturing processes. The same behavior is somewhat harder to adopt in software development because software is not built on a production line. However, software teams utilize repeatable processes to get their software built: Teams repeatedly write code, test their code, automate tests, deploy their code, and so forth. They can apply the stop the line behavior to address problems with any of these processes. Some examples in which stop the line can be applied are broken builds, test automation failures, and setting up an environment for testing. Other examples in which stop the line can be used include making continuous integration work without interruption, ensuring automated provisioning works without failure, or even just addressing a subset of one of these processes.

A somewhat less obvious example in which stop the line behavior should have been applied is the following story: A team Scott and I worked with was just beginning to transition to agile. We explained to the team the importance of whole teams. However, this team told us that its system testers were still finishing the system testing of the previous release (a waterfall project in which system testing was the last phase) and wouldn't be available for several weeks. We suggested that everyone who was available needed to help finish the previous release. For those who couldn't help, they could work on some "agile enablement" items such as improving the automation, introducing continuous integration, learning about and piloting test-driven development, and even lining up customers to participate in an active stakeholder interaction program for the new agile release. However, the organizational leadership chose to have the team start working on the new release immediately—and they didn't do any system testing until the system testers were freed up from the previous release. When the system testers joined the new release, it quickly became apparent that they lacked the knowledge and insights needed regarding how best to test the code that had already been written. Because they missed out on the initial project kickoff, and the associated training, training them in the middle of the project slowed down the rest of the team and, therefore, system testing started even later than originally anticipated. In addition, because system testing started late, the testers found complex problems much later than had they started testing from the beginning. Delays in discovery meant the problems were even more costly to fix.

The desire of this organization to get started "right now" on the new project without having the system testers available is one of those reflexive, waterfall responses that this book is meant to address. And, as you can see from the way the story ended, the team was basically doing a waterfall project and received very little benefit from their initial move to agile.

The obvious stop the line behavior would have been to have *not* started working on the new project and, instead, have helped get the previous project *done*. This would not only have solved the problem where the system testers were not available when the rest of the team started the new release, but it also would have solved the *root* problem, which was that the previous project was not finished and was interfering with the beginning of the next project.

Note that it may not make sense to stop the line for every problem that arises because it is not often clear that solving every problem encountered will, in fact, make a team more efficient or improve the quality of the product. For instance, a team may discover that its design for managing system failures does not work well in some scenarios that had not been anticipated. Its design may be sufficient for the anticipated usage, but the code will likely become more brittle over time if the design flaws are not addressed. If the team decides to stop the line or, said differently, stop any additional coding and immediately fix the design issues, it may not hit the project deadline. If it makes business sense to do so, it may decide to compromise by using the design that is currently in place and add the necessary redesign as technical debt that needs to be paid back in the next release. Teams need to determine, in a mature way, when to apply stop the line behavior.

Stop the line behavior can be applied in other ways—ways not associated with process issues, defects, or other problem areas. In some organizations there may be products that are no longer delivering a profit. Business managers can apply stop the line behavior by discontinuing development of new releases of these unprofitable products. Like other root-cause fixes, there may be short-term costs, but the long-term gains (in this instance) will be that more resources will be available to work on products that are making money.

Why Is Stop the Line Hard?

Does the following scenario ring a bell? "*We started to have build problems, but when we stopped to fix the build problems, it became evident that our build software needed to be updated, which was going to take more time than we had. The new build software also required an update to our operating system, but that required that other software on the machine be updated as well. Of course, if we were going to go to the trouble of updating all the required software on our build machines, we needed to consider an upgrade to our hardware as well."* When addressing interrelated problems, the number of problems can quickly feel insurmountable, and stopping the line to fix any one problem might feel like a useless drop in the bucket. As a result, it can become habitual to avoid fixing hard problems by arguing that the cost to fix them is too high, even though teams tend to know better. One of the biggest reason why stop the line behavior does not occur that often is that teams get used to living with pain—and they can even begin to find ways to justify it.

Another reason why stop the line behavior is hard is that stopping the line can be prohibitive *in some cases* because the cost of the fix is too expensive. For example, I live in the northwestern part of the United States and, if you're familiar with the area, you know there are a lot of trees. We get several winter storms each year that produce enough wind to regularly blow down trees. Consequently, we lose our power several times each year—and it tends to happen on the coldest days. Every time this happens, the power company spends days or even weeks repairing the downed power lines. The power company is fixing the symptoms of the problem, but it is not solving the root cause. The root cause of the problem is that the power lines are above ground and near trees. Fixing the root cause would entail moving the power lines underground so they will remain unaffected during windstorms. But the cost of doing so is always deemed to be too high. Updating the infrastructure, and getting the lines underground, is just too expensive. In these situations, the longer term gains need to be considered.

And, finally, let's face it, would you rather fix an old, tiresome problem or work on developing some new, fun code? This is the "shiny new toy" syndrome that many engineers tend to suffer from. I was a developer on an old client-server product that was built to run on multiple platforms. Back in those days we had a large makefile that managed all our platform builds. Completing the builds successfully on all the platforms took many hours, so build breaks were costly. When a broken build would require makefile changes, developers often found a "quick and dirty" fix to get the build to work. However, such "solutions" invariably made the build process ever more fragile. One of our senior engineers would get annoyed with this "quick and dirty approach" used by his teammates. He would often sit with an offending developer for hours to fix a build problem at its core. And it often took hours because the issues were complex and tremendous domain knowledge was required to get it right. I once had the "opportunity" to sit through one of these sessions and, although definitely grueling, having him show me how to do it right was liberating and made me a believer in fixing problems at their root.

It is not necessary to convince engineers that when a problem has been solved at its root, the problem is not likely going to occur again. Knowing when to do this, and how to apply this thinking, is where it can get hard. When is a problem significant enough to have the team actually *stop* what it is doing and shift gears to fix a problem? Unfortunately, only you and your team can answer that. What we can do is to provide you with some practices and some breakthrough thinking to help you gain insights to answer the questions correctly for your situations when they do arise.

Practices

Fix Blockers

A great place to start practicing stop the line behavior in a small way is to fix blocking issues that are surfaced during the daily team meeting. It is during these meetings where team members identify any blocking issues they may be encountering. It is the duty of the team to address these blockers and to try to remove them before the next daily standup. This is stop the line thinking—and it is a good place to start. What may not be baked into this practice initially is discovering the root cause of a problem and tackling it at that point instead of just addressing a symptom. Try to adopt the notion of removing blockers in such a way as to not let them occur again. This behavior may cost the team some time upfront, but it will prove its worth in the long run as the team starts to "get it" by no longer accepting a "band-aid" fix now, only to see a problem come back to haunt them in an even bigger way later.

Reflections as a Guide

Agile teams use reflections to identify problems, discuss solutions, and brainstorm on actions. (See Chapter 11, "Continuous Improvement," for more on reflections.) For stop the line behavior, agile teams should use reflections as a tool to review their behavior when it comes to blocking issues. Ask the following questions as part of your reflections:

- Was the root cause of a blocking issue eliminated? If not, why not?
- If the root cause was not eliminated, how is the team going to deal with the same problem in the future? ("Pay me now or pay me *more* later.")
- Is there a set of problem types that occur over and over? (If so, these are good candidates for applying stop the line thinking.)

What if the Problem Is Too Big to Stop the Line?

The most challenging aspect of stop the line behavior is that it requires teams to remove the root cause of a problem so that the problem does not happen again. It is important not to lose focus on this aspect in your quest to get blockers out of your way. If you decide that you cannot immediately fix a problem at its root cause because it is too big, consider the mechanism described next.

What happens if a team hits a problem that is too large to solve *right now*? For instance, what if a team determines that the way it is building its software does not easily accommodate a new technology that needs to be added to the product? To solve this problem correctly might involve a costly update or rework to their build system. And the team has no choice but to solve the problem somehow. In such cases, a team may use shortcuts to solve the problem, but by continually using shortcuts the team incurs more and more project debt until the problem gets so big that it can no longer be ignored. The cost of solving the problem at this point can be significant—either that, or the problem is irreparable and the team has to start over from scratch.

We suggest using user stories to manage these scenarios in which the team assumes the stakeholder role. (Typically a customer role is used in user stories because the team normally works on features that are important to customers. In this case, however, the team is, in essence, its own customer.) Determine what value fixing the problem at its core provides and include that in the stories. When a team starts a new release, these stories are considered as part of the backlog for the new release. The stories should be sized and rank-ordered right along with the rest of the stories for the new feature work the team is planning on doing. Putting such user stories on the backlog provides the best means to ensure the needed work is visible to everyone in the organization, thus ensuring that it does not get neglected nor that the team is somehow just expected to do this work in its "spare time." This technique is nothing more than leveraging the agile process to address the problem of not stopping the line.

Metrics

Metrics may be hard to apply to stop the line behavior because the goal of the behavior is to handle the problem when it occurs, *not* track it. But the following metric may help when a team discovers problems that are too large and/or too numerous to fix *right now*.

Before Scott and I start a formal coaching engagement with a team, we do short interviews with a broad cross-section of team members to discover how the team operates. In the course of these interviews, we usually discover barriers to successful agile adoption (or, as we call them, *inhibitors*). Many of the typical inhibitors should have been fixed when they first occurred, but the teams have left them festering. Inhibitors tend to be large problems that teams know they need to fix but the pressure to do new stuff is typically intense, so the inhibitors linger. In fact, they can at times almost completely prevent teams from adopting agile. Here are a few examples of inhibitors we have seen:

- Severe and/or recurring build problems
- A build process that can take a day or more
- Complex setup procedures that are manually repeated regularly
- Inadequate or broken test automation

Stop the line behavior should be used to fix these kinds of problems, and when they occur it's exactly what we recommend to teams at the outset of their move to agile.

To help teams actually address multiple inhibitors, such as those mentioned, we have them write user stories and prioritize them on their backlog. As part of this effort, and to ensure that teams actually eliminate their inhibitors, we've devised the following technique to make teams aware of the total impact that their inhibitors are having, as well as the benefits gained when they are addressed:

- Create a backlog of inhibitors that adversely affect team efficiency and effectiveness.

- Estimate the number of people that are affected by the inhibitor on a yearly basis.

- Estimate the time that each person spends on the inhibitor on a yearly basis.

- Roughly estimate the cost to fix each inhibitor. (Risk can be a factor in the estimate if the team so chooses.)

- Evaluate the return on investment (ROI) for removing the inhibitor. The ROI is calculated by subtracting the cost estimate to fix the inhibitor from the yearly cost of the inhibitor. The yearly cost is calculated from multiplying the monthly cost per person times the number of people affected (accounting for 12 months in a year). An additional 25% of the total cost is added to the total cost to account for the cost of multitasking.

- If an inhibitor results in regularly distracting team members from doing real work, add in an additional 25 percent to the cost to account for the inefficiencies of multitasking. (See Chapter 4, "No Multitasking," for more discussion on how multitasking hurts both team and organizational efficiency.) In essence, multitasking requires more cumulative time to complete the work (we suggest using the estimate of 25 percent more time) because you add time in the process of switching tasks to reset your context. When teams get into the habit of solving problems as a part of their daily operations, their net efficiency actually improves. They can often leverage what they learn to solve the next problem *and* avoid future problems, thus making the team even more efficient.

- Use that evaluation to prioritize the investment against the product backlog items.[1]

The following example conveys the overall process from identifying inhibitors, assessing the current costs, determining the ROI of fixing the inhibitors, rank-ordering the inhibitors from those that provide the most ROI down to those that provide the least, and then tracking the actual ROI using a burn-up chart as inhibitors are removed. Table 9.1 shows the calculation of ROI to remove a single inhibitor (automate build results feedback) as 120 person days. Table 9.2 shows the same calculation but includes an additional 25% to account for the benefits of eliminating the task-switching overhead, resulting in an updated ROI of 157.5 person days. Table 9.3 shows an example where removing the inhibitor frees up more person days than fixing the inhibitor but only if the gains realized from eliminating the impacts of the constant task-switching are factored in.

---

1. Scott and I first published this approach as part of IBM's intellectual property activities via IP.COM. You can download the entire publication from their fee-based website here: www.ip.com/IPCOM/000220881

Table 9.1   A Typical Attempt at Determining the ROI of Fixing an Inhibitor

Inhibitor	Monthly Person Cost (Days)	Number People Affected	Yearly Cost (Person Days)	Estimate of Cost to Fix (Person Days)	ROI (Person Days)
Automate build results feedback	2.5	5	150	30	120

Table 9.2   An Updated ROI for the Same Inhibitor Using the 25 Percent Efficiency Improvement Gained from Eliminating Multitasking

Inhibitor	Monthly Person Cost (Days)	Number People Affected	Yearly Cost (Person Days)	Yearly Cost (including 25 percent Task-Switching Overhead)	Estimate of Cost to Fix (Person Days)	ROI (Person Days)
Automate build results feedback	2.5	5	150	187.5	30	157.5

Table 9.3   A Separate Example Showing How Adding in the 25 Percent Efficiency Calculation Moves a Given Inhibitor from the Realm of "Not Worthwhile" (minus 50) to "Worthwhile" (plus 100)

Inhibitor	Monthly Person Cost (Days)	Number People Affected	Yearly Cost (Person Days)	Estimate of Cost to Fix (Person Days)	ROI (Person Days)
Remove build breaks due to inadequate build hosts	1	50	600	650	- 50

Inhibitor	Monthly Person Cost (Days)	Number People Affected	Yearly Cost (Person Days)	Yearly Cost (Including 25% Task-Switching Overhead)	Estimate of Cost to Fix (Person Days)	ROI (Person Days)
Remove build breaks due to inadequate build hosts	1	50	600	750	650	100

Table 9.4 shows which inhibitor to work on first, as well as indicating that the last item would not be one to pursue at all (due to the negative ROI). Note also that Automate Test Review and Defect Assignment would likely be one that teams would typically work on first because the "cost to fix" is so low by comparison with the others, but the table clearly shows that this should be the last of the inhibitors to address because the overall ROI is so small by comparison with the others:

Table 9.4 Sample Rank Ordering of Inhibitors with ROI Calculations for Each.

Inhibitor	Monthly Person Cost (Days)	Number People Affected	Yearly Cost (Person Days)	Yearly Cost (Including 25 Percent Task-switching Overhead)	Estimate of Cost to Fix (Person Days)	ROI (Person Days)
Hardware provisioning—Windows.	2.0	35.0	840.0	1050.0	50.0	1000.0
Remove build breaks due to inadequate build hosts.	1.0	50.0	600.0	750.0	30.0	720.0
Move all defect tracking to RTC instead of having two defect repositories.	1.0	30.0	360.0	450.0	35.0	415.0
Automate build results feedback.	2.5	5.0	150.0	187.5	15.0	172.5
Automate build launch.	2.0	4.0	96.0	120.0	15.0	105.0
Automate build results feedback.	1.0	50.0	600.0	750.0	650.0	100.0
Automate test review and defect assignment.	2.0	3.0	72.0	90.0	4.0	86.0
Hardware provisioning—AIX	1.5	10.0	180.0	225.0	625.0	-400.0

Figure 9.1 clearly shows the overall progress of the team toward achieving ROI based on inhibitors already fixed with ROI yet remaining. Table 9.5 provides a visual demonstration of the progressive ROI that will be realized.

Table 9.5　The Final Table Showing the ROI for All the Inhibitors and Ranking Them by Highest ROI.

Inhibitor	Monthly Person Cost (Days)	Number People Affected	Yearly Cost (Person Days)	Yearly Cost (+ 25 Percent Task-Switch Overhead)	Estimate of Cost to Fix (Person Days)	ROI (Person Days)	Total Savings Realized When Completed	Completed?	Actual Savings
Hardware provisioning—Windows.	2.0	35.0	840.0	1050.0	50.0	1000.0	1000.0	X	1000.0
Remove build breaks due to inadequate build hosts.	1.0	50.0	600.0	750.0	30.0	720.0	1720.0	X	1720.0
Unify defect tracking tool.	1.0	30.0	360.0	450.0	35.0	415.0	2135.0		
Automate build results feedback.	2.5	5.0	150.0	187.5	15.0	172.5	2307.5		
Automate build launch.	2.0	4.0	96.0	120.0	15.0	105.0	2412.5		
Automate test review and defect assignment.	1.0	50.0	600.0	750.0	650.0	100.0	2512.5		
Automate test review and defect assignment.	2.0	3.0	72.0	90.0	4.0	86.0	2598.5		

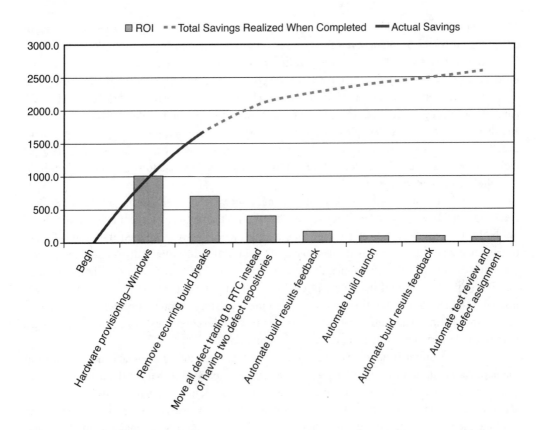

Figure 9.1   Burn-up chart showing the increasing ROI in person days recovered (y axis) as each of the inhibitors (x-axis) is removed.

Breakthrough

Until now, I've been discussing stop the line for issues that typically confront development teams and sometimes the overall organization. This breakthrough technique shifts the focus to your customers. With this in mind consider trying this mechanism: Remove the biggest inhibitor is to customer success. And by inhibitor I do not mean a missing feature; I mean identifying an aspect of your product that is currently problematic for your customers. Talk to your customers, your customer support teams, product managers and market managers, sales representatives, and others in your organization that regularly interact with customers. What's the biggest inhibitor identified that prevents customers from being happy with your product and/or from receiving expected value? You will be tackling a nagging customer issue at its core.

I understood the value of stop the line when my team did this by prioritizing the solving of a nagging customer problem, even though we could have "gotten by" without doing anything. Our product was successful; however, we knew that there was an obstacle that made it hard for our customers to truly get the most from the product. Our installer was difficult to use, a bit temperamental depending on the environment, and bugs tended to surface right after we shipped. An agile coach suggested that, for our next release, we prioritize the installer first in the backlog, and then use it every day to deploy our own software. For many traditional enterprise products, installers are the first part of the software product that most users see, so this is where they get their first impressions of a product. With that in mind, it made sense to stop overlooking problems and fix them at their root.

When I first suggested this idea to my team members, they were not in favor of it. Reflexive, waterfall thinking kicked in. They reasoned that until the software was completed, they could not build a complete installer. This felt like a stall tactic, so we discussed the option further because we knew that our existing approach of building the installer at the end of the project was not working. Finally, after much discussion, they decided that they could build the baseline installer in the first several iterations. It would install only the part of the code that was "working." For the remaining iterations, they updated the user story "Done!" criteria to include successful installation. The team established the rule that the installer must be kept up to date each iteration and everyone on the team had to use it every day.

After the initial installer was developed, the team got into a regular cadence with this method. As the iterations progressed, the installer was expanded to handle the additional code. The exercise proved to be not as difficult as the team had anticipated. As the team members used the installer regularly, they started to discover ways to make it easier to use and more robust. By the time the product shipped, the installer was working extremely well; many of the kinks had been removed and it was easy to use. By the end of the release, this approach seemed like the obvious thing to have done even though the team had discounted it early on.

Determine what is the most significant barrier to customer adoption of your product and prioritize fixing it to the top of the backlog. Do that work first and then find a way for the team to exercise the updated code constantly. If the team has to suffer the customer pain, then it will "get it" and find creative ways to reduce or eliminate such pain.

For this breakthrough, you do not actually have to stop the line when you first hit the problem, but it does require that you prioritize fixing the problem to the top of your backlog and fixing the problem at its root. After you experience fixing a problem that your customers stumble over constantly, and enable them to be delighted, it can be quite liberating! When you get to this point, continue on—consider using stop the line for smaller, lower-profile problems.

Summary

Being agile requires that teams stop the line to solve critical problems at their core so that they do not lose time by dealing with the same problem again and again.

- Stop the line is a lean practice that comes from manufacturing and means anyone on a production line can stop the line when a problem is encountered. The root cause of the problem is identified and fixed before the production line is restarted. The end result is higher productivity. Stop the line is also used in software development, which means that when a problem is encountered, the team stops the work, finds the root cause, and fixes it before continuing.

- Stop the line can be applied to a wide range of problems including broken builds, broken test automation, repeatedly fixing defects associated with poorly architected code, and even continually shipping new releases of unprofitable products.

- Stop the line behavior can be hard for teams to adopt because they get into the habit of deprioritizing problems and living with pain, especially if the problems seem to be too many, too hard, too costly, or not interesting enough to fix.

- Fixing blockers that surface at the daily standup allows teams to practice stop the line behavior. Be sure to find and fix the root cause of a problem; do not just fix the symptoms. If problems take too much time to solve with stop the line behavior, they can be added as user stories to the team's backlog.

- Prioritize problems that are too large to tackle as stop the line problems with the following technique: Create a backlog of inhibitors that adversely affect team efficiency and effectiveness; estimate the number of people that are affected by the inhibitor on a yearly basis; estimate the time that each person spends on the inhibitor on a yearly basis; estimate the cost to fix each inhibitor; evaluate the return on investment (ROI) for removing the inhibitor (using the 25 percent efficiency improvement realized by eliminating the real but often unnoticed multitasking that occurs because of handling a recurring problem); and use that evaluation to prioritize the investment against the product backlog items. Track the cumulative ROI of fixing the inhibitors.

- Apply stop the line behavior by prioritizing the fixing of your most significant customer inhibitor.

Agile Leadership

Being successful with agile requires leaders who learn, participate in, and experiment with agile so that they lead with an agile mindset and react with agile instincts.

By Leslie Ekas

Unlike the rest of the book, this chapter on agile leadership is not about a specifically agile principle or practice. That being said, a successful transition to agile requires leadership—leadership that understands how agile is supposed to work, and supports, enables, and guides the organization as appropriate. My goal for this chapter is not to go through all the research that has been done on what makes a "good leader," whether leaders are born with natural leadership talents, if those talents can be trained into a person, or any such thing. If you're in a leadership position, or even aspire to one (whether technical leadership or management), there are certain things you have to be willing to do if you want your teams to be successful with agile.

I got my first opportunity to try agile because my senior vice president understood agile and wanted my organization to try it. He funded the necessary education of our team leaders on lean and agile—which was a great start. But, more important, he wholeheartedly supported our adoption of agile. His sponsorship gave me (as a middle-level manager) the ability to fully engage all the different parts of our (then waterfall) organization. Getting the entire organization engaged was required to successfully make our move to agile. Thinking back on our first year, our agile adoption would not have been as resolute as it was without our executive's support. His visible support of our efforts sent a clear message to everyone in the organization—he wanted us to make it work. Had his encouragement not been there, our determination to be successful would likely have diminished over time, and I don't think we would have ultimately succeeded. His encouragement and visible support kept us always wanting to try to get better.

After we started with agile, all the teams learned that they not only had to work differently than they were used to doing, but they also all had to work together from the first day of the project. We reported our progress differently and even tried new tools to manage our backlog of work. From the beginning, no one was sure that we would be successful delivering a release, and

I was not sure how forgiving our other executives would be if we failed. But we had the senior executive support needed to do our best, overcome inhibitors, and be aggressive in our approach.

Our executive kept telling me that he was going to listen in to various standup meetings just to see how it was going. I am not sure if he ever did because our meetings were by phone and we did not take attendance. But just knowing that he might be in attendance was enough to encourage the team to try hard to make our agile transformation work. We never took his comments about attending our meetings as a threat—instead we believed that he was actually showing his support.

After about 8 months, the senior executive asked me to give a presentation on our progress to the general manager of our division. I reviewed our agile adoption approach with the general manager and discussed where we had successes and failures. Being relatively new to IBM at the time, I did not realize how timely this presentation was. Agile was new, and we were one of the first teams in the company adopting it. It was a great experience and, looking back on it, I cannot believe how naïve I was in thinking that everyone "got" agile. At that time, almost no one did. It was not because our leaders were not extremely bright and well versed in software development, but because agile was *new*, and it encompasses a large set of principles and practices that are often not quickly grasped, especially by folks who have spent 20 years, 30 years, or even more developing products using waterfall.

My immediate management was curious as to how this "agile thing" would go. To its credit, it was supportive of my requests for help when needed. The first challenge we hit was that our whole team was not dedicated to the project. In particular, our product documentation writers were allocated only part time and this immediately gave us trouble. I asked that our writers be dedicated full time for the duration of the release, and my upper management complied—even though doing so put other projects under duress due to our limited resources in this area.

In our first release we learned a lot about whole teams, productive standup meetings, good tooling, and getting regular customer feedback. However, we were terrible at getting to "Done!" and, frankly, we were still doing "waterations." But we experienced enough success to entice us to continue, and our management was willing to continue to support us going forward. That is not to say it was all smooth sailing—because it was *not*. The more we learned, the more we wanted changes in our organization, our operations, our resources, and more. With progress came new challenges.

I have seen teams struggle with their adoption because their management "supports agile with words" but is unaware, first, of their need to actually understand how agile changes the way teams work and, second, how they need to enable and participate in the transition. In fact, I will simply say that unless teams have the support of their organizational leadership—an organizational leadership that truly understands agile—then they barely have a fighting chance to adopt agile and make it stick.

Principles

Agile Leadership

What is agile leadership? Is it leading in a manner that aligns with agile principles? Is it leading agile teams that are implementing agile practices? Actually, it's both—and a lot more. Scott's experiences and mine have both shown that, for an agile transformation to be successful, the leaders must understand the agile principles, be willing to put them into practice in their organizations, be supportive of their teams, and be willing to make changes in their own behavior. This is where it all starts.

Leadership, for the purposes of this chapter, includes management as well as technical leaders who do not have management roles. Technical leaders are often the product domain experts and experienced practitioners that other team members look up to. Agile adoption is not a developer-only thing; it is an organization-wide transformation that includes all engineers responsible for doing the day-to-day work as well as the organizational leadership.

Being successful with agile requires leaders who both learn and participate in the agile transformation. Doing so engenders an organizational leadership that can lead with an agile mindset and react with agile instincts. Leaders that resist learning and making such changes, or who resist participating in the transformation, unwittingly sabotage their team's efforts to transform. Leaders who maintain traditional, waterfall mindsets and expectations will negatively influence team behavior, thus preventing many of the benefits of adopting agile from actually occurring. Leaders that are "OK" with agile but who do not align their thinking and actions accordingly will be lucky if their teams succeed. Leaders that jump in with both feet will be in a much better position to enable their teams to succeed. It is really that simple—leading agile teams with an agile mindset is an agile requirement for leaders.

In the same way leaders need to jump into agile with both feet, they also need to encourage their teams to jump into agile with both feet. Experience has shown that teams who slowly wade into agile do not get many benefits early on, and that tends to cause enthusiasm for change to quickly wane. Teams that aggressively adopt agile, making necessary changes quickly, tend to reap significant benefits earlier, thus making the transformation more likely to be permanent. A note of caution, however: When teams do aggressively adopt agile, it can feel somewhat chaotic. This is especially true because agile surfaces problems much earlier in a product release cycle than has ever been true for waterfall projects, and this is *a good thing!* It's always better to find problems earlier than later. The chaotic feelings come from the different team structures (whole teams versus teams split by discipline), new ways of working (small user stories, small tasks, and getting to "Done!" every iteration), different measurements ("working software" versus lines of code counts, test case completion rates, pages of user documentation, and so on), as well as the fact that problems are discovered earlier and are dealt with immediately. Leaders need to understand that this is going to happen and prepare both themselves and their teams for it. After the "chaos" is past (and it usually doesn't take *that* long for it to pass), the natural cadences of agile will take over and the benefits will be noticeable to all.

Why Is Agile Leadership Hard?

It may be fair to say that leading agile teams is harder because as a leader you have to put your skin in the game and not rely on the organization or the process to define success. The key challenge in successfully leading agile teams is understanding agile well enough to lead with the right instincts. Protect the team, keep the team focused, provide a safe zone for failure, encourage learning, set clear boundaries, delegate appropriate responsibility, and insist on a culture of continuous improvement.

If you "grew up" using agile, leading agile teams should not be a problem. However, if you did not, leading agile teams may be as hard for you as it will be for your teams to adopt agile. Agile is so fundamentally different than traditional waterfall style approaches that you cannot "fake it" as a leader. You have to understand agile, you have to experience agile, and you have to think in an agile way.

If you do not have agile experience, you need to learn with the team. It is crucial that you are willing to get experience. I was never a developer in an agile team; however, the first team in which I was a developer behaved much more like an agile team than most of my later teams. That was because it was early in the days of software development, and we did not have a rigorous process in place, so we all learned as we went. We sat within a few feet of each other; we completed small batches of work across our technology stack; and we were good at *not* collecting project debt. In addition, we had a customer that wanted to see our progress constantly. The customer required that our software work 24 hours/day, 7 days/week, 365 days/year, and if it did not, we were going to be fixing any problems at the customer's site on a live system. Working on that team was demanding, exhausting, educational, fast-paced, and *incredibly fun*. As the industry grew up, the teams I worked with had typically adopted waterfall approaches. It seemed logical and worked well enough, and we developed and shipped good software.

But I started to grow frustrated with how we built software. I got tired of the "hockey stick" increase in work as the project progressed; I grew tired of our siloed teams not working well together; I became weary of our defect backlogs, and I thought we could do a better job for our customers.

GET MORE FROM YOUR AGILE ADOPTION

To get more from your agile adoption, it might be helpful to evaluate the shortcomings of your current development practices. Figure out what needs to be fixed or improved and determine where agile can help address those pain points. When Scott and I first work with teams that want to move to agile, we do an assessment of all facets of their current development practices to see what's working and what's not. For those areas we see that are problem areas, we recommend specific agile practices to address and fix the problems. For those areas in which things *are* working well, we try to show how those areas already align with some agile practice or thinking. If teams see that something is going well because of some underlying agile concept that they were unaware of, it often helps "grease the skids" for consciously adopting agile to overcome their problem areas.

When I learned about agile, I was already a development manager. That meant that as I learned about agile, I did so as a manager. I read every book I could get my hands on and encouraged my teams to try new agile practices. I listened to most of their daily standups and met with the team leaders to figure out what we did well and what we could do to get better. The point is that I had to jump in with both feet and not sit back and watch. The reason that agile leadership can be hard is because it is hard to "get" agile without actually "doing it" at some level. Be willing to get better, try something new, and give it a chance. Your attitude *will* influence the team's attitude.

Practices

Learn Agile, Experience Agile, Develop Agile Instincts

As an agile leader you have special responsibilities. You need to protect your teams, encourage them to get better, delegate responsibility where appropriate, and enable teams to take responsibility for their outcomes. To understand why these responsibilities are important, and how to act on them, you need to learn agile. There is no way around it. Leaders play a role in agile adoption—leaders are not spectators. Read as much as you can. There are great books, lots of presentations and experience reports on the Internet, and lots of forums, blogs, and educational sites that you can reference.

Listen to the team while they're at work. Standup meetings are a great place to understand how well the project is progressing each day and how well agile is being integrated into the team's thinking. End-of-iteration demonstrations give you a good opportunity to evaluate how well your teams are getting to "Done!" Listen to the customer feedback. Find out what the most critical problem is based on the output from a team's reflection and how they are trying to solve it. This may provide a great opportunity for you to jump in and help if resolution is beyond the team's scope. Please adopt the practice of playing "fly-on-the-wall" if you listen to or attend any of the team's meetings. As an agile leader you do not direct the team on a day-to-day basis—you go to these meetings to observe and understand.

Get some experience. Learn a practice and teach it to the team. When my first team started with agile, I read Michael Cohn's book, *User Stories Applied.*[1] I put together a primer on what I learned, taught it to my team, and said, "Let's get started." I barely knew what I was doing, but neither did the team. So we gave it a try, and eventually, we made user stories work pretty well.

To be a successful agile leader it is important to develop a set of instincts that drive your behavior:

- You have to want to create whole teams because you understand how effective they are, even if it means a reorganization of your area.

---

1. Cohn, Mike, *User Stories Applied: For Agile Software Development*. Boston: Addison-Wesley, 2004. Print.

- You have to be frustrated if your teams do not get to "Done!" in short iterations because you do not want to see teams start waterfalling backward. You know that having working software every iteration is the best way to validate progress, find problems quickly, and get continuous feedback from customers.

- You have to insist that your teams improve their build capabilities, even encouraging them to adopt continuous integration because you know the tremendous benefits continuous integration brings and how it paves the way for DevOps.

- You have to protect your team from interruptions because you know that when the team loses focus, they are less productive.

- You have to want to scream if you see your teams ignore a problem over and over.

- You have to want your teams to get better because if they do not the competition will likely push you out of the market.

- You have to want your team to be agile because it is a better way to create products and deliver value to your customers.

These have to become your natural instincts if you want to successfully lead in an agile way.

Enable and Protect

One of the principles of the Agile Manifesto is to *"Build projects around motivated individuals. Give them the environment and support they need, and trust them to get the job done."*[2] This principle encapsulates the primary agile leadership mandate.

The first chapter of this book discusses the importance of enabling and protecting whole teams as a means to enable agile success. The chapter on whole teams also describes why protecting teams from interruptions enables teams to focus on and complete work every iteration. Agile leaders need to build cross-functional teams that include highly trained and skilled individuals to complete design, code, build, and test cycles every iteration to deliver value to the customer. These teams need the skills and tools to get their work completed. And if they do not have the necessary skills, leaders need to ensure that they have time dedicated to obtain the skills. Agile encourages team members to deepen their domain knowledge as well as expand their skill set so that they can be highly productive team members with ever-widening responsibilities. "Skills-silos" are a relic of waterfall.

In many traditional software teams, managers were encouraged to squeeze as much work out of a team as possible. This philosophy is not a part of agile thinking—actually it is opposed to it. Keeping such a waterfall mentality will result in the team's inability to make agile stick. Allow teams to establish a velocity and then use that to understand the team's real capacity for getting work done.

---

2. http://www.agilemanifesto.org/principles.html

RETHINK WORKING ALL FEATURES AT ONCE

We see situations in which managers push teams to get started on new features before other features are complete. This strategy is in conflict with agile thinking and seems to be motivated by a fear of not getting features done. The thinking is that a new feature has to be started no matter what or else the new feature may not get completed by the end of the release. What this behavior actually results in is *not* getting stuff done, which simply pushes teams into excessive overtime at the end of the project. Starting on a new feature before a previously started feature is done means that defect fixes get pushed until later, automation gets delayed, code refactoring isn't done, and so on—all because of the urgency to show progress on the next item at the expense of getting the previous feature "Done!" This is waterfall thinking. If you are in a leadership position, Chapter 3, "Queuing Theory," and Chapter 4, "No Multitasking," can help you to understand how having your teams focus on one thing at a time and get it "Done!" can enable your teams to succeed.

Recently I heard a team describe its struggles understanding its velocity after four iterations because team members were not fully committed during each iteration. The members talked about their growing defect backlog and their need to add "test iterations" to the end of the project. After more of the same, this is what they concluded about their project status: "Everything is cascading to a single date." In other words, everything was piling up to the end of the project. If that is not a description of waterfalling backward, I don't know what is. In another scenario, I heard a team complain that it had more work to complete than it had people. Everyone on the team was trying to do five things at once because they "just had to get all this work done." If this sounds familiar, and you are in a leadership role, then this is your cue to jump in and help. Help get such a team back on track by protecting them, stopping new work until the project debt has been addressed, stopping the multitasking, and so on. Failure to do so will allow the problems to compound and will virtually guarantee that the team will not get much in way of benefits from its attempts at moving to agile.

Help Your Team Learn, Let Your Team Fail

In addition to agile leaders getting education, they need to encourage their teams to continue to learn and improve. Teams need to try new practices to find out if they work so that they can incorporate successful practices into their processes to make them better. Teams may not be inclined to try new practices because the effort may distract them from their regular work, and if something new fails, they do not want to be penalized.

Here's a situation I know of in which a manager wanted his team to learn about and try test-driven development (TDD), but he ran into resistance. Team members didn't really appear interested in investing in this technique because they thought the effort required exceeded the value they would realize. The manager did not agree with their conclusion, so he tried a different approach. He gave a young developer a 2-week assignment to learn TDD. He was required to apply the approach with his new code. Not excited about the idea, but willing to accept the challenge nonetheless, he learned TDD, figured out how to use it with his own software, began to understand its merits, and showcased what he learned to the rest of the team at the end of the iteration. He was so impressed with what he had learned that he became an advocate for TDD and encouraged the rest of the team to try it. After his initial foray into TDD, he was bemoaning that the team had not tried it sooner. He saw that the quality of his code was so much better by having adopted TDD.

However, not all new initiatives will succeed, so the organizational environment has to be risk-free, without penalty for failure. Only leaders can ensure this environment actually exists. If teams veer away from trial and error because they get penalized for failures, they will never try to get better. As a leader you do not want to stand back and watch your team fail, but you also do not want to get in the way of learning—this is a fine line that leaders need to walk.

The following story concerns a team I managed that had to deliver a small release to a new market quickly to determine if we could satisfy the customer base with our technology. The team lead was a seasoned developer who was excited about agile. He went off on his own and created a large number of user stories and then reviewed them with the team. I was not happy that he essentially wrote all the stories on his own, but that was already history when I got involved.

The next problem was that the stories did not embody thin, vertical slices of functionality that crossed the architecture stack. The stories were fat slices of almost complete functionality. I talked with him about this, and he felt that they were thin enough and could be completed in an iteration. So I sat back and watched.

Initially the team tackled a user story that required building the code using a new technology in the context of old software with old build technology. This story did not close for several iterations, which quickly put the entire team hopelessly behind. At the earliest signs of trouble, the team did not stop the line and solve its problems. Instead, the team tried to continue to write more code even though the builds were not working.

Well, the good news is that they did finally fix their problems, and they delivered the functionality to customers. The team leader laughed and told me that he finally understood that the initial approach was flawed. He had a great attitude, and I thought the experience was useful because I am sure the team members will never repeat the same mistakes. In the end, it was not only clear what went wrong, but also exactly when the problems started. It was a satisfying learning experience for all of us. Sometimes letting a team fail can be a good learning experience for the team. Failure has a wonderful propensity to make lessons learned the hard way *stick*. If a team is trying something new (like user stories in the preceding example), leaders have to be willing to take the chance to let a team fail—in the context of a penalty-free environment. Part of being willing to take a chance on letting a team fail means that the team has to take responsibility for figuring out how to accomplish a task. I discuss this practice in the following section.

Set Priorities, Provide Boundaries, and Let the Team Figure Out How

"The wicked leader is he who the people despise. The good leader is he who the people revere. *The great leader is he who the people say, 'We did it ourselves!'*" [sic] Thus says Lao Tzu.

This quote highlights a critical aspect of agile leadership: Leaders set the direction and establish the priorities, but the teams need to "own the execution," meaning they decide how to get the work done and hold themselves accountable for their commitments. For agile teams, and leaders of agile teams, this means the days of the micro-manager are over.

That being said, there is still that fine line that a leader needs to walk to enable teams to take ownership, while still providing leadership. In the previous story, I let the team take ownership of the user stories that had been written. I didn't tell the team to scrap the stories and start over. I had a strong belief that there would be problems, but I also needed the team to "get" user stories, and allowing them to experience the difficulties that inevitably come with poorly written stories was the right decision.

The flipside is that leaders can't continue to allow a team to fail. Teams have to be given plenty of opportunity to figure things out, and perhaps fail, so that they learn and get better. If failure is a recurring theme, or a team doesn't seem to be learning from its mistakes, leaders need to step in. Here's a story where I had to do just that.

I managed a team that was adopting agile but struggling to get to "Done!" every iteration. The primary reason for the struggles was that the team was responsible for the next release as well as the maintenance work for previous releases. High-priority maintenance work always trumped new development, so it was difficult to know if the team could complete its user stories within a given iteration. I encouraged them to form two separate teams—one for new work and one for maintenance work—but they resisted. They were concerned that members of the maintenance team would get behind on learning new technologies, and that the new development team would lose touch with how customers were using the product and also what areas of the code were problem areas.

We discussed and discussed the problem, but the team continued to resist my recommendation, believing it could get new development and maintenance work completed within an iteration, despite its lack of success up until that time. After many discussions and too little progress, I finally insisted that the team try the new approach. I understood at the deepest levels the agile principles of *working on one thing at a time* and *preventing disruptions,* but my team leaders did not. After a virtual edict on my part they finally agreed to split into two separate teams. The team leaders decided how to implement the changes. To ensure that everyone got experience with doing both new development and maintenance work, the team decided that, from time to time, a few team members would rotate between the two teams. Having a small group of engineers that rotated every once in a while ensured relative team stability from iteration to iteration. The engineers who did rotate were different every time. Everyone would rotate at least once over the course of the release.

Success was slow at first because it quickly became apparent that few members of the team could work outside their own domains. Immediately this approach made it obvious how dependent the organization was on few people. One of the areas with an obvious lack of skills was the server technology side of the product, so the team decided to train the engineers with client-only experience to work on the server technology as well. As time went on, more team members handled a greater variety of tasks. The team started to get more efficient, and both teams found themselves far better able to make their goals. Eliminating the constant interruptions that occurred when there was only one team made the organization much more productive. And even though I was the one who decided to make the team changes, the leaders "owned" how to make it work. For instance, they came up with the idea of rotating team members at iteration boundaries and how to address the skills issues that surfaced.

It is critical that leaders establish the priorities and help teams achieve them. But teams have to be accountable to complete the work. Figuring out where one responsibility ends and the other starts can be tricky. Leaders have to let teams figure out how to get the work done so that the teams can hold themselves accountable. But, as the above illustration shows, if the teams don't understand agile or are not adopting the agile practices in the right way, leaders need to have enough understanding of agile themselves to see those situations and be willing to step in as necessary.

How Can You Help?

Scott grew up near Dayton, Ohio. At that time, Dayton had a large concentration of General Motors' assembly plants. Scott's next-door neighbor worked at GM as a senior industrial engineering manager, responsible for the part of the assembly lines that took care of applying paint to the vehicles. He made the plans for how the painting portion of the assembly lines interacted with the other parts of the assembly line and was responsible for determining what paint application technologies would be used as well what types of paint had to be used. These were complex decisions, and the deep knowledge needed to make good decisions came with significant amounts of engineering study and experience. However, the reason we include this story is because this manager did not tell the folks on the assembly exactly how to do their jobs. Instead, he explained the main concepts of the assembly line, showed why certain paint-application technologies had to be used, and why only certain types of paint could be used (primarily due to the electrostatic way in which the paint was applied). When the assembly lines were running, Scott's neighbor was constantly on the floor asking how to make the painting process better, faster, more efficient, and so on. He didn't just sit in his office; it was the assembly line workers that had the day-to-day, intimate knowledge of working with the various machines and the various paints. And he wasn't on the floor telling the assembly-line workers how to do their jobs; he was asking them how *he* could do *his* job better!

If you are not letting your teams decide, you might be micro-managing. This is about the worst path a leader can take. If teams are not equipped to do the work, leaders need to train, get training, or find people that can do the work. Micro-managing will quickly defeat agile.

A Single, Visible View of the Truth

Information hiding and protection has long been a practice in organizations, whether intentional or not. The thinking is that the more *you* know, the more power you have. However, this idea leads to mistrust, an inability to successfully delegate, and most important, a failure to deliver the best results due to inadequate information on the part of others. Successful agile leaders need to be visible and open, and "share the same truth" with their teams. One of Scott's former executives, with this concept in mind, told his organization that he would share everything he knew with them, at least until they proved that they were not worthy of such trust.

Jeremy Hope and Robin Fraser studied several companies to understand how they could improve their businesses by abandoning the typical annual budgeting process and implementing a more "adaptive" budgeting process. As a result of their research, they report that one of the six principles that leaders should adopt to make decentralized organizations work is the following:

"To promote ethical behavior, leaders should support open information systems that provide one truth throughout the organization rather than having middlemen filtering information and making available on a need-to-know basis. Best practices include

- Make information fast and open.
- Set high ethical standards for information flow."[3]

Agile teams need to make decisions every day to deliver on their commitments. Having the most current and accurate information is required to make informed decisions. As a leader, make sure your teams are informed and that everyone has the same information. One way that information is made visible in agile organizations is through the use of "information radiators." Alistair Cockburn describes information radiators on his website:

"An **Information radiator** is a display posted in a place where people can see it as they work or walk by. It shows readers information they care about without having to ask anyone a question. This means more communication with fewer interruptions.
A good information radiator

- Is large and easily visible to the casual, interested observer
- Is understood at a glance
- Changes periodically, so that it is worth visiting
- Is easily kept up to date"[4]

Of course, if you have geographically distributed teams, you need to use some sort of online equivalent of an information radiator.

---

3. Hope, J. and Fraser, R. (2003). *Beyond Budgeting: How Managers Can Break Free from the Annual Performance Trap* (p. 159). Boston, Massachusetts: Harvard Business Review Press.
4. http://alistair.cockburn.us/Information+radiator [emphasis in the original]

Metrics

As teams adopt agile, their leaders are often asked, "How is it going? Are you agile yet?" Well, Scott and I do not believe that you ever stop becoming agile. But how do you know you are on the road to success and not waterfalling backward?

Here is one idea that we have tried with coaching teams. Determine what problems you want to solve by adopting agile. For instance, many teams try to ship releases on time; many teams try to ship with improved quality; some teams hope to increase efficiency by doing more with less while they maintain and improve quality; and so on. Decide what your initial goal is for adopting agile; then evaluate after the first release to see if you achieved the goal. If not, figure out what problems you have and work on fixing them in the next release. If you did achieve your goal, set a new target for your next release.

For example, your organizational goal for your next release may be to ship on the targeted date with zero defects. Agile can help you get there via having a good backlog of user stories and a pattern of getting to "Done!," having a debt intolerant behavior, and so forth. If the team ships on time with zero defects, declare victory, celebrate the success, and target the next challenge. If you meet your goals, your team is likely getting better at agile.

Breakthrough

Give up status meetings. Yes—give up status meetings.

Does the thought of giving up status meetings alarm or annoy you? If so, you may be more wedded to waterfall thinking than you're aware. The primary purpose of status meetings is to share information so that the people attending the meeting can stay informed, get help if required, and act as a focal point for their teams. Although these needs and desires do not go away in agile, there are more effective ways to get the same results.

Status meetings require that someone collect status, compile it into a meaningful presentation, and deliver the findings. Project teams are constantly in motion and, thus, the "status" is always changing. If you are reviewing a team's status, chances are that the status presented is likely already out of date.

Sharing information is critical and solving problems is essential, but this can be done without requiring a *formal* status meeting. One general manager in IBM is well known for saying, "Don't review a bunch of slides with me; I can read them. Tell me how I can help you."

Experiment with other ways to get better results. As both a developer and a manager, I despised status meetings because they took precious time, required preparation for information that would soon be stale, and rarely benefited me in any way other than telling me "what everyone else is doing." As a manager I get more out of attending a team's daily standup meetings, planning meetings, customer demonstrations, and reflection meetings than I ever did from status meetings. By attending the team's working meetings, the information covered was live and being provided by the team "on the ground." I could listen to any of these meetings and get a feel for whether the project was in trouble. Problems always came up, but I felt compelled to get involved only in extreme cases when problems festered.

Make the project "status" available via a wiki, a dashboard, or some other tool. By status, we mean the data that is used by a team to define and track their progress, for example, builds, defects, backlogs, burndown charts, and so on. The best way to manage this data is in a live system that can be automatically kept up to date. Thus anyone can see project status on a minute-by-minute basis at any time, day or night, from practically anywhere in the world. Status is useful if it is up to date and you can get it anytime—and good tooling can help.

Good tooling is also useful to manage the product backlog and associated work, providing access to information like release burndown charts and other valuable information. Continuous integration systems provide data on builds. They can also provide information on test results, software deployments, and more. And this information can be reflected in real time in team dashboards. Wikis are good forums for sharing information when the sharing cannot take place "live." Adopt tools that display live information to ensure that anyone can get a handle on what's currently going on.

As a leader, you can help teams successfully move to agile—and make it stick—if you start working in a more operational manner like agile teams do. By eliminating status meetings and, instead, using agile teaming tools to keep you informed and help your teams achieve their goals, you can execute more effectively along with your teams. Consider problem solving meetings like a scrum of scrum so that you focus your energy on high value work.

The Swedish bank Svenska Handelsbanken *"...inverted the organizational pyramid in which the center now serves operating units that, in turn, are focused on serving and satisfying customers' needs."*[5] This was the behavioral change they made to keep customers from leaving. Previously, the operating units were focused on serving the organization instead of the customers, and this caused customer satisfaction to plummet—thus the need for the inversion. This same thinking can be applied to moving from a team culture in which reporting status seems to be the team's whole purpose to an organization where teams are focused on serving their customers. Management in this case needs to stay focused on ensuring operational efficiency and team effectiveness. To do this, managers need to stay engaged and informed on how their teams are working versus waiting for teams to report status.

Summary

Being successful with agile requires leaders who learn, participate in, and experiment with agile so that they can lead with an agile mindset and react with agile instincts.

- Effective leadership is required to make agile stick. It is critical that leaders understand agile well enough to help their teams move forward. Otherwise, they inadvertently risk sabotaging their team's efforts to transform because their traditional behavior patterns and responses *will* get in the way.

5. Hope, J. and Fraser, R. (2003). *Beyond Budgeting: How Managers Can Break Free from the Annual Performance Trap* (p. 35), Boston, Massachusetts: Harvard Business Review Press.

- Successful agile adoption requires that leaders transform their behavior to allow teams to hold themselves accountable. Excellent technical leadership ensures teams have the skills and the appropriate tools to succeed.

- Adopting agile slowly makes it hard for agile to "stick."

- Leading agile teams requires that leaders equip themselves by learning and gaining experience as well as demonstrating a willingness to give new things a try.

- Agile leaders need to protect their teams from interruptions so that the teams can stay focused and deliver on their commitments.

- It is critical that leaders set the direction and establish the priorities, while the teams need to own the execution, the methods by which they get the work done, and hold themselves accountable for their commitments.

- Agile leaders must encourage their teams to continually learn and improve by trying new practices in a penalty-free zone. One of Scott's son's basketball coaches was fond of saying, "If you're not making mistakes, you're not trying hard enough!"

- To determine whether you are successfully adopting agile, identify what you want to achieve from your agile adoption, and use these goals to guide your evaluation of progress.

- Stop having status meetings so that teams can spend their time on more productive activities—like getting software "Done!"

CHAPTER 11

Continuous Improvement

Being agile requires continuous improvement because teams that continue to learn, adapt, and grow are more productive and competitive. Agile is a never-ending journey of getting better.

By Scott Will

I regularly reach out to teams that have adopted agile on their own to see if they need any help and to see if they have any questions or issues regarding their agile adoption. I admit to being surprised at the some of the responses I get. Although many of the teams welcome my overtures, some have responded by saying something like, "Thanks for the offer. We know we're not 100 percent agile, but we've done the best we can so there's not much you can do to help."

Such responses trouble me because those teams seem to have thrown up their hands and admitted defeat. They're saying, in essence, "We can't get better" or, even worse, "We don't want to get better." My concern is that this sentiment is the result of years of waterfall experiences. Let me explain: I've been in the software industry for many, many years. By way of background, my first exposure to writing code was typing a few simple lines of Basic into a terminal that also had a "ticker-tape" contrivance. As I typed, holes were punched in the tape as it moved along. The tape was then fed into a tape-reader and sent for compiling to a mainframe computer via a rudimentary modem. A year or two later, I had "moved up in the world" and was using punch cards in my programming classes in college. By now you're probably thinking, "Dinosaur!" Well, as this book has hopefully shown, even dinosaurs can learn new tricks...

Waterfall was the entrenched way of developing products throughout my early career. I've worked on many waterfall software projects over the years as a developer, chief programmer, test manager, quality engineering manager, and even as a customer support team lead. Invariably, at the end of every release, we would set some time aside and conduct a "lessons learned" meeting (also sometimes called a *post-mortem*—which, when translated from Latin, is a more fitting term, but I digress). We'd spend a day, or 2 days, combing through our recollections of the project, identifying things that didn't go so well, and making plans for how we were going to change them in the next release. After going through this exercise multiple times, and rarely seeing things get better, I stopped calling them "lessons learned" and instead called them "lessons recorded" because we never made any of the changes we said we were going to—we never actually *improved*—we just wrote our improvement ideas on a piece of paper, put a check-mark in the box stating we held a lessons-learned meeting, and moved on to the next release. The pressures of the next project rarely afforded us any opportunity to fix problems from the previous release. We just kept living with pain, release after release after release. And why? Partly because there was a latent fear among both engineers and management that if we took time to fix problems, or even learn some new practice, we wouldn't have enough time to do all the new functionality that we were being asked to do in the next release: "We've got to get started now!" I certainly hope your experiences don't match mine, but having consulted with many, many teams over the years, both externally and internally (including numerous acquisitions), I'm expecting your experiences with lessons-learned efforts from waterfall days will probably be depressingly similar to mine.

At the risk of perhaps making you feel uncomfortable, let me ask a few questions of you regarding improvement. When is the last time you, personally, tried something new in an effort to improve? You've likely heard about pair-programming—have you tried it? The same with test-driven development—have you tried it? How about automated provisioning? These (and others) are well-known techniques in software engineering with good track records of actually helping individuals and teams to improve. Do you know about "set-based design theory" in relation to making project design decisions? I know of engineers who haven't picked up a book on software engineering since graduating from college—and for some, that was more than 20 years ago. As our media options improve, so do our learning options. There are blogs, podcasts, wikis, online videos, and many other options that engineers can avail themselves of to keep current. Although these statements likely do not apply to you (because you are reading this book after all), you know who I mean.

Principles

Why Is Continuous Improvement Important?

So why the emphasis on continuous improvement in agile? There are many reasons, not the least of which is that competition is part of the business landscape. How many companies have gone under because they couldn't keep up with the competition in terms of innovation and improved efficiencies? And apart from the business aspects, it's much more gratifying to not only work for an innovative company, but to also have a personal goal of not stagnating.

Think back to the "Introduction," where Leslie recounted an early discussion she had with the Poppendiecks. You might recall that Leslie mentioned her frustration with the conversation because the Poppendiecks believed her team was "doing fine" while she felt quite the opposite. As Leslie pointed out, what the Poppendiecks did not tell her was that a team that was *trying* to improve was exhibiting the attitude that would ultimately enable them to *actually* improve. Leslie's team eventually had its first breakthrough with bullpens, and it was this breakthrough that proved to them that adopting agile could provide compelling results. After the team won its first battle, it wanted to keep trying to improve. And this proved the Poppendieck's assertion that the team was "doing fine." At the heart of agile success is the idea of continuous improvement, and I would argue that getting this point is the most critical breakthrough a team can have. When this point sinks in and permeates a team's day-to-day endeavors, the team *will* succeed with agile.

Let me say this again: Leslie and I believe that continuous improvement is at the heart of agile success. All the other agile principles and practices are important, but this one is essential. It is what will enable you to realize the tremendous value of agile. Being agile requires continuous improvement because teams that continue to learn, adapt, and grow will be more productive and competitive. In addition, they'll have more *fun!*

Why Is Continuous Improvement Hard?

Apart from the obvious problem mentioned earlier (that is, the fear that devoting any time to fixing problems and/or learning new practices will negatively impact project schedules), I believe there may be another reason why adopting a continuous improvement mindset is hard. In this case, though, it's more subtle. Like any other discipline, software engineering has seen its fair share of fads. Throughout my career I had seen so many fads come and go that, when I first heard about agile, I didn't want anything to do with it. I assumed it was just the next fad, and if I held my breath for 6 months or so, it would go away just like all the others. Even now that agile has been in the mainstream for more than a decade, and its successes are well documented, I still run into people who think it's nothing more than a fad. My question for them is, what about up-and-coming practices in the agile space? Is *continuous deployment* a fad? How about *transparent development*? What about *DevOps*? To make an informed judgment about new things, one first has to be aware of new things. As described next, learning is key for supporting continuous improvement. However, setting time aside to learn can be just as hard as setting time aside to fix nagging problems. This is another reason that cultivating continuous improvement can be hard. However, Leslie and I want you to push through these deterrents and start reaping the benefits! The aim of this chapter is to provide you with motivation to do so.

Now let's look at how you can accomplish continuous improvement in agile. The following principles and practices are how I lay it out for our teams.

There Is No Such Thing as "100 Percent Agile"

There seems to be this idea that there is a "gold standard" regarding what constitutes agile. If you meet the standard, then you're "100 percent agile." I'm guessing some of this thinking stems from the Extreme Programming (XP) world in which there is a list of "rules" documented as part of the XP approach,[1] and some folks may take the term "rules" to mean they cannot be broken. Personally, I don't believe there is such a thing as "100 percent agile" or an "Agile Gold Standard." As you've hopefully seen by now in this book, agile is built on many principles, which lead to various practices—and most of the principles and practices have a lot of intersection with

---

1. See: http://www.extremeprogramming.org/rules.html

each other. Adopting a particular agile practice will often have the side effect of pulling in other agile practices. Thus there is typically some consistency between teams regarding agile adoption (that is, the use of iterations, writing user stories, engaging regularly with customers, and so on). But, *if you really want to be agile*, you need to adopt the mentality of *continuous improvement*.

I was listening to a webcast of a well-known agile speaker recently and one of his comments gets right to the heart of this matter:

> "If you can't tell me you're better this month than you were last month, don't tell me you're *agile*."

If you agree with his sentiment (and I certainly do), you can see why there can be no such thing as "100 percent agile." Agile then, by definition, encompasses the idea of *continuous improvement*. The Principles of the Agile Manifesto support this: "At regular intervals, the team reflects on how to become more effective, then tunes and adjusts its behavior accordingly."[2] There is no point at which you can sit back and say, "We've arrived!"

Realize That You Will Learn New Things as a Project Progresses

When do you know the absolute least about the project you're working on? The obvious answer is *at the beginning of the project*. At the beginning of the project, everything about the project lies in the future. All you have is speculation and estimation, and a significant dose of wishful thinking. The corollary is that you know the most about the project at the end, when the project is complete—everything that was going to happen has already happened by that time. Needless to say, knowledge about the project, the process, the people, the customers, the environment, the competition, the technologies, and so on is gained constantly throughout a release—so agile recommends strongly that teams capitalize on this ever-increasing knowledge *during* the release instead of waiting until after the project is complete. Getting better at the practices discussed in this book will enable your team to apply what you learn as you progress, to the work that you are doing now. Capitalizing on new information, new insights, and stepping up to new, unforeseen challenges as soon as possible is a significant part of successfully adopting a continuous improvement mentality.

You Need to Set Time Aside to Sharpen Your Axe

You've no doubt heard the story about the two lumberjacks, each given the task of chopping down a tree, and who both had rather dull axes. The first lumberjack, seeing that the time frame given to chop down his tree was short, immediately started chopping. He made some progress but, given that his axe was dull, it was slow going, even though he was working extremely hard. The other lumberjack grabbed a sharpener and spent a good portion of his allotted time sharpening his axe. The first lumberjack thought to himself, "There's no way he's going to cut down

---

2. See: http://agilemanifesto.org/principles.html

his tree in the timeframe given; he's spending too much time sharpening his axe. I'm glad I got started when I did. At least I'll be able to show progress by the time my time is up even if I don't get the tree completely cut down." Well, you know how the story ends. The lumberjack who took time to sharpen his axe was able to fell his tree quite quickly, whereas the first lumberjack didn't get his tree cut down in the allotted time.

This principle of setting time aside to get better should not surprise you. You'll get more work done in a shorter amount of time if your axe is sharp, so you need to regularly sharpen the axe. If you don't, your axe will continue to get duller and duller, and you'll accomplish less and less even though you're working harder and harder. And this is the Catch 22 that most teams find themselves facing; they're spending so much effort trying to compensate for a dull axe that they don't think they can take any time to stop and sharpen their axes. In the context of software development, make sure your skills are current, that you are using tools that make you more efficient, that you are leveraging the best technology for the job, and so forth.

Focus on Small, On-Going Improvements

As discussed in earlier chapters, Leslie and I work in the part of the software industry that develops enterprise-level software, so it's not too surprising that people are swayed into thinking that for something to be useful, it has to be *big*. And such thinking extends into the realm of identifying areas for improvement. Teams will identify problems and come up with big, grandiose ways of solving them, usually envisioning long periods of time and lots of money. Recalling my opening paragraphs, you can see why such plans rarely make the light of day. "No time!" and "No money!" are the usual responses. With deference to Fred Brooks,[3] I call these plans "Silver Bullets," which usually envision the solutions to all the team's problems via big improvement plans.

Instead of the "boil-the-ocean" plans (which teams seem to love but which are rarely acted upon and, when they are, rarely produce the results envisioned), agile recommends teams focus on small, ongoing improvements (lots of little "silver bullets" if you will). The cumulative effect of numerous small improvements over time often exceeds the envisioned benefits of the big, grandiose action plan. We just need to recalibrate our thinking: Bigger is not always better. Note that there may be times when the team does experience a big improvement, and if so, that's great! We don't want to belittle big improvements, we're just cautioning against the attitude that the only option is to "boil the ocean."

3. Fred Brooks, head of the OS/360 development project for IBM and subsequently a professor of software engineering at the University of North Carolina, wrote an essay titled, "No Silver Bullet" where he gently chides the software industry for continually looking for some magical solution that will increase productivity by orders of magnitude. He writes that, "Although we see no startling breakthroughs, and indeed, believe such to be inconsistent with the nature of software, many encouraging innovations are underway. A disciplined, consistent effort to develop, propagate, and exploit them should indeed yield an order-of-magnitude improvement. There is no royal road, but there is a road." In essence, he's telling us to stop looking for "the next big thing" and just continuously improve on what we already have. You can read this essay in his book titled, *The Mythical Man-Month*—a book we believe should be on every software engineer's bookshelf (Addison-Wesley Professional, 1995).

In addition, the psychological benefits of continually showing improvement cannot be overestimated. Although I can't point to any data that specifically supports this claim, it stands to reason that as people begin to see *real* improvements—no matter how small—it will become a motivator to continually make additional ongoing improvements.

Learn from Your Mistakes; Don't Make Them Again

Years ago there was a story about a new executive at a large company who was given charge of an important project. The project failed, and the executive was called into the CEO's office. Expecting to be fired, the executive opened the conversation with the CEO by stating that he knew that the project failed, that he was ultimately responsible, and that he would be cleaning out his desk that day. The CEO responded, "I'm not going to fire you; I just spent several million dollars on your education!"

Whether a true story or not, I don't know, but the point is that people are going to make mistakes, and the best way to respond to mistakes is to learn from them and prevent them from occurring again. The only time mistakes should be "punishable" is when they're made again and again, without any evidence that real learning took place after the first occurrence.[4] Accept that you, your team, and your company will make mistakes—and sometimes big mistakes—but realize that tremendous benefit can be obtained *if* people learn from their mistakes, and not only keep them from happening again, but also use them as catalysts for improvement.

Fail Fast

Closely related to the notion that there will be failures is the idea of "failing fast." This is, in reality, just a pithy way of describing the trial and error process that most of us go through. Who hasn't written a little bit of code, looked at it, and then quickly come up with a better way of writing it? You probably wouldn't have come up with a better way unless you had initially written the poor code. The process of writing the poor code ("failing") is what allowed you to gain the insights needed to rewrite it better. The key idea with failing fast is that you start with an idea on how to tackle some area that needs improvement, take some initial steps toward making the improvement, and then check to see if the steps you've taken are actually helping. If not, then stop—don't keep going down a wrong path. Use the information you've gained about what's not working as input for coming up with a better approach.

Management Needs to Actively Promote Innovation

I almost titled this section, "Management needs to actively enable agile." In the experiences that Leslie and I have had with various teams, it's often management that unwittingly forces teams to "waterfall backward." These managers have not taken the time to learn about agile, nor do they understand how adopting agile requires a significant shift in thinking. Too many times managers force teams to conform to the old, waterfall ways of doing things because that's all they (the

---

4. Wasn't it Albert Einstein that said something like, "The definition of insanity is doing the same thing over and over and expecting different results"...?

managers) have ever known, and they haven't embraced the continuous improvement mindset. As one example, such managers tend to ask for waterfall-oriented metrics such as KLoC estimates, defect "S-curves," how many test cases have been executed, as well as others. Managers should, instead, be looking at release burndown charts and learning that "working software is the primary measure of progress."[5] Simple transitions like these on the part of management can keep teams from becoming frustrated with the "impedance mismatch" between what they're trying to do (adopt agile) and what they're being asked to do (waterfall). Such frustrating situations rarely give rise to innovative thinking. If managers don't demonstrate a willingness to learn, to change, and to improve, teams aren't likely to learn, to change, or to improve.

Conversely, a management team that shows that it's willing to learn and change will be setting a great example for its teams. In addition, a management team that encourages teams to try something different will likely see continuous improvement in the teams. The following story comes from a situation that Leslie faced on one particular project she was managing. Basically, her teams had to decide on whether a proposed merger of a set of products should use either Dojo or Faces as its web user interface. One of the products used Dojo and another used Faces. In addition, there were strong advocates for both in the organization. Leslie had been reading about "set-based design"[6] and decided to give it a try. I'll let her explain:

> It is hard to get anyone to try set-based design because it seems to take more resources and time than current practices. We tried it when we were merging two different teams that were using different technologies for the same client problem with similar applications. It was our hope that we could standardize on one of the two web UI technologies. We decided to try a twist on set-based theory: Each team took over the other team's code for two, 2-week iterations, and each team implemented the same user story in the iteration. That way, each team had to learn about the other technology to help reduce biases against the other technology. By doing the work to complete the user story using the nonfamiliar technology, they could then decide which technology provided a better solution.
>
> The teams learned a lot—fast—and came to a common agreement on the benefits of both technologies and where each was weak. They thought it was a great way to evaluate the technologies because their biases were muted and they were able to validate the relative merits of each technology by doing valuable work. In addition, they were better able to find weaknesses in the technologies they had adopted and potential solutions.

This is a good story on not only how a set-based design approach proved to be both informative and successful, but also how management actively promoted a new technique within the organization. This wouldn't have happened unless Leslie had been keeping current with industry advances.

---

5. See: http://agilemanifesto.org/principles.html

6. For more information on this practice, a short article with simple examples and additional references can be found here: http://xp123.com/articles/set-based-concurrent-engineering/

Practices

What are some of the ways teams can ensure that they actually are continuously improving? We'll touch briefly on a few practices, the first of which is probably quite well known to you already. The other practices addressed have also worked well for many teams.

Reflections

I pointed out earlier in this chapter that one of the principles of the Agile Manifesto was "At regular intervals, the team reflects on how to become more effective, then tunes and adjusts its behavior accordingly."[7] Given this, it should come as no surprise that these meetings that take place at "regular intervals" are called "reflections." (You may have heard them called "retrospectives" elsewhere—I view the two terms as synonymous.) I recommend that these "regular intervals" should occur at the end of every iteration. Here's how I suggest a team conduct a reflection meeting.

First, it's not a gripe session. Yes, people love to complain and, at times, it can even be cathartic to do so. However, the goal of a reflection meeting is actual improvement, so a team must stay focused on the end goal. Sure, some complaining from time to time may actually be helpful and lead to a better solution, but if the meeting devolves into nothing more than a gripe session, then not only will it fail to help the team improve, but it will also be a waste of time and drive down team morale (which will probably entail even further griping later on).

Regarding the format of the meeting, I recommend the team go around the table (virtually, if necessary) and give each member of the team the opportunity to state what is working well. After everyone has had the opportunity to provide input, then the team can review the list of items mentioned and do a little brainstorming on whether there's an opportunity to *expand* the positive impact from any of these items. Often, one of the best ways to improve is to capitalize on something you already know is working well—just figure out how to drive it into more of the process, or the product, or the development environment, or wherever it makes sense to do so. For example, say a team member has been experimenting with adding static code analysis to a "sandbox" build and has achieved some positive benefits. The team member can discuss the benefits during the reflection meeting and then the team can discuss whether instrumenting the production build with static code analysis is something worth pursuing.

The next thing the team does is to, again, go around the table where everyone provides input on what's *not* working well. One of the toughest things (initially) for teams to do during this part of the meeting is to NOT jump in and start brainstorming as soon as the first problem is mentioned. We engineers tend to be so conditioned to solve problems that, as soon as a problem is mentioned, everyone wants to jump in and help solve it. The caution against doing so here is that you may hear only about one problem—brainstorm on it, and then run out of time—before any other problems are brought up. The problem you focused all your attention on may not be the biggest problem the team faces. So, our recommendation is, after everyone on the team has had the opportunity to identify problem areas, the team *then* decides which item on the list is the biggest

7. See: http://agilemanifesto.org/principles.html

problem that the *team* faces. We like the idea of having the team "vote" on the various items that have been raised—with the item receiving the most votes being the one (the only one) that the team agrees to address. An additional option for this approach is to set a time limit on this part of the discussion, that is, something like 10 minutes to surface problems and decide on which one to focus on. Spend the remainder of the meeting brainstorming and identifying specific actions to begin to solve this one problem. When some definitive, concrete actions have been identified, the team adds these to the planned work for the next iteration (thus ensuring that there will actually be time to implement the actions).

At the end of the next iteration, the first question raised during the reflection meeting is, "Did our improvement actions solve the problem?" If not, then come up with some more actions to take the next iteration. Do *not* move on to another problem until you get the first one fixed, even if it takes multiple iterations to solve the problem. Work on one thing at a time, get it off your plate, and then move on to the next item on the list. You'll note this refrain is fairly constant in agile: *Work on only one thing at a time.* This means one release at a time, one user story at a time, and only one improvement action at a time. Actually solving problems is the key to making reflections valuable and to continuously improving.

If you did solve a problem, or make some notable improvement, then celebrate! It doesn't have to be a big, involved celebration, but the team should acknowledge that it has improved and gotten rid of some pain point. Nothing breeds success like success.

Now, assume that you and your team have gotten rid of all your problem areas. (Yes, I realize that this may be some time in coming.) If this happens, should you stop having reflections? I would recommend *against* doing so. Shift the focus of the reflection meetings to looking for new practices and techniques that you can adopt. Remember, the goal is continuous improvement; you don't get to stop improving if you're agile. If you haven't tried, for example, test-driven development, or pair-programming, use your reflection meetings to coordinate a pilot on one of these techniques. Or perhaps try to move further into the agile build practice of continuous integration, or try adopting automated provisioning in the test environment. How about continuous delivery? There are a lot of ways that teams can continue to improve, so don't rest on your laurels.

Just a few small points to keep in mind about reflections: First, they are meant for the team; they're not designed as a way for the team to "turn itself in" to management if something is wrong, nor should managers be asking the team for the results of their reflections. Managers can ask if the team is holding reflections, and if they're actually helping, but managers shouldn't try to learn about any "dirty laundry" from the team. Such actions on the part of management quickly squelch open discussion within the team about needed areas of improvement. Furthermore teams should occasionally "reflect" on how they are doing reflections and try new ways to move to the most useful approach.[8]

8. One reference that was recommended to me is Patrick Kua's book titled, *The Retrospective Handbook: A Guide for Agile Teams* (CreateSpace Independent Publishing Platform, https://leanpub.com/the-retrospective-handbook). You may find that Patrick approaches the practice of reflections (retrospectives) from a different angle than covered here—and that's OK! The goal is to make these meetings beneficial so that the team can continually improve. Learning about other ways to be successful is always a *good thing!*

Value Stream Mapping

From the lean world comes a practice known as *value stream mapping*. A value stream map (VSM) is a way of mapping out a process, determining where value is being added and where delays are occurring. As an example, say that you're part of a software maintenance organization that's using waterfall. When a customer defect comes into your queue, and you look at it and determine that Bob is the best person to work on it, that's something of value. However, the time it takes from when you pass the defect to Bob, and Bob starts working on it, is not valuable; it's a delay. After Bob gets to work on the defect, he's doing something of value. When he finishes the fix, it goes into the tester's queue and waits until the tester can run the necessary testing. That's another delay. When the tester finally finishes testing, and says the defect fix is ready to send to the customer, the fix is routed to the final build and packaging process where it may sit for a while, which is another delay. Yes, people may be working on other things, which is preventing them for working on this defect, thus incurring the delays. But from the perspective of the customer who opened the defect, a delay is a delay. A value-stream map for the simple example just given might look something like the chart shown in Figure 11.1.

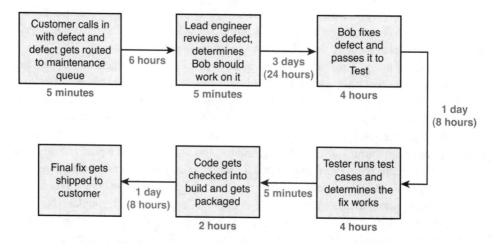

Figure 11.1   A simple Value Stream Map showing the flow of a process where work is being done and how long it takes (below boxes) and where delays (waste) are occurring (with arrows).

Note that "days" in the previous example are based on 8-hour business days. So the total time from when the customer called in to when he received a fix was 56 hours and 15 minutes (or 56.25 hours). Of that total time, only 10 hours and 10 minutes (10.17 hours) is where actual work was done (*value*). The remainder of the time was delay (*waste*). Thus, the overall efficiency of this process is 18 percent. What a team should do is look at the value stream map, specifically at the point in which the biggest delay occurs (in this case, it's the time from when the defect goes on Bob's queue to when Bob actually starts working on it) and then brainstorm on ways to drive that time down. After improvements have been made there, then look at the next biggest delay (in this case it's a tie between the time when the tester is sent the fix and when testing actually begins, and also from the time the final fix is packaged and ready to when it is sent to the customer) and brainstorm on improvements for one of them, implement some improvements, and then "lather, rinse, repeat" for the remaining areas where large delays occur. Note that this sample value stream map is a very, very simple one for a waterfall team. Other processes will result in much more complex value stream maps, especially when alternate paths and loop-backs (repeated steps) are factored in. Nevertheless, value stream mapping is an excellent tool for teams to use to look for areas for improvement.[9]

A few notes regarding value stream maps: First, do not over-engineer them. Usually looking at the most common route through a process is good enough to find areas in which significant improvements are needed. Second, don't give yourself more than two meetings to finalize a VSM. Next, make sure all the people involved in the process participate in the VSM activities. Finally, be careful that your VSMs do not miss the "bigger picture." In other words, don't focus exclusively on an isolated portion of a process when focusing on the surrounding processes can lead to better overall improvements. In the previous example, the VSM started with support, moved to development and test, and then back to support. What we're cautioning against is, for example, looking only at a "support-only" VSM, a "development-only" VSM, or a "test-only" VSM when the interactions among all three disciplines is what needs to be focused on because it is the entire process that is used to respond to a customer issue. It's this overall process that should be the focus.

Addressing Reluctance

There can be a fear of trying new things because of the possibility of failure—and no one likes to fail. However, failure is an opportunity for learning and can spawn other ideas that ultimately more than make up for any initial "failures." Additionally, trying new things imlies change and many people are uncomfortable with change. As long as you're taking small steps (that is, "fail fast"), failures shouldn't cause any major ripple effect in the project or in the organization and the apparent change may not look so daunting. As my son's varsity basketball coach used to tell the team, "If you're not making mistakes, you're not trying hard enough!" Agile teams should live in a mature, penalty-free environment in which any failures that occur as part of the effort of trying something new and innovative are not only tolerated, but also *expected*.

The "Art" of Continuous Improvement

There's no specific, universally agreed-upon process regarding how to continuously improve. What I offer here is a simple approach for continuous improvement:

---

9. See the following links for more information on Value Stream Mapping: http://en.wikipedia.org/
   wiki/Value_stream_mapping and http://agiles2008.agiles.org/common/pdfs/
   Poppendieck%20-%20Value%20Stream%20Mapping.pdf

- **First:** Stop living with pain.

Although this may seem like a simple concept, it can be a trying exercise. First, you're probably aware that there are problems facing your organization, many of which have probably been pain points for years, and the organization has just gotten "comfortable" living with the pain. Think about that for just a minute—*gotten comfortable living with pain*. Such words should cause all sorts of lights and sirens to go off in your head. We want to help you squelch those alarms by helping you to begin eliminating the pain. Refer to Chapter 9, "Stop the Line," for an overview of how to handle this situation.

- **Next:** Benefit from the agile practices you've already adopted.

Teams frequently tell me about the various agile practices they've adopted, but when I ask if the practices are actually providing any benefit, I often get blank stares. Putting a "check mark" next to the practice seems to be the goal instead of ensuring that the practice is actually providing benefit. So be rigorous in your assessments of whether you've gained benefits from the practices you've adopted. For example, assume you've adopted the practice of daily standups. Are these meetings nothing more than status meetings? If so, they're most likely hurting the team. These daily meetings should not only be short (I recommend limiting them to just 15 minutes) but they should also be used to ensure team communication and coordination are taking place. That's where the real benefit of these meetings lies. One question to ask is, "Do you feel like you can miss your daily meeting and not be worse off?" In other words, do you find the daily meeting *useful*? If not, then perhaps the meeting is more of a "check mark" than something of value. If the meeting doesn't seem to be useful, this would be a good topic to bring up during a reflection meeting!

- **Finally:** Keep getting better; exceed your expectations.

You've gotten rid of your pain and you're seeing real benefit from the practices you've adopted so far. At this point it may be tempting to rest on your laurels. Don't. My encouragement for you here is to continue to look for opportunities for improvement so that you can, in essence, make your lives easier and better. Why do something that takes 20 hours when you could pursue some innovation and drop it to 10 hours? You'll have 10 hours available that you didn't have before, which should translate into a positive impact on your daily life, both in the office and out. Brainstorm with the team on ideas. To come up with a good idea, you need lots of raw material to begin with. Look at an area that hasn't changed in quite some time and brainstorm on ways to improve it—even if it's never been singled out as a problem area. When you can start making improvements in areas that you'd never even considered before, you'll start exceeding your expectations regarding what continuous improvement can do for you!

Share

It is often said that, "Experience is the best teacher"—and this is true! But what this does not mean is that *you* have to actually experience something to learn from it. If you can learn from others' experiences without having to go through them yourself, then you'll be that much better off. We recommend that teams set up regular sessions where they share information on what is working for them and why, as well as what they've tried and not had success with. Some of the best ideas Leslie and I have encountered came from other teams because those teams provided a perspective that was different than ours. We've seen teams try new ideas that resulted in unexpected but valuable results. Cross-learning is a beneficial practice for helping teams to get better.

As important as continuous improvement is, sharing your increasing knowledge with other teams is also important. There are many ways to achieve cross team sharing; the explosion of social media should provide fertile ground for coming up with ways to do so in your organization. But whatever you try, do not underestimate the value of live conversations when you the share the information. Live interactions allow teams to advance the ideas through the discussion, increase networking opportunities, and also encourage a little friendly competition to keep the ideas sharp. As I tell folks all the time, "If a picture is worth a thousand words, then a conversation is worth a thousand emails."

Metrics

Given the widely disparate areas that teams can focus on for improvement, there are no common metrics that cover every possible instance. For teams that try value stream mapping, you can see if the efficiency of a given process increased after you took action by creating another VSM of the same process and generating new data. If you try improving your builds, you can track build success rates and time required for builds. You can track automation coverage improvements and more.

Lastly—and I know that this is not really a metric—but celebrate your improvements! Making improvements usually takes hard work, so post a team board that displays your improvements for all to see. As I previously said, nothing motivates more success like actual success!

Breakthrough

To get into the habit of continuously improving, add an "inter-release" improvement iteration. Earlier I covered some of the reasons teams give for not embracing continuous improvement, many of which are carryovers from waterfall days. An inter-release improvement iteration is a simple technique to begin to build a culture of continuous improvement in your organization, especially if there's been reluctance or a lack of enthusiasm for it in the past.

The improvement actions taken *during* a release will often focus on alleviating immediate pain points and perhaps on gaining some small "wins." The focus of this technique is setting apart some time *in between* releases—the length of one iteration. Calling this time *an iteration* should help ensure it receives the appropriate priority; having just a nebulous "time between releases" could make it easy to deprioritize it. For example, following this technique, a team would dedicate 2 weeks' of time between the end of one release and the start of a new release just to learn about and pilot a new practice. Some possible examples: Learn about and pilot test-driven development, or continuous deployment, or moving the test environment to the "cloud." This technique will help prevent you from "waterfalling backward" to the point in which the team does not pursue improvement activities or gives up on them.

Dedicating just the time of one iteration during which the whole team can focus on trying something new, investigate a proposed technique, or whatever—without the distraction of being expected to work on a project—can pay big dividends in the life of the next project and be a morale booster. It will ensure the team has confidence that organizational leadership is bought into the idea of continuous improvement since the leadership is willing to dedicate time to allow the team to explore ways to improve. Such confidence can be a big motivator for the team to continue to try new things and get better and better. It is a simple, effective, and a powerful way to start down the path of continuous improvement.

Summary

Being agile requires continuous improvement because teams that continue to learn, adapt, and grow are more productive and competitive. Agile is a never-ending journey of getting better.

By now, you've probably realized that Leslie and I *strongly* recommend a number of agile practices. You might be thinking, for example, that we'd state that "whole teams" is the most important concept. After reading other chapters, you might be tempted to say that "no multitasking" is the most important, or "working software," or perhaps even "leadership." Truth be told, we want to impress upon you just how important each of these concepts is to successful agile adoption.

However, the reason we decided on having "Continuous Improvement" as the last chapter in the book is that the final impression we want to leave you with is that we consider continuous improvement to be *the most important facet of successfully adopting agile*. If you really *get* the idea of continuous improvement, and really begin to act like you get it, the other concepts, principles, and practices covered in this book will likely follow—and probably sooner than later. The desire to improve, and to do so *continuously*, is that important.

Being agile requires continuous improvement because

- Teams should always be progressing.
- No one's perfect.
- There is no such thing as "100 percent agile."

Hopefully you see the need for always trying to improve, and hopefully we've also provided you with a good basis for ensuring continuous improvement actually takes place. Here's a recap of what we covered:

- The "art" of continuous improvement
  - Teams should always be progressing.
  - No one's perfect.
  - There is no such thing as "100 percent agile."
- "If you're not making mistakes, you're not trying hard enough...."
  - I believe it was Edison who famously said, "I have not failed. I've just found 10,000 ways that won't work." Compare his "failures" with his nearly 1,100 patents.
- Some thoughts on areas to target for improvement:
  - Development processes:
    - Test-driven development (TDD)
    - Pair-programming
    - Refactoring
    - In-house deploys/continuous deployment
    - Evolutionary architecture and emergent design
  - Development environment:
    - Automation (including automated provisioning and use of cloud technologies)
    - Builds (including static code analysis and continuous integration)
    - Minimizing interrupts (for example, creating dedicated maintenance team)
    - Team communication (including "bullpens"—see Chapter 1, "Whole Teams," for more information)
    - Customer interaction (including the practice of "Transparent Development")
- Closing thoughts:
  - A helpful comment regarding continuous improvement: An often over-looked aspect of learning involves "unlearning." This is normally referred to as breaking old (bad) habits, but it's a little more nuanced than that. Here's a quote from Edgar Schein that captures this thought: "Changing something implies not just learning something new but unlearning something that is already there and possibly in the way. What most learning theories and models overlook are the dynamics of unlearning, of overcoming resistance to change. They assume that if you can just get a clear enough vision of a positive future, this is motivation enough to get new learning started."[10]
  - And another: "The only way to win is to learn faster than anyone else."[11]

10. Edgar Schein, *The Corporate Culture Survival Guild*. San Francisco: Jossey-Bass, 1999: 117–118.

11. Reis, Eric, *The Lean Startup: How Today's Entrepreneurs Use Continuous Innovation to Create Radically Successful Businesses*. New York: Crown Business, 2011: 111. Print.

- And, finally, if you'd like to read an insightful work on continuous improvement, consider Matthew May's book titled, *The Elegant Solution*. Matthew does a great job of showing how some improvement approaches are better than others, and he also conveys a great sense of encouragement showing that continuous improvement is a great practice with usually great results.[12] I would especially recommend his chapter on "Kaizen," which is just a Japanese term for an idea that originated in the United States, but which we in the United States have lost over the years.

12. May, Matthew E., *The Elegant Solution*. New York: Free Press, 2007. Print.

Appendix

By Scott Will

Exploring Your Agility: A Brief, Annotated Questionnaire

Wait until you've read the book and then check out the following annotated questionnaire. This short exercise is meant to give you a quick "read" on whether there are some lingering waterfall tendencies that may need some breakthrough thinking.

To begin, we ask a few probing questions and have a little fun providing "agile answers" and "waterfall answers masquerading as agile answers." After those, we ask a more serious question about what agile practices you've adopted that you might be willing to give up and why. Finally, we ask a few questions about particular practices and give our take on each of those practices for your consideration.

How did adopting agile change your team dynamics? Did it improve your productivity?

What waterfall thinking, operating under the guise of agile, would answer:

"Our agile development team writes code for several iterations and then our agile test team gets involved in the project. Our productivity has not improved."

What we'd like to hear:

"We found out that 'being agile' required us to adopt the whole team approach because the synergy that resulted from cross-disciplined, cross-component teams working together helped us be more productive than when the disciplines worked in isolation."

How has adopting agile enabled you to deliver value to your customers?

What waterfall thinking, operating under the guise of agile, would answer:

"We perform demonstrations for managers, product managers, executives, and team members on a regular basis, but we've never included customers in our demonstrations."

What we'd like to hear:

"Being agile required us to engage in regular, active stakeholder interaction because only our stakeholders can tell us what actually meets their needs as we're developing the product."

What agile practice do you use to ensure that your team achieves a manageable and consistent workload?

What waterfall thinking, operating under the guise of agile, would answer:

"Each person on our team works on his own user story."

What we'd like to hear:

"Being agile required us to adopt the principles of queuing theory because we achieved greater efficiency and throughput by leveraging a steady flow of small batches of work. In addition, our agile team uses small tasks to ensure that we can all work together on one user story at a time and get to 'Done!' before moving on to a new user story."

What Would You Be Willing to Give Up?

The following is a list of practices that teams typically adopt when moving to agile. For each one that your team has adopted, assume the opportunity arises to stop engaging in the practice.

Put a "*yes*" next to each practice that your team would be willing **to give up**.

Put an "*n/a*" next to each practice that your team is not currently using.

_____ Having "whole teams" (that is, teams that are both cross-component and cross-discipline)

_____ Having daily standup meetings

_____ Creating user stories

_____ Sizing user stories with story points (using relative sizings) using planning poker to assign story point values

_____ Creating small tasks at the beginning of each iteration for the user stories targeted for completion in the iteration

_____ Continuous integration as a build practice

     _____ Getting to "Done!" every iteration

     _____ Holding reflections at the end of each iteration

     _____ Demonstrating completed user stories to customers at the end of each iteration

     _____ Using "working software" as *the* measure of project progress

     _____ Keeping project debt at or near zero throughout a release

     _____ Continuous deployment

What Leslie and I have seen is, when a team is willing to give up on a particular agile practice, it's usually because the team is not getting any benefit from the practice. In such instances, it's likely that the team has just "gone through the motions" without understanding the practice itself and/or because the team doesn't exactly know *how* to derive benefit from adopting a given practice. Either way, for every practice that has a "yes" next to it, we would suggest spending time understanding *why* the team would be willing to give it up. Use the brief overview of the principles included in each chapter to understand why and how particular practices are meant to provide real benefits.

For those practices that have an "n/a," consider how you might adopt those practices in the future. Each of the currently unused practices makes for a good discussion topic at upcoming reflection meetings.

Questions on Various Agile Practices

How Long Are Your Iterations?

In general, we recommend iterations that are no longer than 2 weeks as a starting point. There are many benefits from adopting such short iterations, including how well they help teams break typical, waterfall habits. Many of the other benefits are covered throughout the book.

One of the engineers on an IBM team I worked with sent me an email discussing some of his efforts to encourage shorter iterations. I really like the thinking behind a list of indicators he came up with that point out situations in which teams have adopted iterations that are too long:[1]

"In general, your sprints are too long:

- If you are having stakeholder requirements change more frequently than your sprint duration

- If you have stakeholders wanting code drops more frequently than your sprint duration

- If your sprints have a cadence that doesn't gel well with other teams (such as one team on the project using 4-week sprints versus another using 6-week sprints)

- If you are having problems estimating the work, such that at the end of the sprint you

---

1. This list was taken from an email sent to me by Matthew Stave. Leslie and I appreciate Matthew having granted permission to include his list here.

have a good amount of work left over

- If you are not great at execution from a project perspective and would benefit from more opportunities to practice [Note: This idea comports with the agile idea that, if something is hard to do, do it a lot—it'll get easier the more you do it.]
- If tasks are sized such that nothing is ready for long periods, then a massive amount of work drops toward the end of a sprint
- It's hard to get status in the middle of a sprint, and waiting until the end is 'too long to go dark'
- If changing people/assignments midsprint affects delivery of too much stuff"

How Often Do You Build?

If you don't have the capability of completing *at least* two "production-level" builds every day, then you will struggle being successful with agile. The effort to put in place a robust continuous integration environment and practice gets everyone "on the same build" all the time and will result in a large productivity boost. Short iterations are almost impossible with anything less than the ability to create two builds a day. Otherwise, a build break can mean at least a day (or longer) between good builds. Continuous integration is also a key enabling practice for DevOps.

What Disciplines Are on Your Teams?

If development, test, user experience, and product documentation skills are needed, but are not part of each of your teams, you're still working in a waterfall way. In agile, teams should be "whole teams," where all necessary disciplines are represented on the team (as well as all necessary component skills). And for those situations in which all necessary disciplines are not on the team, the team members that do make up the team have to step up and tackle the needed work—even if it's outside their typical domain or expertise. For example, if performance testing on the product is needed, just because you may not have skilled performance testers available doesn't mean you get to skip performance testing. The engineers on the team should step up and do performance testing (see the story of how Leslie's developers learned how to do performance testing—and the benefits they realized from doing so—in Chapter 8, "Release Often").

Keep in mind that whole teams should have all necessary product component skills on the team as well. (Whole teams are also cross-component teams.) It is difficult to get to "Done!" each iteration if teams are built only around product components.

Do You Carry a Defect Backlog?

If your answer is "Yes," then you need to ask yourself "Why?" If defects are put off until later, they almost always come back to haunt a project. It's much tougher to resurrect quality at the end of a release than it is to keep quality at "ship-ready" levels throughout the release. In addition, delaying the fixing of defects is almost always a less-efficient approach than fixing them as soon as they're found.

If you are in the habit of delaying the fixing of defects, and allowing a backlog to accrue, stop creating new functionality and get rid of your current backlog. If you know you have to fix the list of defects, the highest-quality and most efficient approach is to fix them *now*. When fixed, you can resume building new functionality. And, even here, endeavor to not let any new defects accumulate from this point forward—don't dig the hole twice.

What Do You Automate?

Like continuous integration, automation is another critical practice for agile success. If you're not in the habit of automating, may I recommend in the strongest terms that you start putting significant focus on automation beginning *right now*? Teams should start with automation that can occur as close to when the code is being written as possible (that is, automated unit-testing). Next up would be automated build verification testing and reporting, followed by automated functional testing. After that, automated provisioning is a great practice. Finally, automated system testing should be pursued—assuming it makes sense for your project. (Sometimes system test environments are set up and used just once, so automating testing for these situations may not make as much sense as just doing the testing manually.)

In sum, to make sure you continuously have working software, you need to have your repeatable processes keep up with the pace of verification required:

- Before you check in.
- Builds need rapid validation and fast responses if a build fails.
- Regression testing needs to constantly validate that new code changes have not created problems with existing code.

Without automating these constantly repeated processes, it will be difficult to maintain working software and you will quickly waterfall backward.

Do You Conduct Status Meetings?

We're not opposed to status meetings *per se*. However, in the majority of instances, status meetings are just a waste of time. Think in terms of operational meetings where problems are addressed.

Anything useful that is covered during a status meeting should be available on a project dashboard. If a project dashboard is available, status meetings are redundant. If you hold regular status meetings just because "we've always had them," stop. Everyone needs to share the same truth at all times. Visibility is critical.

Are You Delivering Value to Your Customers?

Of course, the first question that needs to be asked is if you are actually doing customer demonstrations? If not, you're missing out on one of the most important benefits of agile—continuous feedback from customers.

Assuming you conduct regular demonstrations to customers throughout your project, the next question that arises is if you are getting good feedback from your customers? If not, you should first focus on that. We provide some tips on how to get good feedback in Chapter 2, "Active Stakeholder Interaction."

Assuming you get good feedback from customer demonstrations, you should use it to ensure you make changes to your feature-set that helps your product more closely align with your customers' needs. If you just write it down somewhere, with plans to "get to it in the next release," it's a rather pointless exercise—you don't get the benefit from your customers' input, nor do your customers get the benefit from their participation with you. It's just "going through the motions"—you've adopted the practice without getting the benefits promised.

If you know that your stakeholders will buy and use your product when it ships, you know that your stakeholder interaction efforts have been very productive.

Do You Get to "Done!" Each Iteration?

Getting to "Done!" every iteration is critical because it ensures that you are doing your work in small, manageable batches, that you are not collecting debt, and that you are producing working software every iteration. And it is the only way to have working software continuously—period.

If you are not getting to "Done!" consistently, fixing this problem should be one of your top priorities. Getting to "Done!" is an important practice that encompasses many of the agile principles. Many techniques for getting to "Done!" are discussed throughout the book.

Are You Getting Better?

Becoming agile is a journey that will not end. Use continuous improvement as your "GPS." Reflections and resultant improvement actions need to be baked into your thinking and behavior. There are no perfect agile teams, but agile teams are teams that keep getting better.

Concluding Thoughts

Well, Leslie and I had some fun pulling this questionnaire together. I trust that you got an occasional chuckle out it, but I also trust that it gave you some additional encouragement toward getting real benefits from adopting agile—and even more encouragement to continually seek to improve.

As a reminder, we encourage you to join the agile conversation on our blog: "Being Agile." You can find it at www.ibm/developerworks/community/blogs/beingagile/?lang=en.

Index

A

active stakeholder interaction
breakthrough: "2, 2, 2, 2"
technique, 39-40
IBM case study, 25-26
metrics, 39-40
practices
compelling interaction,
35
customer support teams
as stakeholders, 38-39
development
organization as
stakeholder, 37-38
epic reviews, 33
expectations, 33-35
foreign customers, 39
regular demonstrations,
35-36
response to feedback,
36-37
stakeholder
identification, 31-33
principles
challenges to
active stakeholder
interaction, 27-29
doing what is needed,
30
explained, 26-27
importance of
stakeholder
communication,
29-30
stakeholder interaction
in XP (Extreme
Programming), 28-29
summary, 42
addressing reluctance, 167
Advanced Release Burndown
Chart, 89
agile instincts, developing,
147-148
agile leadership
breakthrough: giving up
status meetings, 154-155
metrics, 154
overview, 143-144
practices
developing agile
instincts, 147-148
enabling and protecting
whole team, 148-149
General Motors (GM)
case study, 152
helping team learn,
149-150
learning agile, 147
letting team fail,
149-150
setting priorities and
boundaries, 151-152
single, visible view of
the truth, 153
principles
challenges of agile
leadership, 146-147
nature of agile
leadership, 145
promoting innovation,
162-163
summary, 155-156
allocating people, 60

architecture, evolutionary,
86-88
"art" of continuous
improvement, 167-168
automation
assessing, 177
continuous integration and
automation, 84-85
avoiding multitasking
breakthrough: nuclear
option, 61
inefficiency of
multitasking, 53-55
metrics, 60
practices
100% dedication to
project, 57-58
becoming a "firewall,"
58-59
calendar ruthlessness,
59
one project at a time, 58
pair programming/pair
testing, 59
principles
efficiency, 55-56
flow, 56-57
"stop starting; start
finishing," 57
summary, 62

B

backlogs
defect backlogs, 75,
176-177
reviewing at end of
release, 124
upfront backlogs, 125-127
becoming a "firewall," 58-59
"Being Agile" blog, 7
betas, 28
big problems, handling,
133-134

big-batch (waterfall) thinking,
43-45
blockers, fixing, 133
blogs, "Being Agile," 7
boundaries, setting, 151-152
breaking
habits, 171
silos, 21
breakthroughs
bullpens, 21-22
"Fix It Now!" approach,
89-91
giving up status meetings,
154-155
"inter-release"
improvement iteration,
169-170
nuclear option, 61
queuing theory, 51
removing the biggest
inhibitor to customer
success, 139-140
time-boxed iterations,
76-77
"2, 2, 2, 2" technique,
39-40
upfront backlogs, 125-127
zero-gravity thinking,
103-107
example, 106
explained, 104-105
Brooks, Fred, 15, 161
Brook's Law, 15
Bruch, Heike, 52
building quality in, 71-72
builds, frequency of, 176
bullpens, 21-22

C

calendar management, 59
capacity, ensuring sufficient,
46-47

Cockburn, Alistair, 153
code drops, frequency of,
123-124
Cohn, Mike, 94
commitment, deferring,
114-115
communication in teams,
17-18
continuous improvement, 178
breakthrough:
"inter-release"
improvement iteration,
169-170
metrics, 169
overview, 157-158
practices
addressing reluctance,
167
"art" of continuous
improvement,
167-168
reflections, 164-165
sharing, 169
value stream mapping,
166-167
principles
"100 percent agile"
fallacy, 159-160
challenges of
continuous
improvement, 159
continuous learning,
160
failing fast, 171
focus on small,
on-going
improvements,
161-162
importance of
continuous
improvement,
158-159
learning from your
mistakes, 162

promoting innovation, 162-163
setting time aside to get better, 160-161
summary, 170-172
continuous integration and automation, 84-85
conversations, 17-18
coordinating teams, 19
credit on teams, 19-20
critical decisions, deferring, 114-115
cross-component teams, 11-12
cross-cultural teams, 13-14
cross-discipline teams, 12-13
cross-geographical teams, 13-14
Cunningham, Ward, 65
customer demonstrations, feedback from, 178
customer interaction. *See* stakeholder interaction
customer success, removing biggest inhibitor to, 139-140
customer support teams as stakeholders, 38-39
customer value, focus on, 72-73

D

daily standup meetings, 18
dashboards, 19
debt
    project debt, 67
    removing, 69-70
    technical debt, 65-66
decisions, deferring, 114-115
dedication
    to projects, 57-58
    of teams, 14-16
defect backlogs, 75, 176-177

defects
    avoiding writing defects, 74-75
    defect backlogs, 75, 176-177
    defect resolution process, 76-77
    "Fix It Now!" approach, 89-91
    latent defects, handling, 74
    prioritizing, 76
deferred commitment, 114-115
delivering value
    breakthrough: zero-gravity thinking, 103-107
        benefits of, 106-107
        example, 106
        explained, 104-105
    metrics, 103
    overview, 93-94
    practices
        acceptance criteria, 99-100
        "so that" clause, 97-98
        velocity, 100-103
        vertically sliced stories, 98-99
    principles, 94-97
    summary, 107
demonstrations
    feedback from, 178
    performing, 35-36
deploys, in-house, 88-89
design
    emergent design, 86-88
    evaluating design decisions, 125
    evolutionary product design, 119-120
developing agile instincts, 147-148
development organization as stakeholder, 37-38

"do just enough" approach, 113-114
documentation, 18
"Done!," getting to
    expanding "Done!" criteria, 73
    self-assessment, 178

E

efficiency and multitasking, 53-56
The Elegant Solution (May), 171
eliminating waste
    breakthrough: time-boxed iterations, 76-77
    metrics, 75-76
    overview, 63-64
    practices
        avoiding writing defects, 74-75
        building quality in, 71-72
        expanding "Done!" criteria, 73
        focus on customer value, 72-73
        handling latent defects, 74
        removing debt, 69-70
        small tasks, 70-71
    principles
        challenges, 67-69
        importance of waste elimination, 65
        project debt, 67
        technical debt, 65-66
    summary, 77-78
email
    communication failures, 18
    managing, 60

emergent design, 86-88
enabling whole team,
    148-149
end users, 31
ensuring sufficient capacity,
    46-47
epics
    epic stories, 117-119
    reviewing with
        stakeholders, 33
evaluating design decisions,
    125
evolutionary architecture,
    86-88
evolutionary product design,
    119-120
expanding "Done!" criteria,
    73
expectations, setting, 33-35
ExpertThink, 104
Exploring Your Agility
    questionnaire
        questions on various
            agility practices, 175-178
        waterfall answers
            masquerading as agile
            answers, 173-174
        What Would You Be
            Willing to Give Up?
            checklist, 174-175
Extreme Programming (XP),
    stakeholder interaction,
    28-29

F

failing fast, 171
feedback
    from customer
        demonstrations, 178
    frequency of, 46
    responding to, 36-37
"firewall," becoming, 58-59

"Fix It Now!" approach,
    89-91
fixing blockers, 133
flow, 56-57
Ford, Neal, 88
foreign customers, 39
frequency
    of builds, 176
    of code drops, 123-124
    of feedback, 46
FTP (Research Triangle
    Park), North Carolina, 47
"full credit and no partial
    credit" concept, 19-20

G

General Motors (GM), 152
generalizing specialists, 11
getting to "Done!," 178
giving up status meetings,
    154-155
GM (General Motors), 152
on-going improvements,
    focus on, 161-162
go-to people, 20
GroupThink, 104

H

help
    helping team learn,
        149-150
    offering, 20
high risk first approach,
    121-123
high value first approach,
    120-121
in-house deploys, 88-89

I

IBM, active stakeholder
    interaction, 25-26, 35
identifying stakeholders,
    31-33
improvement. *See* continuous
    improvement
inefficiency of multitasking,
    53-56
information radiators, 153
innovation, promoting,
    162-163
*The Innovation Killer: How
    'What We Know' Limits
    What We Can Imagine*
    (Rabe), 104
insiders, 31
integration, continuous
    integration and automation,
    84-85
intellectual property
    concerns, 28-29
"inter-release" improvement
    iteration, 169-170
interruptions, tracking, 60
isolation, 27-28
iterations
    "inter-release"
        improvement iteration,
        169-170
    length of, 49, 83-84,
        175-176
    time-boxed iterations,
        76-77

J-K

"just enough," 113-114
Kessler, Carl, 42
Kirn, Walter, 55
knowledge, sharing, 169
Kua, Patrick, 165

L

large problems, handling, 133-134
latent defects, handling, 74
leadership (agile)
  breakthrough: giving up status meetings, 154-155
  metrics, 154
  overview, 143-144
  practices
    developing agile instincts, 147-148
    enabling and protecting whole team, 148-149
    General Motors (GM) case study, 152
    helping team learn, 149-150
    learning agile, 147
    letting team fail, 149-150
    setting priorities and boundaries, 151-152
    single, visible view of the truth, 153
  promoting innovation, 162-163
  summary, 155-156
learning
  continuous learning, 160
  learning agile, 147
  learning from your mistakes, 162
length
  of iterations, 49, 83-84, 175-176
  of release cycles, 117
letting team fail, 149-150

M

maintaining teams, 16-17
managing
  calendar, 59
  email, 60
Maute, Yvonne, 49
May, Matthew, 171
meetings
  daily standup meetings, 18
  reflections, 133, 164-165
  status meetings, 154-155, 177
Menges, Jochen I., 52
metrics
  agile leadership, 154
  for avoiding multitasking, 60
  continuous improvement, 169
  delivering value, 103
  eliminating waste, 75-76
  focus on working software, 50
  for queuing theory, 50
  release often approach, 124-125
  for stakeholder interaction, 39-40
  "stop the line" behavior, 134-137
  for teams, 20-21
  working software, 89
Minimum Viable Product, 65
multitasking, avoiding
  breakthrough: nuclear option, 61
  inefficiency of multitasking, 53-55
  metrics, 60

practices
  100% dedication to project, 57-58
  becoming a "firewall," 58-59
  calendar ruthlessness, 59
  one project at a time, 58
  pair programming/pair testing, 59
principles
  efficiency, 55-56
  flow, 56-57
  "stop starting; start finishing," 57
summary, 62
The Mythical Man Month (Brooks), 15, 161

N

Nass, Clifford, 55
Non-Disclosure Agreements, 28-29
nuclear option, 61

O

offering help, 20
one project at a time, 58
one release at a time, 48
"100 percent agile" fallacy, 159-160
100% dedication to project, 57-58

P

PaaS (Platform as a Service), 80
pair programming, 59
pair testing, 59
partners, 31

Pascal, Blaise, 18
people allocation, 60
Platform as a Service (PaaS), 80
Poppendieck, Mary, 18, 21, 45, 64
Poppendieck, Tom, 45, 64
practices
  active stakeholder interaction
    compelling interaction, 35
    customer support teams as stakeholders, 38-39
    development organization as stakeholder, 37-38
    epic reviews, 33
    expectations, 33-35
    foreign customers, 39
    regular demonstrations, 35-36
    response to feedback, 36-37
    stakeholder identification, 31-33
  agile leadership
    developing agile instincts, 147-148
    enabling and protecting whole team, 148-149
    General Motors (GM) case study, 152
    helping team learn, 149-150
    learning agile, 147
    letting team fail, 149-150
    setting priorities and boundaries, 151-152
    single, visible view of the truth, 153

avoiding multitasking
  100% dedication to project, 57-58
  becoming a "firewall," 58-59
  calendar ruthlessness, 59
  one project at a time, 58
  pair programming/pair testing, 59
continuous improvement
  addressing reluctance, 167
  "art" of continuous improvement, 167-168
  reflections, 164-165
  sharing, 169
  value stream mapping, 166-167
delivering value
  acceptance criteria, 99-100
  "so that" clause, 97-98
  vertically sliced stories, 98-99
eliminating waste
  avoiding writing defects, 74-75
  building quality in, 71-72
  expanding "Done!" criteria, 73
  focus on customer value, 72-73
  handling latent defects, 74
  removing debt, 69-70
  small tasks, 70-71
queuing theory
  focus on working software, 50
  one release at a time, 48

  short iterations, 49
  small task sizes, 47-48
release often approach
  epic stories, 117-119
  evolutionary product design, 119-120
  frequent code drops, 123-124
  high risk first, 121-123
  high value first, 120-121
  shorter release cycles, 117
"stop the line" behavior
  fixing blockers, 133
  handling large problems, 133-134
  reflections as a guide, 133
teams, 16-20
  communication, 17-18
  coordination, 19
  "full credit and no partial credit" concept, 19-20
  offering help, 20
  protection, 16-17
  whole teams, 16
What Would You Be Willing to Give Up? checklist, 174-175
working software
  continuous integration and automation, 84-85
  evolutionary architecture and emergent design, 86-88
  in-house deploys, 88-89
  short iterations, 83-84
  vertically sliced stories, 85-86
principals (stakeholders), 31

principles
  active stakeholder
    interaction
      challenges to
        active stakeholder
        interaction, 27-29
      doing what is needed,
        30
      explained, 26-27
      importance of
        stakeholder
        communication,
        29-30
  agile leadership
    challenges of releasing
      often, 146-147
    nature of agile
      leadership, 145
  avoiding multitasking
    efficiency, 55-56
    "stop starting; start
      finishing," 57
  continuous improvement
    "100 percent agile"
      fallacy, 159-160
    challenges of
      continuous
      improvement, 159
    continuous learning,
      160
    failing fast, 171
    focus on small,
      on-going
      improvements,
      161-162
    importance of
      continuous
      improvement,
      158-159
    learning from your
      mistakes, 162

    promoting innovation,
      162-163
    setting time aside to get
      better, 160
  delivering value, 94-97
  eliminating waste
    challenges, 67-69
    importance of waste
      elimination, 65
    project debt, 67
    technical debt, 65-66
  queuing theory
    big-batch (waterfall)
      thinking, 43-45
    ensuring sufficient
      capacity, 46-47
    frequent feedback, 46
    small batches of
      coordinated work,
      45-46
  release often approach
    advantages of release
      often approach,
      112-113
    challenges of releasing
      often, 116-117
    deferred commitment,
      114-115
    "do just enough"
      approach, 113-114
  teams, 10-16
    cross-component
      teams, 11-12
    cross-discipline teams,
      12-13
    cross-geographical,
      cross-cultural teams,
      13-14
    dedication, 14-16
    protection, 14-16
    stability, 14-16
    whole teams, 10-11

working software
  challenges, 82
  definition of working
    software, 80-81
  extending test suites,
    82-83
  shippable software, 81
prioritizing
  defects, 76
  setting priorities and
    boundaries, 151-152
product design. See design
project debt, 67
projects
  dedication to, 57-58
  one project at a time, 58
  project debt, 67
promoting innovation,
  162-163
protecting teams, 14-17,
  148-149

Q

quality, building in, 71-72
questionnaire, Exploring
  Your Agility
  questions on various
    agility practices, 175-178
  waterfall answers
    masquerading as agile
    answers, 173-174
  What Would You Be
    Willing to Give Up?
    checklist, 174-175
queuing theory
  big-batch (waterfall)
    thinking, 43-45
  breakthrough, 51
  explained, 43-44
  metrics, 50

practices
focus on working
software, 50
one release at a time, 48
short iterations, 49
small task sizes, 47-48
principles
ensuring sufficient
capacity, 46-47
frequent feedback, 46
small batches of
coordinated work,
45-46
summary, 51-52

R

Rabe, Cynthia Barton, 104
Rational Team Concert
(RTC), 89
reflections, 133, 164-165
release burndown charts,
89, 126
release often approach
breakthrough: upfront
backlogs, 125-127
metrics, 124-125
overview, 109-112
practices
epic stories, 117-119
evolutionary product
design, 119-120
frequent code drops,
123-124
high risk first, 121-123
high value first,
120-121
shorter release cycles,
117
principles
advantages of release
often approach,
112-113

challenges of releasing
often, 116-117
deferred commitment,
114-115
"do just enough"
approach, 113-114
summary, 128
releases. *See also* release
often approach
one release at a time, 48
release cycles, length of,
117
reluctance, addressing, 167
removing
biggest inhibitor to
customer success,
139-140
debt, 69-70
Research Triangle Park
(RTP), North Carolina, 47
responding
to email, 60
to feedback, 36-37
*The Retrospective Handbook:
A Guide for Agile Teams*
(Kua), 165
retrospectives. *See* reflections
return on investment (ROI),
tracking, 134-137
reviewing
backlogs at end of release,
124
epics with stakeholders, 33
Ries, Eric, 65
Rifkin, Stan, 21
risk, high risk first approach,
121-123
ROI (return on investment),
tracking, 134-137
RTC (Rational Team
Concert), 89

S

SaaS (Software as a Service),
80
Schein, Edgar, 171
setting
expectations, 33-35
priorities and boundaries,
151-152
time aside to get better,
160
sharing knowledge, 169
shippable software, 81
short iterations, 49, 83-84
shorter release cycles, 117
silos, breaking with bullpens,
21
single, visible view of the
truth, 153
small, on-going
improvements, 161-162
small batches of coordinated
work, 45-46
small task sizes, 47-48, 70-71
"so that" clause, 97-98
Software as a Service (SaaS),
80
sprints. *See* iterations
stability
principles, 26-27
of teams, 14-16
stakeholder interaction
breakthrough: "2, 2, 2, 2"
technique, 39-40
IBM case study, 25-26
metrics, 39-40
practices
compelling interaction,
35
customer support teams
as stakeholders, 38-39
development
organization as
stakeholder, 37-38

epic reviews, 33
expectations, 33-35
foreign customers, 39
regular demonstrations, 35-36
response to feedback, 36-37
stakeholder identification, 31-33
principles
  active stakeholder interaction, 26-27
  challenges to active stakeholder interaction, 27-29
  doing what is needed, 30
  importance of stakeholder communication, 29-30
  stakeholder interaction in XP (Extreme Programming), 28-29
summary, 42
standup meetings, 18
status meetings, 154-155, 177
"stop starting; start finishing," 57
"stop the line" behavior, 89-91
  breakthrough: removing biggest inhibitor to customer success, 139-140
  challenges, 131-132
  metrics, 134-137
  overview, 129-131
  practices
    fixing blockers, 133
    handling large problems, 133-134

reflections as a guide, 133
principles, 130-132
summary, 141
stories. *See* user stories
sufficient capacity, ensuring, 46-47
Sutherland, Jeff, 30, 96
Svenska Handelsbanken, 155
Sweitzer, John, 42

T

task sizes, 47-48, 70-71
teams
  breakthrough: bullpens, 20-21
  dedication, 57-58
  disciplines on teams, 176
  helping team learn, 149-150
  letting team fail, 149-150
  metrics, 20-21
  people allocation, 60
  practices
    communication, 17-18
    coordination, 19
    "full credit and no partial credit" concept, 19-20
    maintenance, 16-17
    offering help, 20
    protection, 16-17
    team dashboards, 19
    whole teams, 16
  principles
    cross-component teams, 11-12
    cross-discipline teams, 12-13

cross-geographical, cross-cultural teams, 13-14
dedication, 14-16
protection, 14-16
stability, 14-16
whole teams, 10-11
summary, 22-23
whole teams
  go-to people, 20
  power of, 9-10
  protecting, 148-149
technical debt, 65-66
test suites, extending with working software, 82-83
testing
  pair testing, 59
  test suites, extending with working software, 82-83
time-boxed iterations, 76-77
Toyota, 130
tracking ROI (return on investment), 134-137
truth, single view of, 153
Twain, Mark, 52
"2, 2, 2, 2" technique, 39-40

U

unlearning, 171
upfront backlogs, 125-127
user stories, 72
  benefits of, 94-97
  compared to requirements, 96
  epic stories, 117-119
  example, 95
  format, 95
  "so that" clause, 97-98
  vertically sliced stories, 85-86, 98-99

writing, 96
zero-gravity thinking,
   103-107
user-experience (UX)
   professionals, 57
UX (user-experience)
   professionals, 57

V

value, delivering
   breakthrough: zero-gravity
      thinking, 103-107
      benefits of, 106-107
      example, 106
      explained, 104-105
   metrics, 103
   overview, 93-94
   practices
      acceptance criteria,
         99-100
      "so that" clause, 97-98
      velocity, 100-103
      vertically sliced stories,
         98-99
   principles, 94-97
   summary, 107
value stream mapping, 77,
   109-111, 166-167
value-driven development,
   123-124
velocity, 47, 100-103
vertically sliced stories,
   85-86, 98-99
VSM (value stream
   mapping), 166-167

W

wait-state, 43
waste, eliminating
   breakthrough: time-boxed
      iterations, 76-77

metrics, 75-76
overview, 63-64
practices
   avoiding writing
      defects, 74-75
   building quality in,
      71-72
   expanding "Done!"
      criteria, 73
   focus on customer
      value, 72-73
   handling latent defects,
      74
   removing debt, 69-70
   small tasks, 70-71
principles
   challenges, 67-69
   importance of waste
      elimination, 65
   project debt, 67
   technical debt, 65-66
summary, 77-78
waterfall (big-batch) thinking,
   43-45
waterfall answers
   masquerading as agile
   answers, 173-174
What Would You Be Willing
to Give Up? checklist,
174-175
whole teams
   benefits of, 16
   breakthrough: bullpens,
      21-22
   challenges, 11
   communication, 17-18
   coordinating, 19
   cross-component teams,
      11-12
   cross-discipline teams,
      12-13

cross-geographical,
   cross-cultural teams,
   13-14
dedication, 14-16
definition of, 10
"full credit and no partial
   credit" concept, 19-20
go-to people, 20
helping team learn,
   149-150
letting team fail, 149-150
maintaining, 16-17
metrics, 20-21
offering help, 20
power of, 9-10
protecting, 14-17, 148-149
stability, 14-16
summary, 22-23
team dashboards, 19
Williams, Laurie, 59
working software
   breakthrough: "Fix It
      Now!" approach, 89-91
   definition of, 80-81
   focus on, 50
   metrics, 89
   overview, 79-80
   practices
      continuous integration
         and automation, 84-85
      evolutionary
         architecture and
         emergent design,
         86-88
      in-house deploys, 88-89
      short iterations, 83-84
      vertically sliced stories,
         85-86

principles
    challenges, 82
    definition of working
      software, 80-81
    extending test suites,
      82-83
    shippable software, 81
  summary, 91-92
writing user stories, 96

X-Y-Z

XP (Extreme Programming),
  stakeholder interaction,
  28-29
zero-gravity thinking,
  103-107
    benefits of, 106-107
    example, 106
    explained, 104-105